Advances in Monastic Archaeology

Edited by

Roberta Gilchrist and Harold Mytum

with contributions by

C J Bond, L A S Butler, T P O'Connor, P H Cullum,
S Moorhouse, D M Palliser, J Schofield, D Stocker,
J Stopford and S H Ward

TEMPVS REPARATVM

BAR British Series 227

1993

B.A.R.

All volumes available from:
Hadrian Books Ltd, 122 Banbury Road, Oxford OX2 7BP, England

The current BAR catalogue, with details of all titles in print, post-free prices and means of payment, is available free from the above address.

All volumes are distributed by Hadrian Books Ltd.

BAR-227

Gilchrist R and Mytum H (Eds) 1993
Advances in Monastic Archaeology

© The individual authors 1993

ISBN 0 86054 746 9

Tempvs Reparatvm Volume Editor: John W Hedges

Typeset in Times Roman using LATEX by Sebastian Rahtz (ArchaeoInformatica)

British Archaeological Reports are published by

TEMPVS REPARATVM
Archaeological and Historical Associates Limited

All enquiries regarding the submission of manuscripts for future publication should be addressed to:

David P Davison MA MPhil DPhil
General Editor BAR
Tempvs Reparatvm
29 Beaumont Street   Tel: 0865 311046
Oxford OX1 2NP   Fax: 0865 311047

Contents

Introduction
Roberta Gilchrist and Harold Mytum

This volume of papers results from a conference on urban monasteries held at the University of York in 1989. It serves as a companion study to an earlier British Archaeological Report on the archaeology of rural monasteries (1989). Both volumes take the archaeology of later medieval monasticism as their subject. In separating urban and rural monasteries, however, contrasting themes have emerged in addition to differing coverage of monastic orders, which through their vocation were sometimes attracted exclusively to either the medieval town or countryside.

Recent work on rural monasteries has emphasised the development and management of the monastic landscape and outer court. In contrast, excavation of urban monasteries is through necessity generally smaller scale and piecemeal and does not encourage landscape studies. Instead recent work on urban monasticism is more often approached in relation to the development of urban topography. This volume of essays is timely in a number of respects. It coincides with an evident resurgence of interest in monastic archaeology, which has been heralded by a number of synthetic works (Coppack 1990; Greene 1992; Gilchrist 1993), and appears in the wake of the excavation of a number of important urban monasteries, among them Shrewsbury Abbey, the Gilbertine priory at York, the Dominican friary at Beverley, St Gregory's, Canterbury, St Anne's Charterhouse, Coventry, and work in London on houses of every type and order.

Several of the papers approach monastic houses as an index for measuring urbanism, or for charting the spatial development of particular towns. Lawrence Butler defines and enumerates medieval urban monasteries, presenting a document-derived approach to be tested on material evidence. He raises the possibility of linking research questions with archive records for evaluation of monastic sites in advance of any threat of destruction. This approach has since been developed as part of the Monuments Protection Programme, for which descriptions are complete for the full range of ecclesiastical monument classes.

David Palliser reviews Yorkshire monasteries in relation to urban development, contrasting cases where monasteries have served as a stimulus to development (for example Selby and Beverley) with cases where monasteries are secondary to existing towns, like York, where they develop outside the core area. Palliser notes that medieval hospitals provide a particularly sensitive indicator for considering a hierarchy of medieval towns because of their predominantly urban distribution. Patricia Cullum gives an account of the history of St Leonard's, York, one of England's premier medieval hospitals, which was an unusually early and large foundation. Cullum outlines the composition and running of this community and discusses its relationship to the medieval town, particularly through the impact of the hospital's charitable activity, which was

not confined to precinct. Despite an increase in work on the history of medieval hospitals (Cullum on Yorkshire; Rubin 1987 on Cambridge; Rawcliffe 1984 on London and currently Norwich Great Hospital), archaeological attention to hospitals has been scant, although a detailed project is underway for St Mary Spital, London, and works of synthesis have begun (Gilchrist 1992).

A longer time perspective is provided for monasteries in London and Chester. Simon Ward presents a summary of the detailed study of the monasteries of Chester based on archaeology, 17th-century plans, and documents. His contribution represents a study of monasticism in a smaller town with reference to the processes of Normanisation and patronage by the earls who dominated the county. By the late 14th century 25% of walled area of Chester was taken up by monastic precincts. Ward discusses the processes by which monasteries, in particular the Carmelite Friary, expanded their precincts through the accretion of property. The monasteries of Chester were subject to much rebuilding in the late 15th to early 16th centuries, and the composition of their precincts continued to influence the town's topography long after the Dissolution. It is the purpose of John Schofield's paper to specifically elucidate the use of religious precincts and buildings in London after the Dissolution. Few of London's monastic churches survived as parish churches because properties were transferred to courtiers or officials of the Court of Augmentations. Schofield outlines two phases of 16th- century redevelopment typical of London's religious houses. In the middle of the 16th century monastic buildings were briefly transformed into urban palaces, interesting for the modifications necessary to the larger house plan in order to accommodate restricted urban sites. By the late 16th century a fragmentation of precincts was evident as they were divided up for smaller housing and industrial premises.

A number of papers provide summaries and detail potential for finds from monastic sites. Among them, papers by David Stocker on worked stone and Jenny Stopford on ceramic tiles, make a plea for standardisation in method and criteria for recording.

Stocker outlines the procedure for the recording of worked stone in order to determine the date and appearance of buildings and to provide insights into the motives of builders. He discusses problems with dating worked stone, particularly with regard to the issues of residuality and the re-use of materials, for example in the footings of later rebuildings. Stocker emphasises that standardised recording is essential for archive purposes, especially where storage problems may result in reburial of less important pieces. Stopford discusses the economy of ceramic tiles on the basis of the identification of production groups, in contrast to approaches which link stylistic groups. She presents a case study of the tiles excavated from Bordesley Abbey, showing the changes in the West

Midlands tile industry over 300 years.

Terry O'Connor outlines the potential for animal bone studies when dealing with a specialised settlement type such as the monastery, a distinct economic unit with formalised use of space. In contrast to specialists dealing with other categories of material, O'Connor makes it clear that new data will be required in order to address this potential. A general paucity of animal bone has been noted for monastic sites even where bone has been targeted for sieving and sampling procedures. He discusses the economic relationships between a monastery and its town which may be gleaned through animal bones from certain sites, in particular Gilbertine York, where indications are that by the 15th–16th centuries the priory shared its source of meat supply with the town.

Stephen Moorhouse presents his own distinctive and innovative approach to finds research, emphasising the study of pottery and glass according to the original function to which vessels were put. Moorhouse makes extensive use of documents, medieval illustrations and archaeological data to provide vivid and novel insights into monastic life. He uses domestic accounts to suggest possible functions for vessels and inventories to link them to the use of particular rooms, in addition to the spatial plotting of particular forms recovered from excavation. He emphasises a study of the 'total assemblage', that is items of different materials employed interdependently.

James Bond contributes a paper on water management, a subject which he has made his own. This survey of urban sites complements an earlier paper on water management in rural monasteries (1989). Bond outlines the problems of survival and study in urban contexts, where a lack of large-scale, open-area excavation necessitates greater reliance on documents. Bond discusses early plans of water systems, provides definitions and descriptions of common features, explains technology, and presents a provisional catalogue of references to water supply in urban monasteries.

Together these papers present a wide range of views and approaches current in monastic archaeology, and from them may be drawn suggestions for future research. In addition lessons may be drawn from our omissions, in particular the lack of comparison with European monasticism (although papers are forthcoming on the Premonstratensians by James Bond, and the Carthusians by Mick Aston), and the absence of perspectives drawn from archaeological theory.

Acknowledgements

We would like to thank the University of York for their co- operation and hospitality, and the authors for their patience in awaiting a publication beset by production problems. Sebastian Rahtz deserves special thanks for rescuing the manuscript from a mainframe and producing camera-ready text for publication.

References

Bond, C J, 1989, Water management in the rural monastery, in Gilchrist and Mytum, eds, 83–112.

Coppack, G, 1990, *Abbeys and Priories*, London: Batsford, English Heritage.

Gilchrist, R and Mytum, H C, eds, 1989, *The Archaeology of Rural Monasteries*, Oxford: British Archaeological Report 203.

Gilchrist, R, 1992, All Christian Bodies and Souls: the archaeology of life and death in later medieval hospitals, in S Bassett and S Esmonde-Cleary eds, *Death in Towns, 100–1600*, Leicester University Press.

Gilchrist, R, 1993 forthcoming, *The Archaeology of Religious Women. Gender and Medieval Monasticism*, London: Routledge.

Greene, J P, 1992, *The Medieval Monastic House*, Leicester University Press.

Rawcliffe, C, 1984, The hospitals of later medieval London, *Medical History* 28, 1–28.

Rubin, M, 1987, *Charity and Community in Medieval Cambridge*, Cambridge University Press.

List of Contributors

C James Bond, 2 Stone Edge Batch, Tickenham, Clevedon, Avon

Lawrence Butler, Department of Archaeology, Micklegate House, University of York, Y01 1JZ

Patricia Cullum, Department of Historical and Critical Studies, University of Northumbria at Newcastle, Newcastle-upon-Tyne, NS1 8ST

Roberta Gilchrist, Centre of East Anglian Studies, University of East Anglia, Norwich, NR4 7TJ

Stephen Moorhouse, Deighton House, 8 Deighton Lane, Healey, Batley, WF1 78B

Harold Mytum, Department of Archaeology, Micklegate House, University of York, Y01 1JZ

T P O'Connor, Department of Archaeological Sciences, University of Bradford, Bradford, BD1 1DP

David Palliser, Department of History, University of Hull, Hull, HU6 7RX

John Schofield, Museum of London Archaeology Service, 1 London Wall, London, EC2Y 5HN

David Stocker, English Heritage, Fortress House, 23 Savile Row, London, W1X 2HE

Jenny Stopford, Centre for Medieval Studies, King's Manor, University of York, York, Y01 2EP

Simon Ward, Grosvenor Museum, 27 Grosvenor Street, Chester, CH1 2DD

1 The topography of monastic houses in Yorkshire towns

D M Palliser

1.1 Introduction

The subject of this brief survey is those medieval monastic houses in Yorkshire (within its pre-1974 boundaries) which can reasonably be described as urban or suburban. Yorkshire has been selected as the largest historic county in England, and my aim is to consider the relationship of houses to urban areas, and to some extent the internal layout or 'microtopography' of the houses. Monastic houses are taken, for convenience if not for accuracy, to include all 'houses of religion' in the medieval sense — houses of friars and of canons regular as well as of monks and nuns. I do not, however, include all 'minsters', which — though the term is a corruption of *monasterium* — meant often a secular collegiate church (e.g. York, Ripon, Beverley) or a mother church with rights antedating the parochial system. These minsters were often of considerable importance as generators of small towns (Blair 1988), and indeed some, like Beverley and Ripon, had been monastic in the strict sense before the Viking invasions.

Despite Yorkshire's size, its urban monasteries were not numerous outside the county town (Table 1.1). That might seem unexpected for a county of which its latest historian has written that 'Yorkshire's greatest medieval glory is its collection of monasteries' (Hey 1986, 57). However, the glory is that of *rural* houses, above all those of the Cistercians. Admittedly remote rural sites were less likely to be plundered for building materials after the Dissolutions, but the real reason is that there never were many urban houses, firstly because there were few towns and secondly because north of the Humber the great urban houses of the south — Benedictine monasteries founded before the Conquest — did not survive the Scandinavian invasions. Of sixty Benedictine monasteries which survived the Norman Conquest, forty 'may be considered urban', but not one of those was in Yorkshire (Butler 1987, 167).

Yet it is possible to exaggerate the lack of urbanisation in the shire. If many of its towns were small and of late foundation, three or four were among the great urban centres of medieval England. If we take the forty wealthiest and most populous communities taxed in 1334 and 1377 (Hoskins 1984, 277–8), they include five Yorkshire towns:

- York (3rd 1334, 2nd 1377)
- Beverley (16th and 11th)
- Hull (27th and 25th)
- Scarborough (28th and 31st)
- Pontefract (36th in 1377; not included 1334).

This ranking of towns by the Exchequer is closely paralleled by the numbers of friaries and hospitals in each town, if not by monasteries proper. Hospitals ought really to be considered first, since the great period of hospital foundations was the early 12th century, a hundred years before the friars, and 'a study of hospital-location can give clear information upon the extent of built-up areas and urban defence lines within the 12th century' (Butler 1987, 175). Dr Butler's league-table of urban complements of hospitals (somewhat higher than previously published figures) gives

York: 24 (just ahead of London's 23)
Hull: 12
Beverley: 10
Scarborough: 6
Pontefract: 5

The figures can be no more than approximations, since hospitals were more prone to disappear, or to exist in unrecorded obscurity, than other religious houses, but the order of urban procedence is not in doubt and is fully consistent with the respective size and wealth of the towns. Altogether hospitals are a good index of urbanisation since they were rarely founded in the countryside; of 90 Yorkshire hospitals listed in the *Victoria County History* survey, 72 were in towns (Hey 1986, 65). Their particularly urban nature can be seen in a 12th-century new town like Hedon; coming late on the urban scene it never acquired a monastery or nunnery, but it numbered at least four hospitals.

Friaries, those characteristic institutions of the 13th century, have long been seen, rightly, as an index of urbanisation (e.g. Reynolds 1977, 51, 63). If we count only the houses of the four main orders and ignore both the short-lived minor orders of the 13th-century (York had *six* friaries, if they are included) and other houses with a short life-span, we arrive at a league-table similar to that for hospitals:

York: 4 (one of only 10 English towns with the full complement)
Scarborough: 3
Beverley: 2
Hull: 2
Doncaster: 2

Friaries were more purely urban than hospitals; of the eighteen 'established' friaries of late medieval Yorkshire (those which endured to the Dissolution) all were located in towns.

Table 1.1 Medieval urban religious houses in Yorkshire (Short-lived houses excluded; some numbers are approximate)

Town	Monasteries	No of Friaries	No of Hospitals
Beverley	Hospitallers	2	10
Bridlington	Augustinian Priory	—	1
Doncaster	—	2	2
Hedon	—	—	4
Hull	Charterhouse	2	12
Knaresborough	Trinitarian Priory	—	—
Malton	(Gilbertine Priory outside town)	—	3
Northallerton	—	1	1
Pontefract	Cluniac Priory	1	5
Richmond	Benedictine Priory (cell to York)	1	1
Ripon	—	—	3
Scarborough	—	3	6
Selby	Benedictine Abbey	—	6
Tickhill	—	1	3
Yarm	—	1	1
York	Ben. abbey (St Mary); Ben. pr. (Holy Trinity), Ben. pr. for nuns (St Clement); Ben. cell (All Saints); Gilbertine pr; St Leonard's Hospital	4	24

1.2 The locations of houses

Monasteries proper, if founded after the Conquest in already existing towns, tended to be sited just outside the core or walled area. York (discussed separately below) is entirely typical: three of its four Benedictine houses, including even the wealthy and early foundation of St Mary's, had to find extramural sites, as did the Gilbertine priory. Holy Trinity priory was the one exception at York, and at Scarborough St Mary's was probably another, for the parish church, which may have been for a short period a Cistercian cell, lay within the defended area between castle and town (Pevsner 1966, 319; Butler 1987, 167). Otherwise the sites were suburban (Pontefract, Richmond, Hull) if not strictly extra-urban (Knaresborough). In the case of St Mary's, York, the suburban location made the abbey very exposed during the Scottish wars. A precinct wall begun in 1266 was not defensive, but in 1318 Edward II granted the monks licence to crenellate. The wall, which survives largely intact and has been fully surveyed (RCHM 1975, 14–22), has been justly called 'probably the most important monastic precinct-wall in England' (Morris 1924, 152).

Where, on the other hand, the monastery was the pre-urban nucleus and the town arose at its gates to service it, the physical relationship was naturally different. A textbook example is Selby, the earliest monastic foundation in the shire after the Conquest. It is clear that before the abbey's foundation c 1070 there was at most a hamlet or small village there, and 'it was only during the course of the 12th century and under the stimulus provided by the new foundation that it developed into a substantial Yorkshire town. According to the Poll Tax returns of 1379, Selby was then the fourth largest community in the West Riding' (Dobson 1969a, 21). The physical evidence is still there of a tight urban core surrounding the magnificent Romanesque church, with the market place to its west and the riverside quays to the north-east. There are no strictly pre-Conquest examples for the reason already given, but at Beverley — where the predecessor of the Minster was a monastery of c 700 — the town clearly developed northwards from its ecclesiastical nucleus in much the same way.

Whitby was the second earliest Yorkshire foundation after the Conquest, of 1077 or earlier. It also dominated the surrounding town, although Domesday Book implies that *Witebi* was already a settlement of some importance and lists separately, as one of its dependencies, a vill of *Prestebi* ('Priestby') which may or may not have signified the abbey site as opposed to the town; certainly the abbey was described as of 'Saints Peter and Hilda of Presteby and Whitby' at the end of the century (Davis 1913, no. 421). Another community which developed into a town under the stimulus of a monastery was Bridlington. Despite the dubious 'burgesses' of Domesday Book, there is no real evidence for urbanism before the priory was founded in or before 1113–14 (Brooks 1966, 25), and it seems clear that the town developed along the High Street from the surviving abbey gatehouse.

Locations of hospitals and friaries varied much more, not surprisingly since both sets of institutions had usually to be fitted into existing towns, though as they usually occupied smaller areas than monasteries they could sometimes squeeze into central sites. Beverley, Hull and York all possessed hospitals in the town centre as well as in the suburbs. Friaries often began in the suburbs, but some were able to move later to more central locations as a result of generous benefactions. This was the case, as will be seen, with the Carmelites at York.

1.2.1 A case-study : York

The shire town not only had a considerable complement of religious houses but has also been subject to recent archaeological investigation which is starting to match its rich documentation. It may therefore justify a separate consideration of house locations (Fig 1.1); the 'microtopography' of their internal layout is considered below alongside those of other Yorkshire houses.

4

York was already a large and densely-packed city by 1066, as Domesday Book and the evidence of recent excavations testify. Whether or not the city was as severely devastated in 1069 as the chronicles allege is doubtful (Palliser 1990, 4, 18, 19), and certainly it would appear from the topographical evidence that the revived Northern monasticism of c 1070 onwards could find little intramural space for new foundations. The one apparent exception (apparent because there is as yet no proof that the Micklegate area was defended before the Conquest) was Holy Trinity Priory, founded by Ralph Paynel in 1089. The explanation is that there was continuity on the site from before the Conquest: Paynel was taking over and adapting to the Benedictine rule Christ Church, an ill-recorded but wealthy college of secular canons, which figures in Domesday Book. This Christ Church in turn may have occupied the site of the lost 8th century archiepiscopal monastery of Alma Sophia (Morris 1986). The only other major religious institution in York with apparent continuity of location from the pre-Conquest period was the cathedral or Minster — apparent only, because the extensive excavations of 1967–72 located no pre-Conquest church although they did reveal a cemetery. The Minster, however, remained a college of secular canons, and was not transformed into a monastic cathedral like Canterbury or Worcester.

The other York monasteries were located in the suburbs except for St Leonard's hospital, which counts as a monastery proper rather than an ordinary hospital, and which is described elsewhere in this volume by Pat Cullum. All, interestingly, seem to have begun with the gift of a pre-existing church, probably parochial, which was made the focus of a monastic and extra-parochial precinct. St Mary's was a foundation of 1086 or earlier in the precinct of *Galmou* or Earlsborough, possibly the site of the palace of the Anglo-Scandinavian earls, and certainly the location of the church of St Olave (Olaf) which Earl Siward had founded and where he was buried in 1055. The church of All Saints, Fishergate, was granted to Whitby abbey, probably in the 1090s, for the construction of an abbey, though it seems to have become simply a cell dependent on Whitby. Clementhorpe, a Benedictine nunnery founded c 1130, may or may not have taken over an existing church of St Clement; excavation in 1976–77 located 'a massive structure of pre-Conquest date' which 'could conceivably have been a church' (Dobson and Donaghey 1984, 5, 8). The Gilbertine priory in Fishergate is a less ambiguous case: it was founded c 1200 with the gift of an existing church of St Andrew.

Alongside the five monasteries in the city (six if St Leonard's is included) were numerous properties belonging to other Northern monasteries. By 1290 at least fifty-one Northern houses had established hospices or acquired other properties in York (Rees-Jones 1987, I 137, 179–80). They were usually located 'near the periphery of the built-up area' in districts convenient for travellers coming from another house — around Monk Bar for east Yorkshire houses, and Micklegate Bar for West Riding and Lancashire houses. Since, however, they occupied more modest plots than monasteries, there was no problem in locating them within the walls, including riverside sites for access by water (Rees-Jones I, 163–7). In 1986–92 it has at last proved possible to identify and investigate one such property, the town house of Nostell priory off Stonegate, which had survived unrecognised within late buildings. Its restoration as 'Barley Hall' has revealed a three-storey timber-framed range of c 1360 at right angles to the street, as well as a second range rebuilt in the 15th century; it may well be the only monastic town house surviving in England.

Of the two dozen or more hospitals in the city very little is known, even in many cases their exact locations. Leaving aside the two with partly surviving fabrics (St Leonard's, and the Holy Trinity hospital in the basement of the Merchants' Hall), the only site recently identified and explored has been that of St Mary's in the Horsefair, a modest suburban house (Fig 1.1). It was founded in 1314 on a disused site which had been the first home of the Carmelite friars (c 1253–95), but the first phase represented what may have been an ecclesiastical building of the late 12th or early 13th century, though the dating evidence is uncertain (Richards et al 1989 13–15). If that is correct, then there might have been a sequence of an unrecorded hospital/church taken over as a friary and then refounded as a hospital.

The sites of the friaries themselves are better known, though opportunities have not yet allowed for much archaeological investigation. The problem for the friars lay in finding sites of adequate size in a central location, and only major landowners could help. The two greatest orders, indeed, succeeded only because of the patronage of the King himself. The Dominicans appear to have been initially content, judging from newly-published evidence, with a modest gift of housing in Goodramgate in the early 1220s (Hall et al 1988, 55, 62), but in 1227 Henry III granted them the 'King's Tofts', a royal free chapel and possible former palace (Palliser 1984, 103). The Franciscans settled on an unlocated York site c 1230, until in 1243 Henry granted them too a central site in his possession, adjacent to the castle. Indeed, one early reference suggests that the site granted was a *bailey*, and the location and shape of the Franciscan precinct as it endured until 1538 is perfectly consistent with that. Henry began rebuilding the castle in stone in 1244, and it would have been an appropriate time to reduce a sprawling earth-and-timber castle of motte and two baileys to that of a keep and one bailey.

The Carmelite friars, as already noted, first settled in the extramural Horsefair by 1253. But in 1295 the gift of a local landowner, William de Vescy, allowed them to move to a central site near Foss Bridge. The map (Fig 1.1) indicates a site of surprisingly large size for a private benefaction at such a date, but the area had been a very marshy one from which the King's Fishpond was slowly retreating in the later middle ages, and much of it may not have been suitable for building before the 13th century. The last of the four main orders, the Augustinians, are not recorded at York before 1272, and they may have occupied their modest two acre site off Lendal from the start. Finally, York briefly possessed houses of two of the short-lived minor orders of friars, the Crutched Friars on

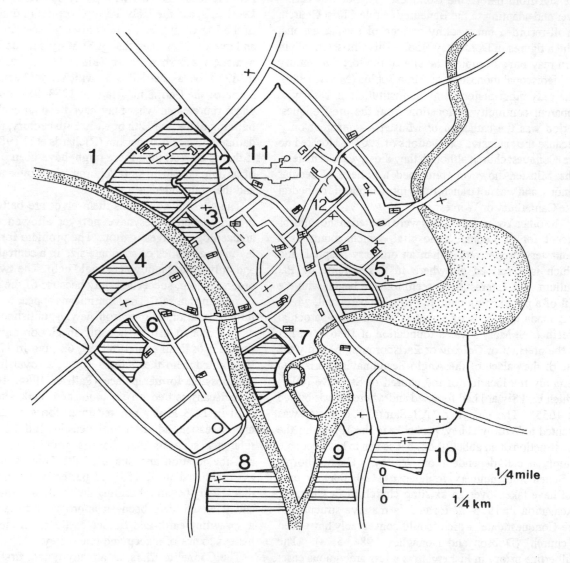

Figure 1.1

a site not yet located, and the Friars of the Sack in Spen Lane.

1.3   Microtopography and the archaeologist

Finally, to return to a consideration of urban houses in the county as a whole, we might enquire how far archaeology, coupled with documentary research, can elucidate their precise location and internal layout.   Documents are in fact remarkably uninformative on the disposition of monastic buildings in the majority of cases, and the best approach is normally to identify the site from either documents or surviving ruins, and then to rely on excavation alone for the plan.

One critical type of evidence, surviving buildings or ruins, depends very much on what happened to the various sites during and after the Dissolutions of 1536–40.   Post-Dissolution ownership and land use, on which documentation is usually informative, decided whether the house was permitted to survive in whole or in part, whether it was demolished but the site left vacant (and therefore archaeologically available), or whether it was built over. Naturally, given the pressures on urban land, fewer vacant sites survived than in the countryside, but there are more partially preserved urban sites than might be expected.

Hospitals sometimes survived in modified form: in York, for example, Holy Trinity Fossgate still survives structurally as the basement of the 14th-century Merchant Adventurers' Hall, while the equivalent hospital of the Merchant Taylors' in Aldwark was rebuilt in 1729–30, apparently on its medieval site (Magilton 1980, 4–5). *Friaries*, in contrast, almost always disappeared rapidly to make way for housing, though their sites can nearly always be located.   The partial exceptions are the Richmond Greyfriars, perhaps not a prime site because of its suburban location, and the Beverley Blackfriars, though the latter is a dubious exception: the surviving building was identified by MacMahon as a dormitory/library block of 1449, but it has now been dated to the 16th century, and may be post-Dissolution (Miller *et al.*1982, 49, 51; Armstrong and Tomlinson 1987, 55–7).

The greater *monastic* sites have had more varied experiences. At Bridlington, Malton, Selby and York Holy Trinity, part or all of the church was retained for parish use, though the other monastic buildings were largely swept away. Pontefract priory, by contrast, was thoroughly demolished for its materials, while York St Mary's is an intermediate case, with much of the church and the monastic buildings surviving in ruins or at least as foundations. The reason there was the unusual retention of the site by the Crown (until as late as 1827), and its use from 1539 to 1641 by the King's Council in the Northern Parts. The abbot's house (the present King's Manor) was retained and extended for that purpose, and renovations started in 1988 have enabled Christopher Norton to undertake an extensive fabric survey which will, when published, substantially modify the standard accounts of that complex building (RCHM 1975, 30–43; Colvin 1982, 355–64). Equally interesting is that a large part of the nave of the church remained standing until the 17th century, as early views testify (e.g. Whittingham 1972, pl. 17; RCHM 1975, pl. 4), and it is possible that the church itself may have been converted for the Council's use.

St Mary's, however, with its extensive survival of plan and foundations and with several published interpretations, is exceptional. More common is the situation where little or nothing survives above ground and where excavated evidence is crucial. The splendid example of the York Gilbertines demonstrated how much of successive phase-plans can be recovered from a previously little-known house even though it had become a factory site in the last century, with all the disturbance that implies. The same is true of Beverley Blackfriars, where again a good deal of stratification mercifully survived modern industrial occupation, and which has been archaeologically examined insofar as limited time and resources allowed (Armstrong and Tomlinson 1987; Foreman Forthcoming).

Clearly, however, open sites hold more hope of intact evidence, and more of them survive, even in towns, than might be expected. Parts of York St Mary's come into this category, despite the building of the Yorkshire Museum on part of the site, as do parts of the precinct of York Holy Trinity, a site retained as a town house and extensive garden until the 1850s. At Pontefract the priory site has remained an open space since the Dissolution, so that the excavations of 1957–72 were able to establish the plan of the church and most of the claustral buildings (Bellamy 1965). This has been an important achievement, because the priory was really the equivalent of a major abbey, the only Cluniac house in northern England, and one of only nine Cluniac houses valued at over £200 in 1535. At all of these three houses more excavation could still be done with valuable results; for the other urban monasteries the case is even stronger.   Rahtz's paper at the 1988 B.A.A. Conference (Rahtz, forthcoming) was a major re-interpretation of excavations of the pre-Viking monastery at Whitby, but it suggests that re-excavation would be helpful. Malton's plan was established by excavation in the early 19th century (as at York St Mary's), but nothing has since been carried out except trial trenching in 1942 (Robinson 1978, 32).   At Bridlington the churchyard preserves the site of the chancel and crossing east of the surviving nave, recorded soon after the Dissolution but not excavated except as part of a 19th-century clearance for burials (VCH 1974, 45). Similarly the churchyard of Selby and the entire site at Knaresborough would appear to be undamaged.

Friaries and *hospitals* represent an even greater challenge than monasteries proper, since so few have been even partially excavated. The one hospital site so far excavated by York Archaeological Trust has shed considerable light on a friary *and* hospital site which was previously very little known (Richards *et al.*1989) A conference on urban friaries was held at York in 1980, when a major excavation of the York Franciscans seemed possible, but in the event little has been possible there except the important confirmation that the friary took over one of the two castle baileys. Indeed, little is known of even the plan of any of the York friaries, and yet their national importance as a group can hardly be exaggerated. Butler has reminded us that 'the 20 houses (of friars) where the provincial chapters were held are likely to be the most substantial and most fully developed. . .where these sites are available a strong case for their excavations could be made out' (Butler 1984, 126, 129): and those twenty key friaries include *all four* York houses. No other English town except Oxford—not even London—is represented in Butler's list by all four of its friaries.

The only substantial excavations of any Yorkshire friary so far are those at Beverley Blackfriars (Armstrong and Tomlinson 1987; Foreman Forthcoming). The fact that Foreman's excavations of 1986–7 unearthed a previously unsuspected second cloister is a reminder that layouts needs to be established and not assumed, whether one is considering a well-known order which may have had a standard plan, or even more so when considering a little-known order like the Order of St Gilbert of Sempringham. At York's Gilbertine priory, it was possible to show that a fairly conventional layout of claustral buildings was established after the foundation in 1202, but that after only a century the chancel of the church, together with the chapter house, was demolished and not replaced (Y.A.T. 1987–8, 25). For 'it is because so many writers have failed to distinguish between century and century and between order and order that almost all the general descriptions of medieval monastic life lack definition, and often also historical accuracy and perspective' (Knowles 1963, xix).

Acknowledgements

I am grateful to Dr Sarah Rees-Jones, for generously allowing me to cite her unpublished thesis, and to the Department of Archaeology at the University of York for rendering my manuscript printable.

Appendix: The dates of the earliest post-conquest houses

Though this paper has been concerned with topography rather than chronology, it became clear in citing dates of foundation that firm evidence was very sketchy for the earliest houses, and that traditional and even demonstrably inaccurate dates were sometimes repeated in standard works. The two most relevant to this paper are Selby and St Mary's, York and these are discussed below.

SELBY The traditional account dates its foundation to 1069, an event commemorated by the Selby Festival of 1969, but it is based on the partly legendary *Historia Selebeiensis Monasterii*. It is not possible to be more precise than 1069–70 (Knowles and Hadcock 1971, 57, 76; Dobson 1969b, 169–70).

YORK: ST MARY'S The traditional date of foundation, 1088 — celebrated in 1988 — is misleading. It is based

on another chronicle tradition, but the earliest charter, of William II, is not more closely datable than 1088–89 and is in any case spurious, though an apparently genuine charter by the same King does show that the abbey had been 'built' by 1093 (Davis 1913, nos. 313, 338; Farrer 1914, no. 350). In any case the 1088–89 charter, if based on genuine tradition, can relate only to a *re-foundation*. Knowles (1963, 170) wrote of a group of monks from Whitby founding St Mary's '*c* 1088', but that takes no account of the presence of the 'Abbot of York' *(Abbatis de Eboraco)* in Domesday Book (fol. 298v). The solution Knowles came to in collaboration with Hadcock (1971, 58, 82) was to start with an Abbey of St Olave founded by 1086 and succeeded by a new Abbey of St Mary's in 1088–89.

References

Addyman, P V and Black, V E (eds), 1984, *Archaeological Papers from York presented to M W. Barley*. York: York Archaeological Trust.

Armstrong, P, and Tomlinson, D G, 1987, *Excavations at the Dominican Priory, Beverley, 1960–1983*, Hull: Humberside County Council (Humberside Heritage Publication No. 13).

Bellamy, C V, 1965, *Pontefract priory Excavations 1957–61*. Leeds: Thoresby Society **49**.

Blair, J, 1988, Minster churches in the landscape, In D Hooke (ed) *Anglo-Saxon Settlements*, 35–38. Oxford: Basil Blackwell.

Brooks, F W, 1966, *Domesday Book and the East Riding*, East Yorks Loc Hist Soc (East Yorks Loc Hist Ser **21**).

Butler, L A S, 1984, The houses of the Mendicant orders in Britain: Recent Archaeological work, in Addyman and Black 1984, 123–36.

Butler, L A S, 1987, Medieval Urban Religious Houses, In J Schofield and R Leech (eds) *Urban Archaeology in Britain*, 167–76. CBA Research Report **61**. London: CBA.

Colvin, H M, 1982, *The History of the King's Works: Volume IV: 1485–1660 (part II)*. London: HMSO.

Davis, H W C, 1913, *Regesta Regum Anglo-Normannorum 1066–1154: Volume I, 1066–1100*, Davis, H W C (ed), Oxford: Clarendon Press.

Dobson, R B, 1969a, *Selby Abbey and Town: a Book Commemorating the 1969 Festival*. Selby: Selby Abbey Church Council.

Dobson, R B, 1969b, The first Norman Abbey in Northern England. *The Ampleforth* **74**, 161–76.

Dobson, R B, and Donaghey, S, 1984, *The history of Clementhorpe Nunnery*, London: C.B.A. for YAT (Fascicule AY 2/1).

Foreman, M, forthcoming, *Further Excavations at the Dominican Priory, Beverley, 1986–89*.

Hall, R A, *et al.* 1988, *Medieval tenements in Aldwark, and other sites*, London: CBA for YAT (Fascicule AY 10/2).

Hey, D, 1986, *Yorkshire from AD 1000*, London: Longman.

Hoskins, W G, 1984, *Local History in England*, 3rd edition. London: Longman.

Knowles, D, 1963, *The monastic order in England. . .940–1216*, 2nd edition. Cambridge: University Press.

Knowles, D, and Hadcock, R N, 1971, *Medieval religious houses: England and Wales*, 2nd edition.   London: Longman.

Magilton, J R, 1980,*The church of St Helen-on-the-walls, Aldwark*, London: CBA for YAT (Fascicule AY 10/1).

Miller, K, *et al*, 1982, *Beverley: an archaeological and architectural study*. London: HMSO (RCHM supplementary series 4).

Morris, J E, 1924, *York* (Little Guide Series).   London: Methuen.

Morris, R K, 1986, Alcuin, York, and the Alma Sophia. In L A S Butler and RK Morris (eds) *The Anglo-Saxon Church*, 80–89. CBA Research Report 60 London: CBA.

Palliser, D M, 1984, York's west bank: medieval suburb or urban Nucleus? in Addyman and Black 1984, 101–108.

Palliser, D M, 1990, *Domesday York*. Borthwick Paper **78**. York: Borthwick Institute, University of York.

Pevsner, N, 1966, *The buildings of England: Yorkshire: the North Riding*, Harmondsworth: Penguin.

Rahtz, P A, forthcoming, Excavations at Whitby Abbey. In Proceedings of the British Archaeological Association Conference 1988.

RCHM, 1975, *An inventory of the historical monuments in the city of York: Volume IV: outside the city walls east of the Ouse*, London: HMSO.

Rees-Jones, S R, 1987, *The Topography and Tenemental History of Medieval York*. Unpublished D Phil thesis, University of York.

Reynolds, S, 1977, *An introduction to the history of English medieval towns*. Oxford: Clarendon.

Richards, J D *et al.*, 1989, *Union Terrace; Excavations in the Horsefair*, London: CBA for YAT (Fascicule AY 11/1).

Robinson, J F, 1978, *The archaeology of Malton and Norton*. Leeds: Yorkshire Archaeological Society.

VCH, 1913, *The Victoria History of the County of York 3*. London: Constable.

VCH, 1974, *The Victoria History of the County of York: East Riding 2*. London: Oxford University Press.

Whittingham, A B, 1972, St Mary's Abbey, York: an Interpretation of its plan. *Archaeol J*, **128**, 118–46.

YAT, 1987–88, York Archaeological Trust, *Annual Report 1987–88*, York: York Archaeological Trust.

2 St. Leonard's Hospital, York: the spatial and social analysis of an Augustinian hospital

P H Cullum

2.1 Introduction

When I visited the exhibition on the *Yorkshire Monasteries* held at the Yorkshire Museum in the summer of 1988, while enjoying the visit and finding much that was new to me, I was disappointed to discover no reference to hospitals anywhere in the exhibition; the absence of St Leonard's Hospital from the display was misjudged. Even at the Dissolution, when much of its glory had passed away, St Leonard's still stood second in value among York houses only to the great St Mary's Abbey which was its neighbour. At just over £300 it was more valuable than Holy Trinity, Micklegate, St Clement's nunnery, and St Andrew's, Fishergate, put together (VCH 1913, 343, 390, 130, 256). Judging by the number of inmates, over 200 for much of the 13th and 14th century, it was possibly the largest hospital in the country, certainly the largest outside London. It was staffed by religious, both male and female, who lived by the Augustinian Rule. The hospital enjoyed the usual privileges of religious status, had a Liberty and occupied a large, and fairly well-defined site within the walls, by 1100. Under the circumstances the omission of St Leonard's from the ranks of York's religious houses is a serious misrepresentation of the monastic presence in York, and a restricted view of the religious diversity of the city.

In this paper we shall examine the diversity of hospital types, before moving on to a specific examination of St Leonard's, York. Confusion about the status of hospitals is not entirely surprising, for they are an extremely diverse group of institutions, and not many can be strictly defined as monastic, in the sense of living by a Rule. Hospitals are probably more variable in size, date, architecture and intended inhabitants than any other form of religious house. Though St. Leonard's was in many ways no different from any substantial monastery, with the exception that it had a major charitable function, it was also in that sense very rare, few hospitals even approached the same size. Most were fairly small, taking a dozen or twenty inhabitants, sometimes fewer. The form they took varied too with date, though until the 13th or early 14th century, and in some cases even later, most imitated either the monastic plan (if large enough) or more commonly simply that of a church, with a chapel at the east end, and the inhabitants living in the 'nave' with ancillary buildings if required, nearby (Clay 1909, 112–15). Leper hospitals probably consisted of small groups of cells clustered around a church or chapel (Clay 1909, 35, 17–19). Later hospitals had other models: wealthier patrons preferred to build on the collegiate plan, as at the almshouse of Noble Poverty attached to the older monastic style, St Cross, at Winchester

(Clay 1909, plate VIII). Guilds built hospitals in the undercrofts of their guildhalls, as with the guild of the Blessed Virgin Mary and Jesus Christ, known as the Trinity, now the Merchant Adventurers Hall, in York. In lesser style individuals might leave their own house, or at least one of their properties, to be used as a home for the poor. Known usually as a maisondieu, these would probably be indistinguishable from ordinary dwelling houses, though perhaps of the better sort. It was not just domestic buildings which might be converted to the use of a hospital: in 1316 the hospital of St Mary in the Horsefair in York was established in the buildings which the Carmelite friars had abandoned upon establishing themselves on a new site by the King's Fishpond (Richards 1989, 6).

Only in the larger hospitals was a Rule generally adhered to, usually, though far from invariably, the Augustinian. Relatively few hospitals were as completely independent as St Leonard's. This was a situation which developed through the 12th and early 13th century as the hospital grew away from York Minster on which it had originally been dependent. A similar development can be seen in the history of St Bartholomew's, London, which was originally dependent upon an Augustinian priory. Many were dependent upon monastic or collegiate churches, or upon town councils, as at Scarborough even from an early date (*Yorks. Inq. III*, 88–90). Where hospitals were dependent upon another monastic house, as was not uncommon in foundations of the 12th and 13th century, if they kept a Rule it would generally be that of the mother-house. Moreover, although the religious — the brothers and/or sisters of the house who cared for the inmates — might be expected to live by some kind of Rule, at least in older foundations, practice varied as to whether the inmates themselves would be expected to adhere to it. On the whole, they would probably not be so expected, though they would be expected to pray: for themselves, for the patrons and founders of the hospital who were their benefactors, and for intercession. In leperhouses, however, it seems to have been more common to expect the lepers to abide by the Rule of the house, with expulsion the punishment for refractory behaviour. Although it was usual for the master or keeper of the hospital to be a cleric, and if a regular, to keep his Rule, it was not unknown for masters to be seculars. At St Leonard's it was explicitly stated in 1245 that the former master had been a layman, and that if another layman were to be appointed he should, like the late master, Hugh, wear the habit of the hospital and live chastely and without property (*H.C.Y. III*, 159). In hospitals of later foundation the master was more likely to be a secular priest, and the following of a Rule less likely to be prescribed though certain prayers, or prayers at certain times of day for both master and inmates, might be required by the patron or founder. All hospitals except the very smallest of the maisonsdieu had a chapel of some form.

The great variety in date, size, Rule, or no Rule, and indeed the different groups of people for whom the hospitals were intended to cater — mostly the poor and infirm, but also the sick, lepers, lunatics, the aged, travellers and children — combine to make it impossible to give any general description of what the layout of a medieval hospital might be expected to be. For those wishing to pursue the subject the best available work is W H Godfrey's, *The English Almshouse*, which contains the groundplans of a large number of medieval and later hospitals. Most of these are of institutions which have survived the centuries and are still operating, sometimes in their original buildings, sometimes in modern buildings on the original site, where something of the original groundplan can be discerned. While these groundplans are very valuable for the main buildings, they are less useful for ancillary buildings which may not have survived so well. There is also the problem that where the hospital has been rebuilt on the old site, as for example at St John's, Canterbury, or the three medieval hospitals of Ripon, the new buildings may have hidden or even obliterated important information about the original buildings. While hospitals, with the exception of the maisonsdieu, tended not to be built in the centres of towns, they were largely dependent upon towns, both as sources of alms and of inmates. Most medieval hospitals were probably suburban, in the sense that often they stood immediately outside the gates of the town, as did the hospital outside the North Bar of Beverley, St Thomas outside Micklegate Bar in York, or St Wulfstan's outside Worcester. Leper hospitals usually stood at some greater distance, on the town or city boundary, which usually ran some way beyond the town walls. Nevertheless, hospitals were usually erected in close proximity to a medieval town, and where they did not survive the Reformation, their sites have often been built over in subsequent urban expansion. This last has been the fate of St Leonard's, though in a less final way than most, and some substantial features do still remain. However, the building of a Georgian crescent through the middle of the site, with a theatre on one side and the city library on the other does not make it easier to interpret what is left, or to hold out hope that there would be anything left for archaeologists to find or interpret. Nevertheless considering the relative frequency with which hospitals were located close to town gates it would be worth keeping an eye out for structures which might be so interpreted when excavating in these areas, particularly on the rare occasions when such an excavation can be made over a large area.

Some use can also be made of antiquarian maps, plans, views of towns, and of engravings and paintings of hospital buildings which have now disappeared. However, a certain amount of care has to be taken here, as maps are not always as helpful as they might be, and engravings and paintings may have been 'romanticised' out of all recognition. In particular we should beware of using maps such as those of Speed and Hollar as accurate representations of buildings, as they may have been intended to be symbolic rather than realistic. Also where such pictures depict still viable institutions the buildings they show may be in part post-Dissolution, may have had radical alterations in their use since the medieval period, or, more commonly, reveal only a partial impression of the medieval buildings, as in the intervening years major parts of the original structure had disappeared through neglect or lack of use. Moreover, antiquaries often did not really understand what they were looking at, which leads to certain problems of interpretation, particularly when all we have is a written rather than a pictorial source. For this witness the frequent reference in Halfpenny, or Sheahan and Whellan to the 'cloisters' of St Peter's or St Leonard's hospital, which would lead to the assumption that rather more of the hospital survived in the early 19th century. It may have done, but it is clear from Halfpenny's engravings in *Fragmenta Vetusta* that what he, and the others were actually writing about were the undercrofts of the two major portions of St Leonard's which are still in existence (Sheahan and Whellan, 1855, 473; Halfpenny 1807, pls. 16, 17). More useful, though only for buildings which have disappeared in the last 140 years, are photographic records. The best idea of how St Thomas hospital outside Micklegate Bar looked is shown in a photograph taken in *c* 1861 just before the building was demolished. Despite being an end-on view and therefore giving no idea of the depth, internal arrangement, or groundplan, the photograph does give the elevation of the street frontage, which would be unlikely to be recovered by archaeology.

We have seen that the form that hospitals were likely to take changed over the centuries, from a monastic or church type, to a collegiate or domestic model. It is likewise probable that older hospitals, like St Leonard's, which was established upon its final site sometime around 1090–1098, also adapted their form over the centuries. Excavation has shown that on many monastic sites, events such as the disappearance of *conversi* after the Black Death led to the abandonment or conversion to alternate use of the laybrothers' quarters, and sometimes the abandonment of parts of the church. Reduction in the size of the community, a tendency for the head of the house to move into independent lodgings, and the relaxations of rules such as eating communally, and the increasing inclusion of meat into the ordinary diet, may all leave traces in the changing architecture of a site, and is likely that similar changes occurred at St Leonard's and other hospitals. In the case of St Leonard's these changes might reflect changing practices in the care of the inmates, the economic fortunes of the hospital, and the increased presence of lay people in the precinct (see below for examples).

Having examined some of the problems of looking at hospitals, let us look in a little more detail at the Rule most commonly adopted by those running hospitals — the Augustinian. The Augustinian, or Austin, Rule was introduced into this country during the reign of Henry I and proved to be popular with a wide variety of patrons wishing to found a religious house. Apart from being the subject of a number of new foundations the Rule was also adopted by a number of pre-existing houses of secular canons which wished to comply with the reforming party in the church which was exerting pressure on houses of secular priests to accept a regular life. It was in this second way that the Austin Rule was adopted at St Leonard's. The hospital was in existence before the Rule was introduced into this country, and those who served it would have been secular priests like the canons of York Minster, of which the hospital was then a dependency. The date at which St Leonard's adopted the Augustinian Rule is unclear, though the period of Archbishop Thurstan (1114–1140) seems to be likely, when the hospital was becoming more independent of the Minster. Thurstan was certainly a proponent of the Austin Rule, and the hospitals of St Gregory, Canterbury, and St Bartholomew, Smithfield in London, which also lived by the Austin rule, date from this period (Nicholl, 1964, 127–29). The Augustinian Rule was based upon a letter of St Augustine of Hippo, in which he advised upon a way of life for a group of women living in community. Like the Benedictine Rule, the Austin did not constitute an order with unified practice from house to house, but each house was autonomous and made its own interpretation of the Rule and its own customs. Like the Benedictines, after 1216 the Austins were organised into a congregation, when heads of houses were expected to meet on regular quadrennial basis. However, not all houses became affiliated to the congregation, so that practice remained diverse. St Leonard's was one of those houses which apparently did not affiliate.

Some of the houses which followed the Austin rule did form themselves into distinct Orders where practice was more uniform: these were monasteries which had been founded respectively by mother houses at Arrouaise, St Victor in Paris, and Premontré, only the last made any impact in this country. The Premonstratensians had a number of houses, but they were influenced by the Cistercians, and were more likely to choose isolated sites than most Austin houses. Nevertheless they did sometimes take on parochial responsibilities, as at Easby, but were less likely to care for hospitals. The Gilbertine order used different rules for different sections of its community, but the canons lived by the Austin rule, and where they did not have a community of nuns to minister to, sometimes took on hospitals, such as the three supervised by Malton (VCH 1913, 314–15). The sisters of the order too, though living by the Benedictine rule, were also involved in caring for hospitals, as the two in Lincoln (Clay 1909, 26).

The tendency of houses living by the Rule to become responsible for hospitals, and more commonly for parish churches, resulted from the comparative laxity of the rule. Austins were required to make the usual vows of poverty, chastity and obedience, but their time and their movements were less circumscribed than that of most monastics; their offices were shorter so that they spent less time in church at their services. They did not do manual labour and they had greater freedom of movement which allowed them out of the cloister. They also had a less restricted diet, being permitted meat, unlike monks; and there was greater freedom of

conversation (Dickinson 1950, 172–94). Despite this laxness Austin houses followed the monastic round and needed the same range of buildings as a monastery. Perhaps because they had borrowed much in the way of customs from the Benedictines, perhaps because it was the most logical arrangement, most Austin houses used the basic Benedictine groundplan of church and cloister, and where they departed from this it was more likely to be because of the constraints of the particular site than for any other reason. Whether this arrangement was also used in houses which were also hospitals is less certain, though it seems likely that in these cases that an enlarged infirmary range, or a hospital building or complex, would be found in addition to the usual claustral range. At St Bartholomew's, Smithfield the hospital house was separate from the church (Clay 1909, 106).

The relative looseness of the Rule meant that it was particularly suitable for a community which had duties other than the simple round of the *Opus Dei* — or to look at it another way, they were free to take up responsibilities in addition to the usual monastic ones. In addition, where houses adopted the Rule at some time after their foundation, having formerly been communities of secular canons, these communities continued to provide pastoral responsibilities for a local parish or parishes. Some of the new houses, too, were established in what had been parish churches of which the founder had the advowson. In the ecclesiastical climate of the 12th century he or she might have found it increasingly difficult to put this to good use themselves. Parish churches provided a sufficient income for communities of Austins, because as canons, they were not required to have the full canonical number of thirteen members, as monasteries were, and many houses were never intended to have more than half a dozen canons. If the canons were given a parish church as the focus of their foundation, they would provide for the parishioners either by giving over part of the nave to the laity or by building a separate parish church in the shadow of their own collegiate church. At St Giles-in-the-Field, London, the lepers had the west end of the southern half of the church, while the parishioners had the northern half (Clay 1909, plate XII). At Dorchester abbey the parishioners had the south aisle of the nave, the canons' cloister being to the north of the church, and at Easby the parish church lies to the south of the main monastic buildings but within the precinct (Cook 1961, 187). If the house had been endowed with a number of parishes, individual canons would be dispatched to minister to each of the parishes, returning home at night if possible. At Healaugh Park the canons deputed one of their number to serve the hospital of St Nicholas, Yarm, which had been given into their care (VCH 1913, 335–6).

Some Austin houses were specifically established to support almshouses or hospitals, as at Malton or Ellerton. In the latter case repeated archiepiscopal strictures in the 15th century that the house should maintain the hospital as required by its foundation document, suggests that this part of the establishment was neglected in later years. Elsewhere Austin houses might be given hospitals to administer, as Yarm was given to Healaugh priory by its founder, or might establish hospitals of their own as part of their wider pastoral responsibilities. One example is St Mary Overie in London which established the hospital which was later known as St Thomas, Southwark (Cook 1961, 179). Austins took on hospitals, or hospitals adopted the Austin Rule, because of the flexibility of the Rule, and because hospital care was seen as an extension of their already established work in parishes.

Moreover it is clear from the customal of Barnwell priory, an Augustinian house in Cambridgeshire, that the work of the Almoner was important. He ran an almonry in which a few poor people were supported, as well as giving alms at the gate, and it was part of his duties to go out of the house in order to visit the sick, infirm, blind and bedridden of the locality. Although, as we have seen, there was no uniformity of custom, as opposed to rule, among the Austins, the customal of Barnwell has generally been regarded as being fairly representative of Austin behaviour (Clark 1897, 172–79). Most Austin houses, then, would have expected to have at least a small almonry. The taking on of a hospital, either of their own volition or as a result of a gift, would simply be an extension in scale of their work, rather than a change.

2.2 St Leonard's

Let us now turn to the Rule as it was observed at St Leonard's. The hospital had originally been a part of York Minster's establishment, which was why it was known until the late 12th or early 13th-century as St Peter's hospital, and it claimed to have been founded by Athelstan in 936. By the 1090s, when its work had probably been considerably enlarged by the results of William the Conqueror's Ravaging of the North in 1069, and rebuilding of the Minster required additional space, the hospital was relocated on land donated by William II, the site on which it remained until the Dissolution (VCH 1913, 336). At this date the brothers looking after the inmates were probably secular priests like those of the Minster. Nothing of the early buildings into which they moved is known except that they were destroyed by the disastrous fire of 1137 which burnt so much of York (Nicholl 1964, 217–18). The grant by Henry I of rights to collect wood in the forest of Galtres for, amongst other purposes, building, might suggest that the early housing was of wood, but is not conclusive (E.Y.C. I, no.167, 142). After the fire the *Historia Fundationis* says that King Stephen built the hospital a new church which he dedicated to St Leonard, and that after the date the hospital was known as St Leonard's, although charters show that the new name was not widely adopted until the later 12th century (VCH 1913, 336). This church was described as being 'in the high street adjoining the hospital' (C.P.R. *1334–38*, 267). If the brothers had adopted the Austin Rule by the date of the fire, or at least by the rebuilding of the church, it is likely that they would have at this time have had the usual Austin cloister built beside it (although this is not specifically mentioned). It is possible that at first the new church of the hospital was used to house the inmates. This was usual practice in hospitals of the church type, where the nave was where the infirm lived, and the chancel where the priests ministered, so that the inmates could take part in the services from their beds. Without knowing the original size of the church or the number of poor that the hospital was supporting in the mid 12th century, it is impossible to know whether this is likely. However by 1220–1255 the inmates were definitely in a separate infirmary, donated to them by John Romanus, the treasurer of the Minster, in which the men and women were housed separately (H.C.Y. II, 409).

Strictly speaking we have for St Leonard's not a Rule but an Ordination and a set of precepts and provisions, both dating from the last quarter of the 13th century, and the report from a visitation of 1364. The first of these was the result of visitation by the Dean and Chapter of the Minster and dates to 1276/7. Although it makes clear that the full complement of staff of the hospital was present by this date: a master, at least thirteen brethren, lay brothers, eight sisters, a number of clerks, and the inmates who are called 'pauperes Christi', it gives no information which could lead to any deductions about the layout of the hospital (H.Y.C. III, 200–03).

The precepts and provision made in 1294 by Walter de Langton, newly appointed master of the hospital, are of more use for working out something of the topography of the house. All the brothers who were chaplains and literate, were to have their own seat and carrel or desk in the cloister. All the chaplain-brothers were to rise for Matins together and to be present at all the hours. After the morning hours at least four chaplain-brothers as well as the chaplain celebrating mass, were to be present at the mass of the Virgin, and then each was to say his own mass. Then until Prime they were to go to their seats in the cloister, to say the psalter and pray. At Prime they were to go into the choir, and afterwards to the chapter for correction of faults. They were then to return to the choir and after the hours and mass of the day were finished, when the little bell rang to assemble outside the door of the refectory, and there sit until all were present, and then enter. A brother should read to them at both dinner and supper, which suggests the presence of a pulpitum in the refectory, and they were not to sit over their meal too long. It is not clear from this whether the sisters were to eat in the refectory or separately, but it is more likely that they ate separately, as they certainly did by 1364. The brothers were then to return to the church and say Grace. In summer after dinner they were to sleep, and then go to the cloister and study until Vespers, for which there would be two peals of the bell. After Vespers of the day and of Our Lady they were to return to their books in the cloister until supper. Then they were to return to the church for Compline of the day and of the Blessed Virgin, followed by the *Salve Regina* or some other anthem in her honour before the altar of the Virgin. Then they should say their private prayers, in choir or cloister until bedtime, when they should all sleep together in the dormitory, the cellarer alone having a separate chamber. They were not to eat or drink after Compline, nor to go into the refectory (VCH 1913, 337).

The cellarer had a separate chamber because he seems to have had much of the responsibility for the day to day running of the hospital. It is also worth noting that the laybrothers who looked after the infirm, had said in 1276 that they were used to being able to ask the cellarer at any reasonable hour for special foods from the cellar for those in their charge. His higher status, and the greater likelihood of his being disturbed, lie behind this separate provision for the cellarer. Even at this date the master would have had his own lodging. There was another chamber in the dormitory which was used for bleeding and shaving. All were to be shaved at the same time, fortnightly. Intervals for bleeding are not stated but were usually set at about seven times a year. If a brother was sick and could not attend the office in the choir he would be allowed to use the chamber (VCH 1913, 337–38). This suggests that there was no separate infirmary for the brothers.

From the provisions as to the locking of the doors it is clear that the church had a number of doors: one by the porch of the Blessed Virgin (possibly near her altar) which was to be used by the secular chaplains and the choir boys; another which was entered through the cloister near the altar of the Holy Cross and was used by the laybrothers to reach their stalls. It is not clear from this whether either of these doors was the same as that by which the chaplain brothers entered the church. As a porch (*porticus*) is specified for their door and not elsewhere, this may have been a completely separate door. It is also unlikely that there would be a porch leading from the cloister to the church. Later in the document it is stated that no brother is to use the door in the nave of the church except for processions. This is presumably the west door. It is also stated that the sisters are to have an honest place set apart from one side to the other for them in the lower (western) part of the church. It is not clear how they were to enter the church, perhaps through the west door as it seems unlikely that they would be allowed to enter through the cloister (VCH 1913, 337–38). This would give an added explanation of the prohibition of the use of the west door by the brothers.

The most logical interpretation of the evidence so far presented is that St Leonard's had a standard Austin cloister, however, one which lay to the north of the church (other evidence for this proposition will be discussed later). It is quite possible that the layout was not completely regular, especially if elements of the pre-1137 buildings survived and had to be incorporated into the new structure. Within the cloister as a whole were distributed the carrels of the chaplain-brothers, most probably being in the east walk where they would be most convenient; from the east walk of the cloister is a door leading into the church, by which the brothers entered; off this walk of the cloister lay the chapter-house and probably other buildings, with the dormitory above, connecting to the church by night-stairs, as at Matins the brothers apparently proceeded directly from the dormitory to the church. The west walk of the cloister would be used by the laybrothers as was standard practice in Cistercian houses, with a door at the south end by which they entered the church. They would thus have their stalls in the eastern part of the nave, and the altar of the Holy Cross would be on the north side of the nave. The sisters would have the western part of the nave and used either the west door or a door in the north nave to the west of the claustral range. It is likely that the nave of the church extended west of the cloister. The door by which the secular chaplains and choir boys entered, that of the porch of the Virgin, if not that of the brothers, would have given them reasonably direct access to the choir. If the cloister lay to the north, this could have been through a door in the south transept, a common location for a ceremonial doorway in large non-monastic churches. The refectory would be in the north walk of the cloister. This would explain why the brothers were in the north walk of the cloister, and why the brothers were to sit and wait by the door of the refectory until they were all gathered together. If the chaplain-brothers were leaving the church by one door and the laybrothers by another, it would be impossible to absolutely co-ordinate their arrival outside the refectory. Seating and possibly a *lavatorium* would thus be expected to be found in this walk of the cloister. Having gathered, the chaplain-brothers would enter at the head of the procession, with the laybrothers following in due order behind. It is clear from the 1364 visitation that the chaplain-brothers had the higher, and the laybrothers the lower part. If the refectory were to take up all of the north cloister range, and run parallel to the church this would give the chaplain brothers the east end, and the laybrothers the west, retaining the same division as elsewhere.

Langton's precepts also make mention of a treasury, though this is not located. It may, however, have been in the church, for greater safety, as at Norwich cathedral. In addition the 1364 visitation made provision for a chamber to be set aside for the imprisonment of brothers who had broken the Rule, though it is not certain that this was in the claustral range. Such of the brothers as were able and willing should also be allowed to attend the theological school in York, once they had celebrated divine service, and a building was to be provided, divided into thirteen studia, where they could study Holy Scripture (VCH 1913, 339). What implications this had for the use of the cloister at that date is unclear. This building is not located. The master had his own lodging, though its location is unknown, but it must have been of reasonable size to accommodate him, a secular chaplain, two *domsels* (pages), and other necessary servants, and men, number unspecified. He was also to have eight horses at the expense of the house, though it is not clear whether he kept a separate stable by his lodging, it seems likely.

Besides the claustral building and the infirmary were all the service buildings, of which there were a considerable number. By 1280 there was a grammar school with a grammar and a singing master and nineteen boys. There was also a guest hall, the cellar, a tannery, a malthouse, a watermill, a workshop in which were a carpenter, a wheel wright and a mason, a smithy, several stables, three ships — though one of these may have only been a ferry and the gatehouse (LJRO, QQ2 and 7). There were two kitchens, a bakehouse and a brewery into which the brothers were not to go, which had been recently repaired in 1377. At about the same date half of the church, cloister and the dormitory, and part of the infirmary of the poor had been roofed in lead (VCH 1913, 340). There was also a cemetery, presumably beside the church. None of the service buildings is located and the one attempt which has been made to reconstruct the actual layout of the hospital, by George Benson, is clearly quite fanciful (Benson 1930, 131–2).

There were two entrances into the precinct: one faced the river and was known at first as the lower gate, later the water gate. This was probably the gate at which alms were given and by here ran the lane known as 'Footless lane'. The second gate was opposite Blake Street and was known as the 'east gate' in the early 13th century (VCH 1961, 363). There was a gatehouse here with an arch over the road in which stood a statue of St Leonard until it was taken down in the 18th century to allow access to the theatre (Sheahan and Whellan 1855, 474). Parts of that gatehouse may be represented by the remains of a small two-storey 13th century building now incorporated into offices of the Theatre Royal (RCHM 1981, 93). In 1299 the hospital was to enclose a nearby lane leading from Blake Street to Petergate in order to enlarge the hospital court (*C.P.R. 1292–1301,*). The line of this lane can still be seen on Ordnance Survey maps showing property boundaries, and emerged somewhere near no.9, High Petergate. In 1308 the hospital seems to have tried to make another gateway directly onto Bootham, but the city protested (*C.P.R. 1307–13,* 86). The precinct did not extend as far as Petergate for there was several tenements whose bounds lay between Petergate and St Leonard's.

Let us now turn to the surviving remains (Fig 2.1). As we have already seen, the infirmary building was built in the mid 13th century. The only free-standing part of the hospital still surviving, a first-floor chapel, with a barrel-vault passageway on ground-level, next to the City Library, has traditionally been identified as the infirmary. Its dating on architectural grounds to the mid-13th century would fit the documentary date of the infirmary, and the identification is probably accurate. What remains of the building is only a part of what formerly existed, and excavation in 1846 revealed the full extent of the range. A plan derived from the excavation is to be found in Benson (1919, fig. 12).

The building revealed consisted of a range running roughly north-west to south-east (parallel to and built onto the city wall), apparently sixteen bays long and four deep. On the north side two chapels extended, one of which survives, the other of which now lies under Museum Street and probably marked the end of the range. This is a most curious arrangement for which I am unaware of any parallels. As shown earlier it was usual for infirmaries to be arranged like a church with a chapel at the east end, and the patients in the 'nave' thereby able to see the altar. It would be expected therefore that a chapel or chapels would be found at the end of the range extending towards the street. Although this would not be perfectly aligned liturgically, it would be considerably less inaccurate than that of the great church of St Mary's abbey next door. An arrangement with the chapels sticking out at right-angles would preclude most patients from sight of the altar and is no more liturgically correct than the expected organisation. This suggests there was some over-riding reason for the alignment of the chapels in this way. One possibility is that space was limited and so rather than encroach on the street the chapels were placed in this unusual location. Another possibility however is that the overriding concern was to orientate the chapels in relation to the existing liturgical arrangement of the site. That arrangement would be set by the alignment of the church of St Leonard. It may thus be that the sole surviving chapel represents the original alignment of St Leonard's church. As the church was also described as being 'on the high street' that would necessitate it being sited with its main axis lying parallel to the street. In that situation it would be impossible to have a cloister in the usual place and it would have to lie to the north of the church.

The infirmary may well have been subject to changing use during its life. From the late 13th century, as well as the sick poor accepted into the infirmary, the hospital was under pressure to take corrodians, who would pay a lump sum, or give some property to the house in return of support for the rest of their lives. The most expensive corrody was that purchased by John and Beatrice de Cundall of Huby in 1394 for £81 (*C.P.R. 1396–99,* 383). The Cundalls were much too grand to live in the infirmary and were to have their own house within the precinct. It is not clear how many other of the corrody purchasers expected the same, for only a few have been recorded in full. Nevertheless it would be interesting to know whether there was a move towards providing more individual dwellings within the precinct at this date, at the same time as there was a move to provide more for the better off. By the Dissolution the hospital was supporting only 44 cremetts (*L. & P. Hen. VIII,* xiv(2) no.623, 227). This number would have rattled around in the old infirmary building, and it is possible that part of this building had already been turned to other purposes by this date. In 1506, the hospital was being asked by the corporation by what right it built its infirmary up to the moat of the city wall, which suggests that alterations may have been made at that date (*Y.C.R.III* 1942, 19).

St Leonard's was the only Yorkshire hospital to provide explicitly for children. In 1255 the church of Newton on Ouse was granted to the hospital 'to assist them in ministering to the poor and sick, and to infants exposed there' (*C.P.L. 1198–1304,* 319). From 1364 they were housed in the 'Barnhous' under the infirmary, but it is not clear where they were before then. The children were to be cared for by one of the sisters, who was to have one or two cows at her disposal. The reference to the cows suggests that some at least of these children were quite small. They were to have a good chimney, and indeed traces of a fireplace do survive in the infirmary undercroft (VCH 1913, 340).

The other fragment of the hospital survives incorporated into the Theatre Royal. This was part of the claustral range, though whether it was part of the church as suggested in the *VCH City of York* (1961, 363) is less certain. Until 1901 this consisted of an undercroft, at least seven bays long, four bays wide at one end, and two bays wide at the other, although this was clearly not the full extent of the original building. In 1887 and 1901 alterations to the Theatre Royal involved demolition of much of this and now only two compartments survive. Fortunately some

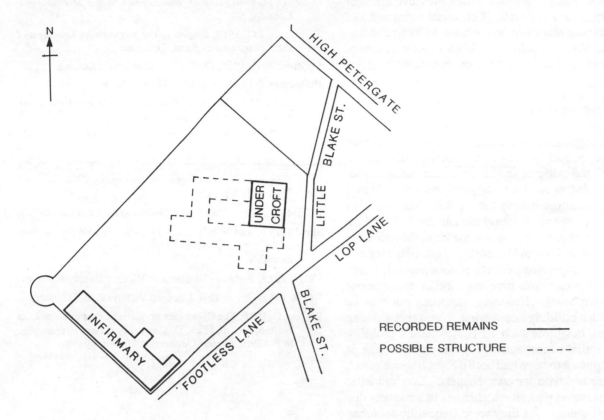

Figure 2.1 Recorded remains of St Leonard's Hospital, York

record, in both photographs and drawings, was made by Benson (1901) to indicate its appearance. The statement that this represents the hospital of William II in *VCH City of York* (1961, 359) is probably based on a suggestion in RCHM pre-publication notes (RCHM York file 60282, 2) that the columns of the undercroft dated to the late 11th or early 12th century. However in the published version it is accepted that the whole building is of the mid-12th century period (RCHM 1981, 93). Christopher Wilson, working from Benson's drawing, thought that the building was datable close to 1150 on stylistic grounds, and was much influenced by Cistercian architecture. Wilson considered it almost identical to the west cloister range of Byland, and very similar to the laybrothers' dormitory at Clairvaux (Wilson 1986, 94). This would be likely since the master of the Hospital, Robert (*c* 1130–62) had close connections with the Cistercians (Nicholl 1964, 242).

If, as has been suggested, the church lay parallel to the street, the building which this undercroft represents cannot have been the church, since it lies at right-angles to the street, but must have been part of the claustral range, and would lie (liturgically) to the north of the church. Wilson's suggestions as to its resemblances might also indicate a claustral use (both parallels are to laybrothers' quarters), moreover it is hard to see why a church should need such an extensive undercroft, nor are there any known indications to suggest that this was a crypt.

There is one other piece of information which might tend to support the identification of this building as part of the cloister. The Theatre Royal was established in 1734

and apparently a map by P. Chassereau of 1750 appears to show the theatre as a rectangular building identical in area to a 12th-century building (RCHM York file 61080 1). This might suggest that the theatre had taken over in its entirety a building which had survived from the monastic complex. As the theatre had been established in what had been a tennis court, this itself would not have required much alteration from a monastic dormitory. Moreover, entrance to the theatre, before the building of St Leonard's Place in 1834, appears to have been through the original gatehouse of the hospital. A photograph of the theatre of about 1865–79 seems to show the survival of a good deal of medieval masonry to second-floor level, and one is given to wonder whether the clearly 19th-century arcade in front of the building was intended to replace a genuine medieval one, as this would probably have been the location of the cloister garth (Murray 1988, 11).

It was customary for all religious houses to give some alms at the gate, but at St Leonard's this had developed into a system of relief which aided a large number of those in York dependent upon charitable giving. Not only did the hospital provide at the gate for number of customary dependents and occasional and itinerant beggars, it also supplied the leperhouses and York Castle with food and drink for the lepers and prisoners. Clearly the hospital was aiding as many outside its gates (there were 300 prisoners in York Castle alone) as it was within them. For this reason it is not possible to see the charitable activity of the hospital being confined solely to the site.

This is true of many hospitals which provided much of their charity to non-residents. The social topography of a hospital cannot therefore be confined to its site, and as many of its clients would have been mobile, it cannot either be entirely located in other dependent sites.

2.3 Conclusion

Hospital topographies are extremely varied, although they can be reduced to three main plans: the church, with chapel and patients in the nave; the college, with separate housing around a courtyard; the leper hospital with small buildings around the church. The first plan is more typical of earlier foundations in the 11th to 13th centuries, and of those caring for the sick; the second is more often found later in the 14th to 16th centuries and for relatively independent, elderly or poor inmates. There is insufficient evidence to give any kind of development plan for leperhouses. However, hospitals can also be found in older buildings converted from a pre-existing use. Larger hospitals such as St Leonard's probably developed entirely independent topographies, though St Leonard's appears to have had both a church with cloister, and an infirmary with its own chapels. Like monastic sites, hospitals also underwent changes in structures due to functional change. As they were frequently suburban in location, often immediately outside town gates, they must be scrutinised for opportunities for excavation.

Primary References

Calendar of Papal Letters, (London, 1893).

C.P.R. Calendar of Patent Rolls, (London, 1893–).

E.Y.C. Early Yorkshire Charters, Farrer W (ed), 1, (1916).

H.C.Y. Historians of the Church of York, Raine J (ed), Rolls Series, **71**, 3 vols, (1963–65).

L. & P. Hen. III Letters and Papers of Henry VIII (London, 1862–1910).

LJRO Lichfield Joint Record Office, MSS QQ2, 7. Copies in York City Archives.

Y.C.R. York Civic Records, Raine A (ed), 3, Yorkshire Archaeological Record Series, **106** (1942).

Yorks. Inq. III Yorkshire Inquisitions, Brown W (ed), III, Yorkshire Archaeological Society Record Series **31** (1902).

Secondary References

Benson, G, 1894–1903, The Hospital of St Peter, York, *Yorks Phil Soc Ann Rep* **9**.

Benson, G, 1919, *An Account of the City and County of York*, pt.2 *Later Medieval York, (1100–1603)* York.

Benson, G, 1930, St Leonard's Hospital, York *Associated Architectural and Archaeological Societies' Reports and Paper* **40**, pt.1.

Clark, J W, 1897, *Customs of the Augustinian Canons*. Cambridge.

Clay, R M, 1909, *The Medieval Hospitals of England*. London.

Cook, G H, 1961, *English Monasteries in the Middle Ages*. London.

Dickinson, J C, 1950, *Origins of the Augustinian Canons and their Entry into England*. London.

Godfrey, W H, 1955, *The English Almshouse*. London.

Halfpenny, J, 1807, *Fragmenta Vetusta*. York.

Murray, H, 1988, *Nathaniel Whittock's Bird's-eye View of the City of York in the 1850s*. York.

Nicholl, D, 1964, *Thurstan, Archbishop of York (1114–1140)*. York.

Richards, J D, Heighway, C, and Donaghey, S, 1989, *Union Terrace: Excavations in the Horsefair*, CBA for YAT (Fascicule AY 11/1).

RCHM, 1981, *York* Vol. V: *The Central Area*. London: HMSO.

Sheahan, J J, and Whellan, T, 1855, *History and Topography of the City of York: and the East Riding of Yorkshire* 1. Beverley.

V.C.H. 1913, *Yorkshire* III. London: Victoria County History.

V.C.H. 1961, *City of York*. London: Victoria County History.

Wilson, C, 1986, The Cistercians as 'missionaries of Gothic. In Norton, E C, and Park, D, *Cistercian Art and Architecture in the British Isles*. Cambridge: University Press.

3 Recording worked stone
David Stocker

The following paper does not deal exclusively with ecclesiastical, let alone, monastic material; but with loose worked stone from all types of ancient buildings, secular as well as sacred. However, since monasteries are often an important source of reused stone, a paper which intendents to discuss approaches to the recording and analysis of worked stone is not out of place in the present volume.

3.1 Definitions

I am dealing in this paper only with loose stone, and because loose it is usually *ex situ*. Occasionally it has been removed from its context archaeologically (that is to say it is a 'small' — or more often a large — 'find'). But much more frequently such loose stonework has become detached from its original setting during the natural cycle of decay, demolition and rebuilding. The principles and methods I am describing are relevant both to stones recovered by excavation and to chance finds resulting from the cycle of decay. Furthermore, much of what follows is relevant to the recording and analysis of *in situ* masonry. Clearly it is important that there be some uniformity of treatment between *in situ* and *ex situ* worked stones, but even so this paper intends to consider only the detached fragments, both because the recording of *in situ* worked stone is relatively well served by the literature (cf. eg Cocke *et al* 1984, Rodwell 1981, ch. 6) and because the immediate post-excavation problem concerns the body of loose, *ex situ*, material.

Pieces of detached worked masonry are usually referred to by archaeologists as 'architectural fragments', or even 'sculpture implies a considerable degree of sophistication in the working of stone which is absent in the great majority of the finds we are discussing. The term 'architectural fragments', on the other hand, is more properly applied to ruins and of course excludes all sorts of worked stones which are not strictly speaking architectural. Large-scale stone artefacts (mortars, cressets, grindstones and millwheels and so on) are sometimes to be found in collections described as architectural fragments and a distinction has to be made between the two classes of find. The same distinction must also be made between architectural stonework and the fragments of gravecovers and other grave-furniture which often form an important component of collections of worked stone from ecclesiastical sites. The approach to recording which I am describing here is appropriate to all worked stone for which records are needed; but in the cases of some of these non-architectural artefacts, other records may be necessary in addition to those discussed here.

3.2 The potential of collection of worked stone

Collections of worked stone may contain potentially important information for a site's interpretation, even when compared with many other categories of find. A good collection of worked stone can add greatly to the understanding of building on a site. The great potential often arises for one of two reasons, both of which are specific to worked stone.

First, particular categories of worked stone can be dated very reliably and with considerable accuracy. fragments from certain types of tracery can be dated as closely as within twenty years: for example, the fragments of tracery from the Shrine of St. Swithin in Winchester Cathedral dated to the 1250s or 1260s on the strength of their mullion sections and on the design of opening there present (Tudor-Craig and Keen 1983). Arguably, some moulding types can be dated even more closely than that, and some moulding profiles have been assigned to particular years in the careers of known master masons (eg. Roberts, 1972a, 1972b, 1977). Such degrees of accuracy are greater than those for many other categories of 'find' and they are available because of the typology of detail. These typologies are relatively well understood (compared with, say, those for medieval pottery) partly because of the many precisely dated examples which are easily available for collection and study. Since the mid-19th century, indeed, there has been massive study of these architectural typologies and at present much of the study of medieval architectural history in the New World is concerned with such typological matters. Some of the most important recent work, however — on the typologies of British medieval mouldings in particular — has been done in this country (Morris 1978, 1979; Rigold 1977).

Close and reliable (or at least thoroughly argued) dating, then, is one category of information which a study of collections of worked stone may offer the interpreter of any site. But such collections will also allow reconstruction of the buildings or of their internal details. There are many examples of such reconstructions of monastic structures (eg. at Bordesley Abbey — Blair *et al*. 1980), but one case will suffice as an illustration of the different levels of information which can be obtained from the analysis of worked stones. Figure 3.1 shows the civic fountain and water-tank in Lincoln known as St. Mary's Conduit. It was built in the early 1540s from assorted stone fragments taken from the church of the dissolved Whitefriary about 200 yards away. The fragments in the Conduit were recorded by the Trust of Lincolnshire Archaeology in 1985 and from a study of them two categories of information arose. First, we were able to reconstruct in some detail the original appearance of the chapel (Fig 3.2), and to date it fairly

Figure 3.1 St Mary's Conduit head, Lincoln.

accurately to the third quarter of the 14th century. This information was particularly useful for the concurrent excavations at the Whitefriars site. But, second, it was possible to say that the masonry from which the Conduit was constructed had been carefully selected and removed during a controlled demolition of the Whitefriary chapel. This was evidently not an opportunistic reuse of masonry by the city council but a quire deliberate 're-erection' of the chapel on the new, 'public', site. I have suggested elsewhere that a commemorative motive may have lain behind this extraordinary building commission by the City Council (Stocker 1990a). Occasionally, therefore, in addition to helping with the date and appearance of the buildings, fragments can also provide more profound insights into the motives of the builders.

Worked stones, then, are potentially important sources of evidence for understanding (in several senses) the buildings for which they were cut. But there are pitfalls. First, I should stress that not all collections will contain worked stones which are very closely datable; and often, even when they do, the stones in question are not from telling contexts. Furthermore, as with other groups of finds, their value as evidence can sometimes be mitigated or confused by problems of residuality. If the building under study has been allowed to collapse and decay as it were 'naturally' then the worked stone recovered from its debris will, of course, be representative of its final phase. This seems to have been the case, for example, with many of the Yorkshire Cistercian Abbeys, where the 19th-and early 20th-century site clearances produced great quantities of masonry from the final phases of buildings because these sites had not been systematically demolished and robbed (Thompson 1981, ch.4; G. Coppack pers. comm). But if, as is much more common, the building has been deliberately demolished and robbed for its materials, many of the key fragments for understanding its final phases will be missing. Bury St. Edmunds Abbey provides a good example. There very little worked stone has been recovered because, as the denuded remains of the wall cores show, virtually all the worked stone facing and details were robbed for reuse soon after the Dissolution. We probably learn more about the date and design of the superstructure of Abbey by excavating the footings of buildings in the town, where the masonry was reused, than we would by further excavations in the Abbey itself (Whittingham, 1951). In many cases, then, what survives is not a group of fragments which are representative of the final phases of the building, but rather a group of pieces which have already been reused in the fabric of the building under study.

In the monastic context, such collections often contain a selection of Romanesque pieces which were reused in a later-medieval rebuilding and they often come from the late medieval foundations in which they were reused. Crowland Abbey in Lincolnshire is a site which illustrates this bias of the sample of worked stone from some major sites. Here a great Romanesque church was comprehensively rebuilt in the early 15th century, but when the ruins of the dissolved monastery were stabilised in 1860 the footings were found to be composed almost entirely of reused Romanesque masonry (Moore 1860). If we imagine that the standing building were demolished tomorrow, and the stone released from the superstructure were removed for reuse in the town, then we would be left with a 15th-century church foundation plan with foundations made almost entirely of 12th-century masonry. In this event we would be able to say little about the final appearance of the monastic church, but quite a lot about its 12th-century predecessor. There is, in fact, a large group of loose worked stone from Crowland, most of which has been collected together in the last century, and the great majority of it is indeed of 12th-century date.

One consequence of the great mobility of stone historically (which is well illustrated by the Bury St. Edmunds case) is that, whilst on an isolated rural site it is a reasonable assumption that worked stones originated in the building under study, in the urban context it is sometimes more difficult to be sure of this. Down to modern times there has been a continuous cycle of reuse of building stone (Stocker 1990b), and, consequently, there is always a possibility that the stone discovered reused in an excavated fabric may come from a second site nearby, having been brought to its present location only for reuse. This is the case, for example, with the large group of stones from the Bedern excavations in York many of which come from 12th-century buildings associated with the Minster; they were brought to the Vicar's Choral site at several dates during the second half of the 14th century for reuse as building rubble (Stocker 1980a). Sourcing the worked stone from a site will always depend on individual circumstances, but it is important that the very great extent to which building stone has been mobile in the past is kept in mind (eg. Stocker 1980b, 1981, 1990b). Even so, it seems that the first rule in reusing building stone is that transportation must be minimised; the Minster stone, for example, was merely transported across the road for reuse at the Bedern.

Although I have said that some worked stones can be highly diagnostic, I have also warned that the great majority in any collection are likely to be less useful. This is particularly true of the simple cut or worked faces which often form the majority in collections. With such plain pieces, dating cannot be accurate to more than a century, even though the simple fragments might give some indication of the type of architectural feature represented. There have been published reports which have dealt only with the more sophisticated worked stones from a site while ignoring the majority, which appear to be of lesser significance. This is clearly unacceptable. Records of some sort should be made of all worked stone from a site, even if only a small percentage are then discussed in print. Records of such pieces are needed because even the least interesting carry information which sometimes relates to the original architectural features for which they were cut, and nearly always indicates something about the methods used to produce them.

In relation to these simple fragments, in particular, a feeling has developed that marks left on the stone by tools used to cut it might be useful in analysing the building from which it has come. Although some progress has

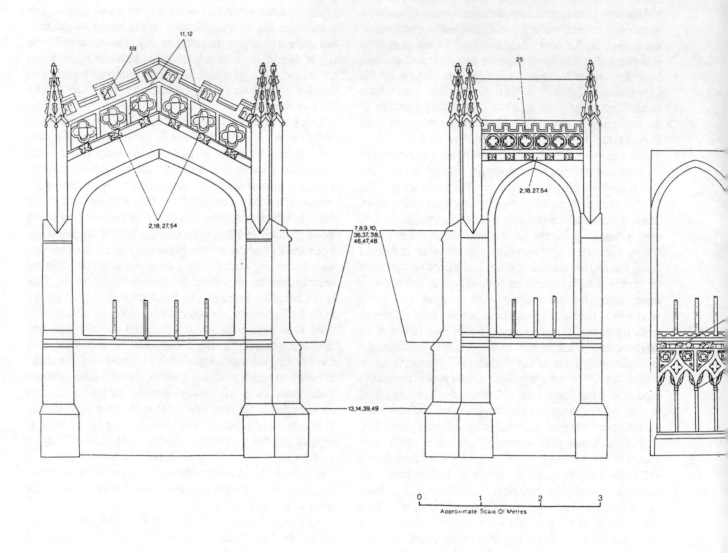

Figure 3.2 Reconstruction of parts of the Kyme Chapel at the Carmelite Friary Lincoln, from fragments reused in St Mary's Conduit.

been made with studies of Roman tooling (Blagg 1976; Hill 1981), little real progress has been made with studies of its medieval equivalent. For example, we do not yet even have an agreed terminology for tooling marks, and much of the analysis available in print is impressionistic in the extreme.

In my view the value of tooling marks as evidence for close dating or for stylistic analysis is always going to be limited, if only because the tools used for dressing stone are almost all of Roman origin and have been in more or less continuous use ever since. It is true, however, that there are periods at which one particular surface finish was preferred to another. In the 12th Century, for example, a fine 'striated' finish (often running diagonally to the bed of the stone) was the norm for all display surfaces (even if they were subsequently to be whitewashed [Fig 3.3]). However, even stones which have this sort of finish on their display surfaces will usually have a cruder finish on their beds and joints which may be indistinguishable from some later-medieval or Roman or modern work. This sort of finish is often called 'axed', but this term is simply inaccurate, as it is easy to demonstrate that this finish can be achieved just as easily with a boaster driven by a mallet as with a hafted instrument. I have therefore taken to calling this finish 'striated'.

The 'striated' finish was superseded towards the end of the 12th century, although it can still be found in the late medieval period. The effect which replaced it, the 'claw' finish, is produced by a toothed or serrated blade (Fig 3.4). It is sometimes said that the transition between the 'striated' effect and the 'claw' effect marks the change-over between the abandonment of the axe as a stone-cutting tool and its replacement by the chisel (eg. Braun 1970, 242). This is also demonstrably incorrect: in the same way that the striated effect can be produced by a driven blade, the claw effect can be produced by an axe with a toothed blade, a tool of which we have contemporary illustrations. It is true, however, that the claw finish is almost always coarser than the striated, and would have taken much less time to produce. It is also a finish which can be easily worked on moulded surfaces in a way which was much more difficult with the striated finish, and so it is not surprising that the change from one effect to another appears to be contemporary with the increase in demand for complex mouldings in the Transitional and Early English styles.

Because tooling studies are still at this early stage, it is not really possible to make more detailed statement than this at present. The evidence has yet to be collected in a sufficiently systematic way. Until then we will not be able to say, for example, how long this later 12th-century transition from one tooling finish to another took; whether it was contemporaneous across the country, or whether it was affected by local geological or other factors; and what (if any) relationship the change in tooling finish had with the development of Gothic architecture from Romanesque. Clearly, in this area, systematic observation and therefore recording are the most pressing requirements.

3.3 The recording of worked stone

Having outlined the potential interest of worked stones both for site interpretation and for their own sake, we should now pursue these desiderata into the practicality of recording such groups of finds.

It seems clear that our records of worked stone ought to fulfil at least two important and sequential functions. They should make a contemporary record of objects, because these may subsequently disappear (through loss, decay, or deliberate disposal); and, subsequently, they should allow analysis to be made, both of the stones themselves and of the buildings from which they originally came. Our record-making therefore has to have these functions in mind, so that the records will be valuable in both respects. They must contain the maximum of recordable information, in order that we loose as little as possible when the original is lost/decayed/disposed of; but they must also present that information in a way which is going to be usable for subsequent workers.

There is no doubt that there is a crisis in this area at the moment. Twenty years of intensive Rescue archaeology have produced large collections of medieval worked stone, as of other types of find. Since several specialists were being pressed to produce guidelines on recording procedures for post-excavation workers in this field, the CBA instituted a Worked Stones Working Party in 1983, which produced a report in 1985 (CBA 1987). Other than the useful leaflet designed for use by parochial church councils (CCC 1985 — arising out of the same working party), this is only advice readily available. The remainder of this paper is intended to establish the background against which the report's recommendations were developed, and so to justify some of its conclusions in greater detail.

In 1983 there was a feeling of urgency because of the lack of space in museum stores for finds of all sorts from reuse excavations. There is no evidence that this crisis has subsided, despite the Longworth Report (Longworth 1982), which was produced in response to the problems imposed on museums by finds from Rescue excavations, and to which the CBA Report is closely related. This perception of crisis was given substance for the museum world when they considered the implications for their storage space of large quantities of heavy, bulky worked stone whose academic significance was not always clear. It was the museums' reaction to requests for storage space which convinced us that, as a first principle, any archive should be able (as far as possible) to substitute for the objects themselves, because it was made clear that a sizeable percentage of the less interesting pieces from worked stone collections would have to be reburied, as indeed Longworth recommended. This position persists, and with such a prognosis, a full archive for all worked stone is clearly essential.

Indeed the policy of reburial of masonry under controlled conditions is underway: for example, at York Minster, where the original masonry from the west window was re-buried in 1987, and at Hailes Abbey and one or two other sites in Guardianship similar disposal is under consideration. The working party was not opposed

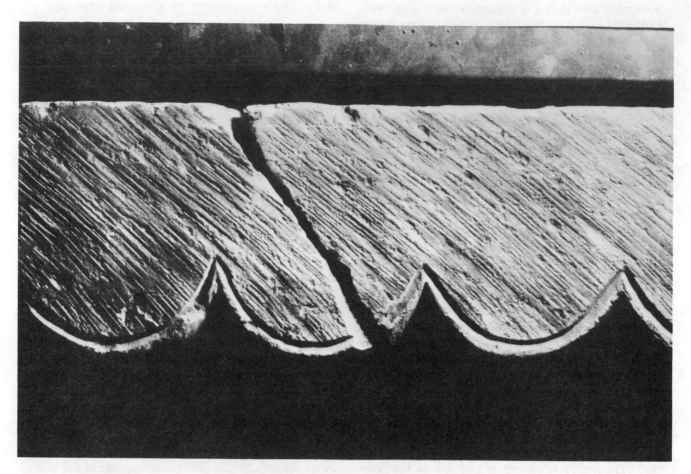

Figure 3.3 'Striated' tooling of the 12th century.

Figure 3.4 'Claw' tooling of the 13th century.

to the idea of reburial of collections of worked stone from excavation, indeed in many instances this seems to be the only practical course. However, we did make recommendations which should govern such procedures (CBA 1987, 22).

As permanent storage by reburial is a likelihood, the whole question of recording methods and quality of archive is of paramount importance, and occupied most of the working party's attention and report. Our first conclusion was that the majority of worked stones from excavations lacked adequate recording. Published reports tended to concentrate on readily comprehensible fragments or pieces with some intrinsic art-historical merit, rather than those with extrinsic importance for understanding the site from which they came. Thus it seemed not only that differing, arbitrary criteria of interest were used to select for archiving and that archives were being produced without reference to common standards, but also that in many cases no archives were being produced at all. The first, and paramount, conclusion of the Report was, therefore, that a full archive should be produced for each collection as the first priority, and that the archive should be completed to a basic common standard. This archive should be, we proposed, entirely independent of any plans for future publication, and would form a component of the total site archive, for which very detailed guidelines are now available (DUA 1986, HBMC 1986).

Which criteria should inform the production of these complete archives that we were recommending? We argued that each worked stone carries different sorts of information worth recording in archive form. Essentially the simplest pieces will have only tooling information (these will usually be fragments with only one worked face). In addition to tooling records, somewhat more complex fragments (which may have two or more faces preserved) will require records of their shape in three dimensions, whilst more complex pieces yet (eg. of moulding and sculpture) may require even more extensive records. To cater for this hierarchy of recording requirements we suggested to hierarchy of recording techniques, the simplest pieces requiring only one or two types of records to be made whilst the more complex pieces may require a variety of record types. In the report we have tried to codify for the non-specialist which types of records will be appropriate for which types of stone (CBA 1987, table 2).

In brief, we recommend that every stone in a collection should have a basic record card (or central record, if the archive is computer based). Most stones will carry tooling worth recording, but although it is possible to obtain scaled photographs of tooling, the time involved (largely in lighting the stone) has made this method quite impractical for all but a few examples (usually for publication) in any collection. Consequently we proposed recording by making rubbing, which preserve all of the diagnostic information — the width of the tool blade, the depth of the draft, the angle of strike and so on — with minimum time and effort. Surprisingly, perhaps, this type of statistical information may eventually prove useful, although I am aware of only one attempt to analyse

it in detail (Stocker 1980).

For the more significant pieces in any collection we regarded a drawn record as essential. We considered the proposal that fragments could be adequately recorded by photography alone, but it was quickly realised that photographs of a stone have many disadvantages in comparison with drawings, and can in no way substitute for the piece should it be lost, buried or destroyed. These disadvantages fall under three main headings.

3.3.1 Scale and consequent ease of reconstruction

Photographs cannot easily be scaled from, and architectural features cannot easily be accurately reconstructed out of a sequence of different photographs of various components.

3.3.2 Legibility

Even when very carefully lit, photographs cannot always distinguish between areas of accidental damages and the critical cut surface. The interpretation of the function of particular stones very often depends on the survival of small details (such as small arrives on the boundary of a break line), and photography simply cannot express such details. Furthermore, photographs cannot adequately depict many moulding sections, yet it is with such sections that the most accurate dates for worked stone fragments can be obtained.

3.3.3 Computerisation

At present photographs cannot be easily converted into a computerised archive, whereas drawings can, particularly when drawn with eventual computerisation in mind.

Although photographs have the advantage of speed the loss of information is such that photographs were not felt to constitute an adequate single record of any but the most basic stones. Photographs will, however, form an important part of the archive both as a valuable additional record showing, for example, surface 'texture' (as opposed to tooling) on sculpted stones. They also make a useful index of collection for rapid reference.

If the archive is to be based on drawn records rather than photographs, however, it is clear that systems of drawing for archive purposes will have to be as cheap and as efficient as possible. For all but a small number of sculpted pieces where such treatment is essential, the sort of drawing techniques which are used in stone finds illustrations in many published reports are quite impractical. Such drawings require levels of time and skill which are simply not available for the numbers of stones in most collections. Drawing techniques for the archive drawings have to be reduced to the minimum acceptable level — a simple and quick drawing style, showing the significant aspects of the piece, is needed.

In the working party, which was informed by the professional draught persons consulted, we felt strongly that, for practical reasons, these archive drawings should be within the scope of the average site recorder rather than necessitating specialist graphics staff. Such drawings will, we propose, be in line and will usually have no stipple shading in their archival form, although shading can very usefully be added to the archive drawing when worked up for publication. Nevertheless there will be a small number (usually sculpted, as distinct from moulded, pieces) where the complexity of the piece requires stipple in the archive drawing. Simplification of drawings, however, should not be taken too far. We are looking for useful depictions rather than diagrams. Since minor recuttings and the pattern of damage can be important both in analysing the original function of a piece and in discussing is secondary uses, we must not exclude incidental detail of this sort.

The geometrical projection used for such drawings is also important. We found a number of otherwise acceptable drawings of worked stones which had been rendered valueless by the choice of an inappropriate projection. Archive drawings (and indeed publication drawings which follow them) ought to observe simple, single-plane, geometry, using more complex projections only when really necessary. For archive purposes it is almost always better to choose several single-plane views than to try and save materials (though not time) by choosing a complex projection which allows several faces to be seen simultaneously.

Sections are also of great value, but sometimes need to be drawn with flexibility. Because of damage, for example, it may be preferable to build up a 'composite' section through a stone (from information taken from various points on its surface), rather than to take a 'single slice' which may miss vital components. Usually the information needed to date stones accurately (like the moulding sequences), or to reconstruct the architectural feature from which they come, can only be obtained from drawings using single-plane geometry. Finally, these single-plane projections are likely to be much more straightforward when the time comes for converting them into a computerised database. Once they are computerised, of course, it will be possible to develop complex projections automatically, but for inputting at present, single-plane projections are likely to be the most convenient (CBA 1987, 43–4).

The archive drawings are best made at 1:1 scale, both for ease of drawing and for ease of comparison and reconstruction. Other than a marginal saving in costs of materials, there is no case to be made for recording worked stones at any other scale. Drawings at other scales take longer to complete, make comparison between pieces more difficult, accurate reconstruction much more difficult, and computerisation more complex.

All of these desiderata have been drawn together in a drawing scheme which I have developed and laid out in our report (CBA 1987, 29–39). There is no reason why its details should not be varied to suit individual circumstances. This scheme has always been used by unskilled personnel — by myself and others — and (with a little practice) it has been used to produce the whole archive, including drawings, for collections of 500 pieces of worked stone in about three months.

Produced according to these principles, archive draw-ings may reasonably substitute for the stones so that long-term storage or disposal becomes an option. Without such records, we submit, disposal would be irresponsible.

3.4 The worked stones report

Fortunately examples of site reports containing unrelated specialist reports presented almost as an appendix to the stratigraphic sequence are becoming increasingly rare. These days writers of conclusions to reports are much more likely to mull over the evidence from all their specialists before arriving at their final conclusions. However, in this movement towards the integrated site archive and the subsequent integrated site report, worked stone studies cannot be said to have been in the lead. It is still possible to find published reports where the evidence clearly available from the worked stone has been overlooked; it is because there is often such a direct relationship between the excavated foundations and the fragments of worked stones which formed the superstructure, that it really is essential that worked stone reports are produced in conjunction with the account of the site structures and not as an afterthought. The conclusions of the worked stone report will often be very relevant to the basic site interpretation.

How much of the archive of the worked stone collection is published will obviously vary from site to site. The writer of the report should state what the relevant archive consists of, where it is, and what method has been used to generate the published report from the archive. In a few cases there may be an argument for publishing all of the drawings with a catalogue and discussion, but in most reports only key stones will be illustrated, even though the catalogue itself should be complete. I have always tried to organise the catalogue in a way which relates to the archaeology of the site, something which serves further to emphasise the connections between this group of finds and the structural history of the site under discussion.

The preparation of the drawings for publication is of course a skilled task, which, in the case of an archive prepared along the lines that we recommend, will usually involve the addition of shading to the archive line drawing. The fact that the archives are drawn at 1:1 means that they can be easily reduced photographically, and publication drawings to the required scale can be worked up from the photographic reductions.

3.5 Conclusion

What, then, is the point of recording worked stone? There have indeed been publications which have made one wonder. But clearly there is information to be gained about the date and appearance of the buildings under consideration and also about more general aspects of architectural history. What is needed is a more systematic approach, and the CBA working party agreed, in particular, to promote the idea that collections should be archived according to approximately uniform principles, independent of the final publication. We hope that the

CBA Report makes practical proposals which will allow this category to find to be more easily assimilated into the final site report.

Acknowledgements

I am grateful to my fellow members of the CBA Working Party for their time and efforts on this topic. The Working Party members were : Dr T Blagg, Mr P Lancaster, Dr R Morris (Warwick), Mr R Morris (York), Mr D Phillips, Ms S Pollard, Dr J West, Dr C Wilson. I am also grateful for assistance received at various stages from Mr P R Hill, Mr A P Davison, Mr A Smith and Dr M C Stocker.

References

Blagg, T C F 1976, Tools and Techniques of the Roman stone mason in Britian, *Britannia* **7** (1976), 152–72.

Blair, J Lankester, P and West, J 1980, A Transitional cloister arcade at Haughmond Abbey, Shropshire, *Medieval Archaeology* **29** (1980), 210–212.

Braun, H 1970, *Parish Churches: their architectural development in England*, Faber, London 1970.

CBA 1987, *Recording Worked Stones: a practical guide*, (eds D A Stocker and R Morris) Council for British Archaeology, London, 1987.

CCC 1985, *Loose stones: sculptural and architectural fragments in churches*, Council for the Care of Churches, London, 1985.

Cocke, T *et al* 1984, *Recording a church: an illustrated glossary*, Council for British Archaeology, London, 1984.

Coppack, G 1986, The Excavation of an Outer Court Building, Perhaps the Woolhouse, at Fountains Abbey, North Yorkshire, *Medieval Archaeology* **30** (1986), 46–87.

DUA 1986, *Museum of London: Department of Urban Archaeology. Archive Guide*, London, 1986.

HBMC 1986, *The design management and monitoring of post-excavation projects* (Circular advice note), 1986.

Longworth, I H (ed) 1982, *The selection and retention of environmental and artefactual material from excavations. A report by a working party of the British Museum.*

Moore, E 1861, Croyland Abbey, *Reports and papers of the Associated Architectural Societies* 6 (1861–2), 20–27.

Morris, R K 1978 & 1979, The development of later Gothic mouldings in England c1250–1400, Parts I & II, *Architectural History,* **21 & 22** (1978 & 1979), 1–48.

Rigold, S 1977, Romanesque bases in and south-east of the limestone belt, *Ancient Monuments and their Interpretation* (eds M R Apted *et al*), Phillimore, London, 1977, 99–137.

Roberts, E 1972a, Thomas Wolvey, Mason, *Archaeological Journal* **129** (1972), 119–124.

Roberts, E 1972b, Robert Stowell, *Journal of the British Archaeological Association,* **35** (3rd. Series) (1972), 24–38.

Roberts, E 1977, Moulding analysis and architectural research: the late middle ages, *Architectural History* , **20** (1977), 5–13.

Rodwell, W 1981, *The archaeology of the English Church*, Batsford, London, 1981.

Stocker, D A 1980a, *The Bedern excavation, York — The architectural evidence* (Unpublished reports, York Archaeological Trust archives).

Stocker, D A 1980b, 'With silver bells...', *Interim, A Bulletin of York Archaeology* **6/4** (1979–80), 3–8.

Stocker, D A 1981, Architectural fragments in York — An outline of the problem, *CBA Churches Bulletin* **15** (1981), 9–13.

Stocker, D A 1990a, From under the Hammer, the afterlife of Lincoln's monasteries. *Dissolution and Resurrection* (ed. L A S Butler), Oxford, forthcoming.

Stocker, D A 1990b, The Life of the Cross; a study of the reuse of building stone in Lincolnshire, *Quarrying and Stone Supply* (ed D Parsons), Royal Archaeological Institute, 1990

Thompson, M W 1981, *Ruins; Their Preservation and Display*, British Museum publications, London, 1981.

Tudor-Craig, P & Keen, L 1983, A Recently Discovered Purback Marble Scuptured Screen of the Thirteenth Century and the Shrine of St. Swithun, *Medieval Art and Architecture at Winchester Cathedral, (Conference Transactions of the British Archaeological Association for 1980)*, 61–72.

Walsh, D A 1979, A rebuilt cloister at Bordesley Abbey, *Journal of the British Archaeological Association* **129** (1979), 42–49.

Whittingham, A B 1951, Bury St. Edmunds Abbey, the plan, design and development of the church and monastic buildings, *Archaeological Journal* **108** (1951), 168–192.

4 Building in religious precincts in London at the Dissolution and after

John Schofield

4.1 Introduction

This paper outlines the post-Dissolution fortunes of several religious houses in the City of London, in particular those of the Augustinian houses of St Bartholomew Smithfield and Holy Trinity, Aldgate. It attempts to show how a new phenomenon, the urban palace, grew out of the monastic buildings; how those creations were short-lived and were themselves overtaken by the forces of immigration and change; and how study of the break-up of religious precincts can throw light on their medieval topography.

A study of the Dissolution in London and its effects upon buildings inside the monastic precincts (Fig 4.1) can be divided into two periods, each of which has a major theme: (a) 1532–1570, the era of the urban palaces and other prestigious uses of the precincts, and (b) 1560–1600, the period of the succeeding fragmentation of the precincts into several tenancies, comprising in some cases industrial premises and smaller scale housing.

4.2 The grand house and the transposed livery company hall

The chronology of the Dissolution in London can be quickly summarised. The suppression of Holy Trinity priory, Aldgate, took place in 1532, fully three years before the general Dissolution. Conventual churches within two monastic houses (St Bartholomew's priory, Smithfield; St Helen's nunnery, Bishopsgate) and within three friaries (the Austin Friars, Blackfriars and Greyfriars) re-emerged as parish churches; but by the end of the reign of Henry VIII, the majority of the religious precincts had been transferred to courtiers or officials of the Court of Augmentations. Thus Austin Friars passed to Sir William Paulet, Lord Treasurer; St Bartholomew's priory to Sir Richard Rich, Lord Chancellor; and to the south-east of the city, Bermondsey abbey passed to Sir Thomas Pope, Treasurer of the Court of Augmentations.

Only one of these urban palaces can be seen today: the Charterhouse, north-west of the city (Fig 4.2). It serves to illustrate many of the plan and decorative features which are less evident among the remains of its more fragmentary colleagues. The Charterhouse was forcibly suppressed in 1537 and the buildings stayed in royal hands until 1545, when the priory was granted to Sir Edward, later Lord, North, a privy councillor. He began rebuilding and transforming the priory into a town house suitable for a courtier who moved in royal circles; it was here that he entertained Queen Elizabeth in 1558 and 1561. His successor Thomas Howard, Duke of Norfolk, continued

building between 1565 and his execution in 1571, and it is difficult to distinguish between the work of the two owners from the existing remains. We can only examine the house as left by Howard in 1571 (RCHM 1925, 21–30; Knowles and Grimes 1954).

The medieval priory consisted of a square cloister surrounded by twenty-six cells, on the south side of which were grouped communal buildings and areas on a west-east axis: the lay-brothers' quarters, recently rebuilt by the last prior, the Little Cloister and the church with the founder's tomb. The lay-brothers' quarters were retained, though the cooking facilities seem to have been extended for the larger company expected at feasts. The Little Cloister was pulled down and widened to form an impressive court of stone buildings to be entered from the south. The church, apart from its tower, was demolished, since the east range of the new court crossed it at right angles. The stonework of the priory buildings, and especially the doorways, was reused throughout the new work; some of Henry Yevele's cell doorways found new homes upstairs in the grand house.

The constraints of developing a restricted urban site, already fairly full of substantial stone buildings, must have severely hampered any attempt to emulate contemporary rural grand houses. At the Charterhouse two courts on the Bridewell and Hampton Court model, with the hall at the back of the inner court, were achieved, but only by placing them at an acute angle to the street entrance. Since the precinct included a large open space to the west, this constraint must have been imposed by the location of the pre-existing lay-brothers' court.

At the back of the new inner court lay the new hall, entered by a porch. A door at the dais end led to a fine stair within a square stairwell — one of the innovations of these decades (destroyed in the last war). This gave access to to the Great Parlour, also damaged in the war, but now resplendent once more with the Howard arms and crest in the ceiling. A long gallery led north conveniently over the cells forming the west range of the cloister; the garth would have made a fine garden to view from the gallery.

Elsewhere, for instance at two of London's three Augustinian houses, the new owner used the prior's lodging as the nucleus of his new residence. At St Bartholomew's priory, Sir Richard Rich moved into the prior's lodging when he took occupation of the house in 1540 (cf Fig 4.3; Webb 1921, ii, xx). In the north-eastern part of the city, the precinct of Holy Trinity priory Aldgate was granted by Henry VIII to Thomas Audley in 1534 (CLRO Repertory 22, f414b; VCH London i, 472). Audley pulled down the church and steeple (the latter possibly a separate bell-tower on the evidence of the plan

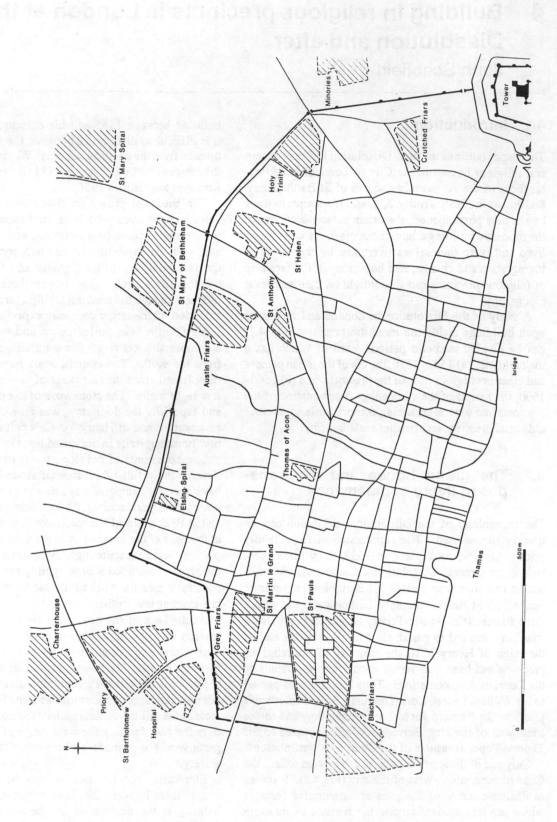

Figure 4.1 Medieval London, showing location of the religious precincts.

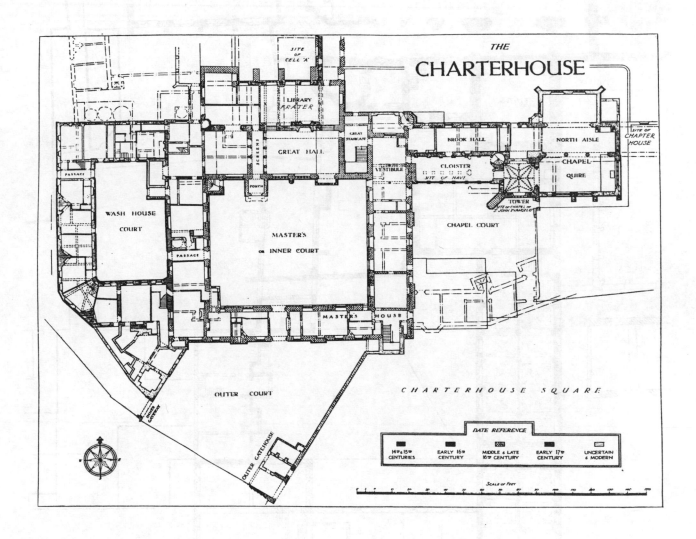

Figure 4.2 Plan of Charterhouse (RCHM 1929).

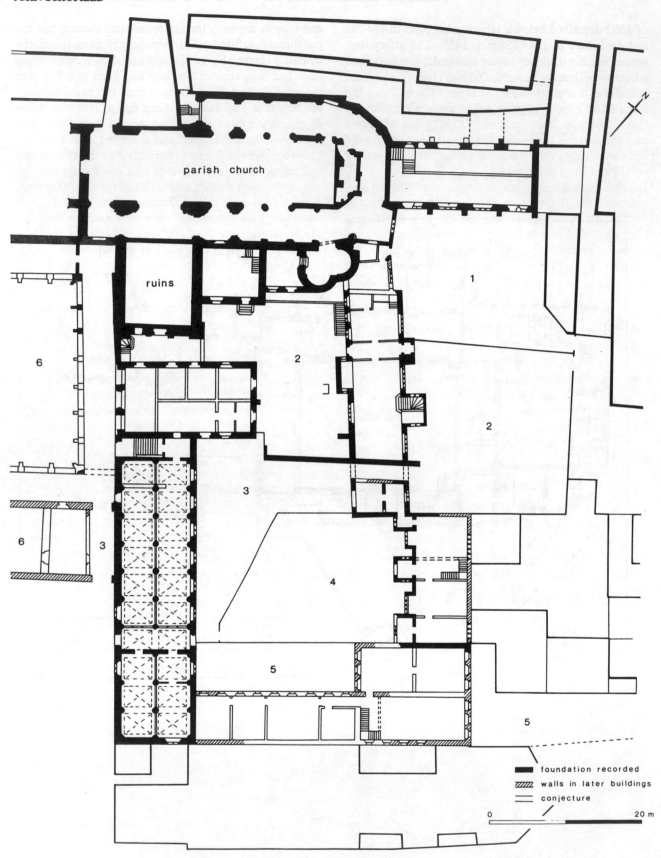

Figure 4.3 St Bartholomew Smithfield: plan of the ladychapel and monastic buildings in secular occupation as described in 1616, a reconstruction based on surviving physical evidence by E A Webb (1921, ii, pl xlix). Rich's house, the former prior's lodging, was then in the tenure of Arthur Jarvis.

of 1592 described below), rebuilt other parts of the site and died there in 1544 (Stow i, 142). The priory then passed via his daughter to her husbands, the second of whom was Thomas Howard, Duke of Norfolk; the main house was thereafter known as Duke's Place. Since the name Duke's Place is given to the western range of the cloister from at least the time of Ogilby and Morgan's map (1677), it is likely that this, the likeliest site for the prior's lodging in the medieval period, was the portion rebuilt and lived in by Audley.

There have been several excavations within the precinct of Holy Trinity since 1977, and the topography of the medieval priory is the subject of a study in progress (Schofield and Lea in prep). The priory precinct as it existed at the end of the 16th century can be reconstructed from a plan by John Symonds [1] of the majority of the buildings in the precinct, probably drawn in 1592, which is now at Hatfield House (Lethaby 1900). John Symonds was a London joiner who carved in wood and stone, employed in the Office of Works from 1567. In 1577 he began a series of commissions got Lord Burghley, and seems to have become his private architect; he was in charge of Burghley's London houses in 1595–6 (Summerson 1957). For the evidence that the survey can be dated to 1592, see Lethaby 1900, 46–7. The Symonds plan (Figs 4.4, 4.5), drawn at both ground floor and first floor levels, shows many different features and we shall return to it several times.

A first inspection of this plan may serve to reveal the outline of Audley's mansion. The name Duke's Place, later given to the whole precinct and even later to the street which still runs along its north side, was originally the name of Norfolk's mansion forming the west range of the cloister; presumably Norfolk's house and Audley's house were the same. Presumably also, as at Bermondsey, the entrance gate, the subsidiary buildings around the Great Court, and the monastic kitchen were simply taken over and kept in use. Beyond these basic outlines the nature of any innovations by Audley or Norfolk becomes increasingly speculative. The main range between the Great Court and the cloister was, on present archaeological evidence, doubled in width to the west in the monastic period. On the first floor, now on the cloister side, lay the hall; by 1592 the range fronting the court was divided into tenements, but its run of bay windows suggests a long room, perhaps a gallery, of some size. Given the reduced circumstances of the priory's final years, one is tempted to suggest that this rebuilding on the first floor was part of Audley's scheme in the 1530s, the date of the nearest analogies for such window-arrangements (e.g. a series of four rectangular bay windows at first floor level forming part of a range built on the east side of New Palace Yard, Westminster, in the reign of Henry VIII (Colvin 1966, 30–1 and pl 11). A further range, called 'the gallery', bordered the southern side of the garden occupying the south half of the main court.

The transformation of the church itself was remarkable. Audley, according to Stow, wanted to extend to Leadenhall Street in the south by exchanging the parish church of St Katherine Cree, originally part of the priory

and now in the way, for the conventual church, but the parishioners refused. He then largely demolished the monastic church. By 1592 the roofs of both chancel and nave had been removed, a way had been knocked into the chancel through the ladychapel, the north transept had fallen or had been knocked down, and two suites of rooms occupied the church on the first floor; one suite over the ladychapel, and a second called the Ivy Chamber, formed out of the crossing of the church and looking down on the one side into the former chancel and on the other side into the ruins of the nave (Fig 4.6). A gallery led from this appartment to the main range of the house. We cannot say how much of this building can be attributed to Audley. We can however conclude that by 1592 a mansion occupied the former prior's range and the western half of the precinct, and that two suites of rooms had colonised the body of the church. Fragmentary building accounts of 1541–2 mention both 'a great gallery' and 'the great chamber next the street side' (PRO E/101/674/24) which may well refer to the gallery along the north side of the church and the Ivy Chamber (or the chamber over the ladychapel), as shown by Symonds in 1592. Recent excavations (Riviere 1985; Schofield and Lea in prep) have located a small amount of evidence from this period, including a foundation within the area of the main house which incorporated two contiguous pieces of window mullion, probably from a large window in the church, and indications of the reuse of a chapel as a cellar, with the ground outside covered with slates, presumably also from the church.

Despite the restrictions of their sites, these new urban palaces may have demonstrated current fashions in the layout of rooms. We cannot yet identify suites of rooms — the great chamber, withdrawing chamber, bedchamber and closet, and long gallery — which are a feature of large houses of this period elsewhere (Girouard 1983, 59). One possibility is that if the Audley mansion originally extended to and included the Ivy Chamber in the crossing of the priory church at Holy Trinity (Fig 4.5), then the high end of the hall would have led via a gallery to a kind of prospect house, the Ivy Chamber itself; an arrangement which first appears in London in the plan of Bridewell Palace, where the prospect house was represented by the range along the Thames, built in 1520–23.

As already mentioned, the large precinct of the Austin Friars in the northern intramural part of the city passed to William Paulet, and the copperplate engraving of London of c 1559 supplies some details of the garden of Winchester Place, built by Paulet in the years around 1550 (Fig 4.7). Here is shown a formal garden, a fountain, and a blocked-up gatehouse in the garden wall which marked the north end of a path through the friary, now enclosed and no longer available for public access (Stow i, 176). Excavations in advance of redevelopment recently took place on this important site, and some remains of the friary were found (*Medieval Archaeol* 1991, **35**, 150).

Grand houses were however not the only occupants of the newly-released precincts. From about 1542 there appeared a new class of buyer who bought and sold estates in bulk, and syndicates or private individuals buying for investment. The church of St Helen's nunnery in

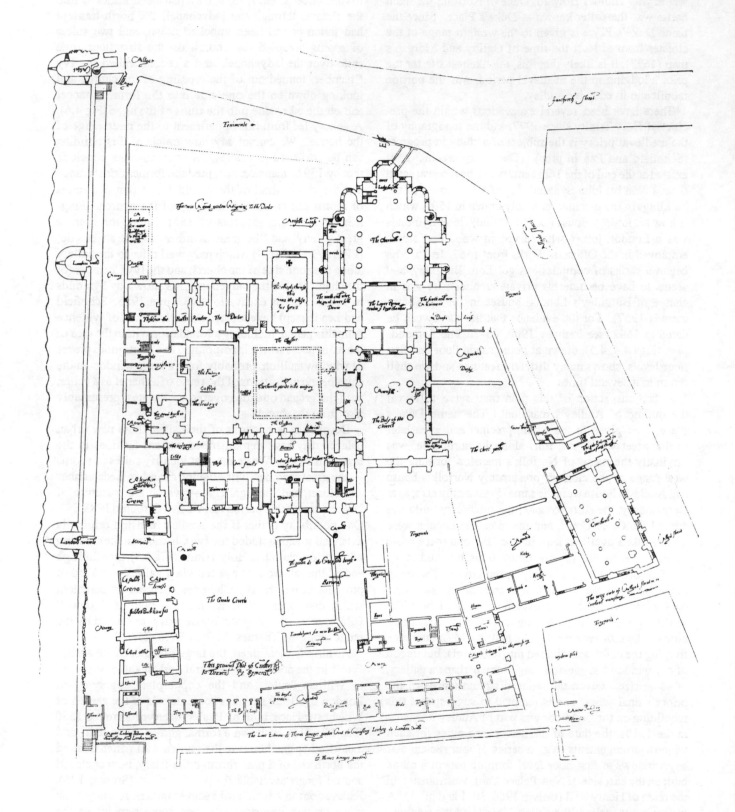

Figure 4.4 Holy Trinity Priory, Aldgate: ground-plan of the priory buildings by John Symonds, probably drawn in 1592 (after Lethaby 1900).

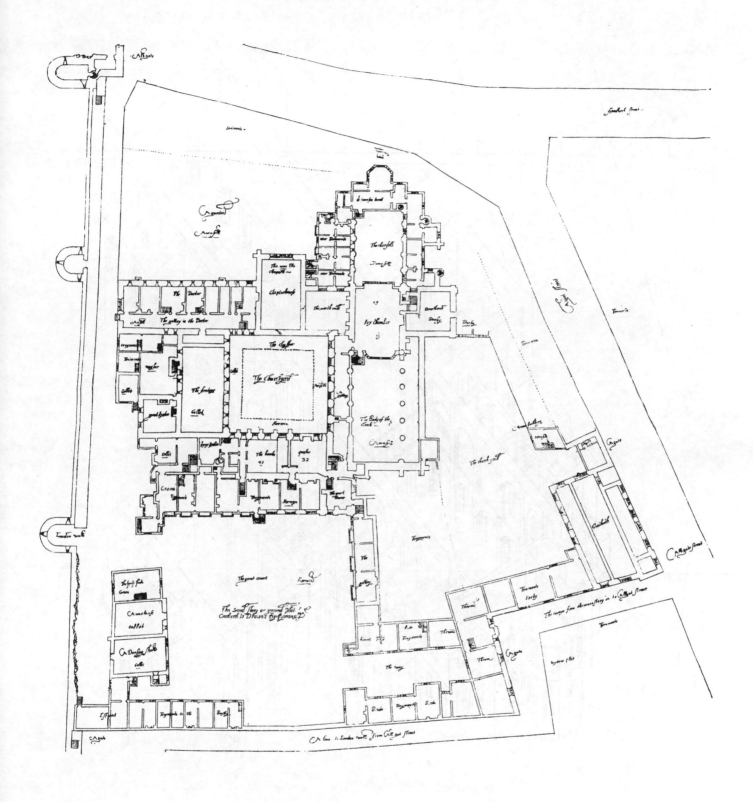

Figure 4.5 Holy Trinity Priory, Aldgate: first-floor plan of the priory buildings by John Symonds, probably drawn in 1592 (after Lethaby 1900).

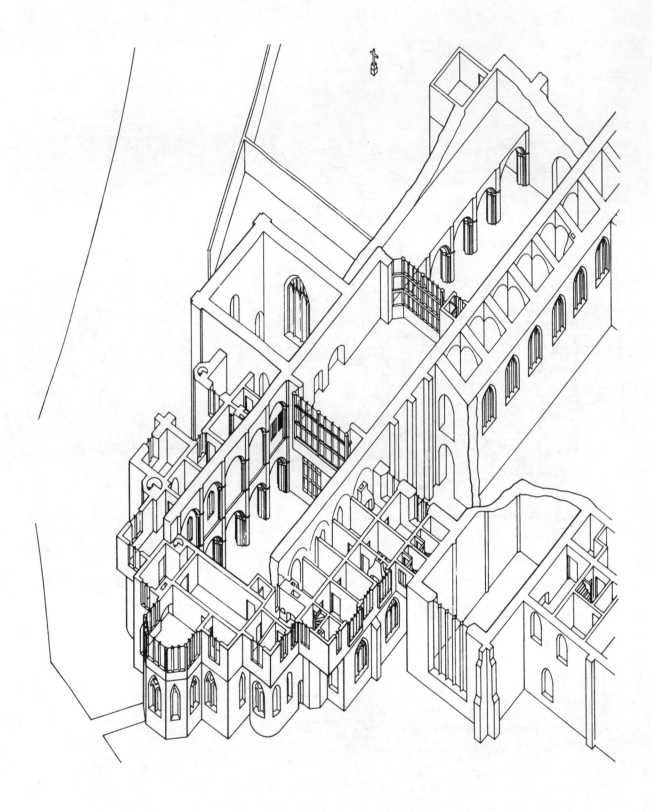

Figure 4.6 Holy Trinity Priory, Aldgate: reconstruction of the east end of the priory church in
1592 by Richard Lea, from the plans of John Symonds.

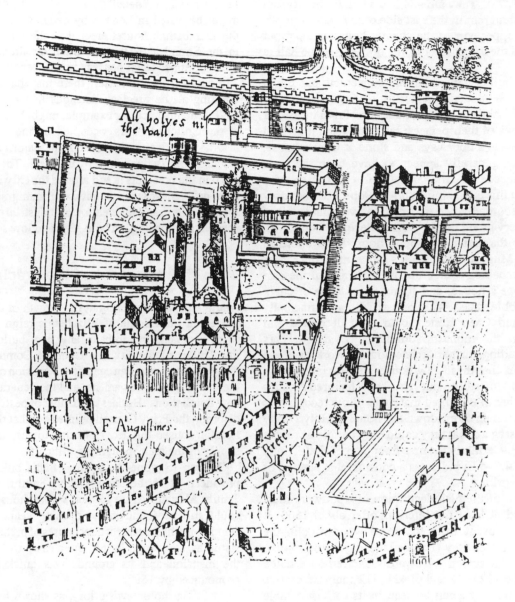

Figure 4.7 Austin Friars, Broad Street: the precinct in the copperplate map of *c* 1559, showing the friary buildings largely intact; but to the north the ranges probably reflect Paulet's rebuildings after 1550, and the former pedestrian gate from the friary gardens to the street on the north has been blocked.

Bishopsgate was kept in use because it was also a parish church. The nuns' hall and other buildings to the north of the church were however sold, first to Sir Richard Williams, nephew of Thomas Cromwell, and in 1544 to Thomas Kendall, leatherseller, who bought at least the east cloistral range, composed of the former dorter and chapter house, on behalf of the Leathersellers' Company (Black 1871, 73). They already had a hall in the city, but moved here and rebuilt the east side of the cloister in two stages: the upper part of the chapter house as a parlour in 1567, and the upper floor of the dorter as a fine hall in 1610.

As far as building materials are concerned, one might expect that the sudden availability of large amounts of stone would make the new grandees careful in its use for the appearance of their palaces; but apart from the frugal re-use of Yevele's doorways and stone at Charterhouse, this does not generally appear to have been the case. The outer facade of Charterhouse is coursed squared ragstone, but this is a facing on brick. Pope's Bermondsey residence, recorded when in decay, shows what is left of possibly a very grand timber-framed design of the 1540s, grafted onto the monastic ground floor. Excavations in 1985 by the Museum of London's Department of Greater London Archaeology have uncovered walls of the east range of Pope's house, and found them to be of chalk and tyle rubble faced with re-used ashlar, principally greensand and Caen stone, some of it decorated and clearly from the monastic buildings (D Beard, pers comm). Pending further archaeological work on these sites, it seems that these new houses did not incorporate large amounts of stone, but may have featured facades either of timber or of mixed materials. Stow records that Audley's workmen threw down the stones of Holy Trinity with such disregard that they could only be sold as rubble (Stow i, 142). Certainly the first-floor plan of Holy Trinity priory (Figs 4.5–4.6) indicates a considerable amount of new timberwork.

The advent of Flemish decoration in woodwork must have affected at least the interiors after about 1560; it is noticeably absent from the fixed woodwork in the interiors at Bermondsey (Pope's building of the 1540s), but present in the screen at Howard's Charterhouse, dated 1571 (RCHM 1925, 25 and pl 42). The main decorative elements of this style can be seen in its earliest datable appearance in London, the screen at Middle Temple of 1562–70; other examples followed in the screens and woodwork of Staple Inn (c 1581), Gray's Inn (late 16th century) amd Lincoln's Inn (early 17th century; RCHM 1925, 59, 54, 50). Elsewhere in the City, Netherlandish influence was most apparent in notable architecture in three buildings of 1563–70: Nonsuch House on the bridge (1563), the Royal Exchange (1567–9) and Gresham's house in Broad Street, later Gresham College. Mark Girouard, writing of the Elizabethan country house, has argued that 'from the death of Henry VIII to about 1570 English architecture is on the whole hesitant, confused and dull' (1983, 28). Perhaps it is inappropriate to compare the purpose-built and constrained houses in London with those on open sites, but the former do display inventiveness, adaptability, ingenuity and vigour. They have also possibly been under-rated because nearly all have disappeared and most are unknown.

Girouard goes on to argue that the years around 1570 were a watershed in the design of grand houses, and in the following 15 years English architecture had its own original flavour, with houses 'no longer direct transplantations from Flanders or weak shake-ups of French and Tudor detail' (*Girouard 1983*, 30). This claim might be tested in London by detailed consideration of the Elizabethan houses erected to the west of the City in the Strand and Holborn, often on sites which were once bishops' town-houses, in the period 1570–1600. Although in the City itself there may have been some building at the precinct mansions in the decades after 1570 (one instance, for example, might be Lumley Place at the Crutched Friars, occupied by the Lumleys who also lived at Nonsuch Palace), the majority has clearly reached a fairly fixed form by this date. The period after 1570 in the precincts in and around the City is interesting for a different reason: the influx of immigrants, many of foreign origin, and the creation of industrial premises and speculative housing, on both high and low social scales.

4.3 The filling out of the precincts

Alarm and complaints about the growth of the city were voiced in the middle of Elizabeth's reign. In 1580 a royal proclamation forbade any new buildings within three miles of the city; the Court of Common Council fought a vain campaign against subdivision of tenements, the building over of gardens, and the general increase in new foundations. Besides the danger of pestilence or civil disorder, the Privy Council pointed out that the growth of London caused the decay of other towns, and made the supply of the metropolis more difficult.

We can examine the nature of this building at two precincts: St Bartholomew's priory Smithfield, and Holy Trinity Aldgate. At the former, several houses of quality could still be found in the opening years of the 17th century, but had streets of new houses of perhaps middling status as company; in the latter case, the break-up of the mansion and its grounds was quicker and more pronounced by 1592.

At St Bartholomew's priory, as shown by a rental of 1616, the stone buildings in the middle of the priory still contained five prestigious lodgings or mansions: Sir Percival Hart held the ladychapel and gallery alongside the church, Arthur Jarvis had the prior's lodging, Sir Henry Carey had the farmery, Sir Edward Barrett the house of the master of the farmery, and Lord Abergavenny was tenant above the chapter house and dorter (*Stow* ii, 77–9, 144, 151, 171–6). Hart and Jarvis were able to enjoy the former monastic water supply, brought from north of the city, as their private privilege (*Stow* ii, 161). But this prestigious enclave was bordered by newer buildings of different character. The third lord Rich, who came into possession of the former St Bartholomew's priory in 1581, began to redevelop the fairground to the north of the priory church and laid out several streets which survive today as Cloth Fair, Middle Street and

Newbury Street (Fig 4.8). Several buildings from this private housing venture remained until the early 20th century. Houses of three or four storeys with garrets encroached onto the site of the demolished nave of the priory church (the choir being kept for parochial use, ensuring its survival to the present day), and others were built against the choir and ladychapel to the east (Fig 4.8; Webb 1921, ii, 293). Here Bartholomew Fair was held, by taking over the shops in the new houses for a week (*Stow* i, 311). Despite this plebeian tone, the houses put up by Rich in the 1580s and 1590s were of substantial character and seem to have been at least respectable, as their situation next to the nucleus of superior residences would suggest. The whole scheme is interesting as being a private speculative property venture on a large scale fully 40 years before the more famous Lincoln Inn's Fields or Covent Garden, further west.

The development at Holy Trinity priory was equally intricate and piecemeal, but was subject to different pressures. In 1579 the City began to talk with appointees of the Lord Chancellor, Sir Thomas Bromley, about his lease of 'Creechurch' from Lord Howard; this may refer to the mansion or to part of the precinct (CCPR Aldgate within, 1579). Lord Thomas Howard sold the site of the priory to the City in 1592 (CLRO, Letter Book AB, 106d; Repertory 22, f.379). This was presumably the occasion of the drawing of the survey by Symonds, then in Burghley's employ, though since Burghley was not directly involved the actual reason for drawing the plan remains unknown; it was probably because Howard applied to the crown for licence to alienate the property (CLRO Repertory 22 f.414b-416). Counterparts of leases issued by Audley and the Duke of Norfolk were included with the sale documents, and they were listed at the time of sale. Six leases dated from Audley's time (1540–4); lists of leases, probably incomplete, also dated from 1564–5, 1582–3, 1586–7 and 1591–2. Of the tenants shown in the 1592 survey, Edmond Auncell appears on the list of 1582–3 and two others, Richard Bedoe and Bryan Nayler, in 1591–2. It is clear that the precinct, like others in London, was subject to progressive fragmentation from shortly after its sale to Audley; eleven main tenants or occupiers are named in 1592, and several areas of Symonds' plan (Fig 4.4) are marked 'Tenements' without further specification.

In 1592 a William Kerwin occupied most of the west range of the cloister (the part most likely to have been the house of Audley and Howard), the western arm of the cloister, and the garden occupying the southern half of the Great Court, in which he was erecting new buildings (Fig 4.4). Apart from the outline of their foundations shown by Symonds, the nature of these buildings is unknown; but by 1677, as shown on Ogilby and Morgan's map, the alley to the south of them was known as Sugar Baker's Yard.

William Kerwin was Master of the Masons' Company in 1579 (GL MS 4318) and as City Mason rebuilt Ludgate in 1585–6 (Masters 1984, xix, 23, 38–9, 179, 181). Kerwin may have lived elsewhere, for he was a churchwarden of St Helen's Bishopsgate in 1570–1 and 1571–2 (GL MS 6836) and was buried in St Helen's in 1594; his tomb survives (RCHM 1929, 23). It is therefore possible that he used part of the priory as his place of work, as a builder's yard; and perhaps as a quarry for building works such as Ludgate, for which he supplied at least some of the stone (Masters 1984, 38).

While no traces of Kerwin's occupation have been found in the recent archaeological excavations at Holy Trinity priory, a watching brief following excavations of 1979 on the west side of the cloister, that is in the range occupied by Kerwin and probably the centre of the Audley mansion, recorded a pit containing delftware wasters (Vince and Schofield in prep). This lay in one of the ground-floor rooms of the western half of the range, fronting onto the Great Courtyard to the west. On Symonds' plan of 1592 this room has, in one corner, a large oven of domestic character. It seems on present evidence unlikely that this was a kiln; the main objection, besides its comparatively small size, is that it lay in the middle of a building complex, and that the flue went up the side of what had been the Duke's Hall. This however was used as the contemporary Woodmongers' Hall (Harben 1918, 318) and by the parishioners of St James Duke's Place for worship, their church (from the Symonds plan (Fig 4.4), the former monastic chapter house) having fallen down in 1572. The occurrence of the wasters may indicate that use of the oven was not successful.

Thirteen immigrant potters are known to have been resident in the precinct of Duke's Place between 1571 and the end of the century (Kirk and Kirk 1902; Britton 1986); something is known of one of them in particular. Jacob Jansen (or Jonson/Johnson), potmaker, came from Antwerp, probably via Norwich, arriving in London in 1571; several other Flemish potters and painters of pots were noted in the alien returns of the same year. By 1576 Jansen had three servants and by 1582 six servants, four with his own surname. He was then assessed as one of the two richest strangers in the parish of St Katherine Cree, which incorporated the precinct in the late 16th century. He is mentioned in the alien returns until 1592–3. His will of 1592 was proved in 1593.

Thus although it seems unlikely that the (probably) domestic oven was involved in pottery production, evidence is growing for the manufacture of delftware within the precinct from the 1570s. It is possible that the notable Rose plate of 1600, now on show in the Museum of London, is from Jansen's pottery or one nearby. The interim conclusion must be that we now have a second industry within the fringes of the Elizabethan city to add to the known glassworks of Jacob Verzelini, established in the hall of the Crutched Friars by 1575, when it burned down; subsequently it was re-established on the site, to the trepidation of the neighbours (Sutton and Sewell 1980).

The precinct of Holy Trinity priory, as shown by Symonds in 1592, was therefore a mixture of a grand mansion and two other suites of rooms which were probably parts of the original mansion, possibly a builder's yard for the City Mason and the living (if not workplace) of at least one immigrant potter. The east end of the church (Fig 4.6) had sprouted timber-framed tenancies above its Romanesque arches. The spaces between the piers were

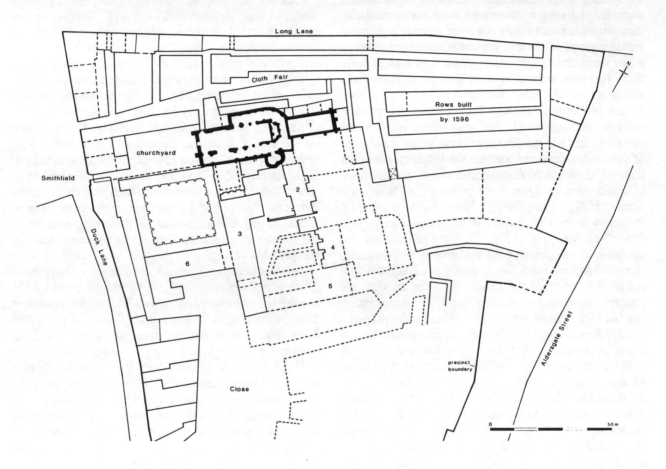

Figure 4.8 St Bartholomew Smithfield: plan of the precinct reconstructed from a rental of 1616 by E A Webb (1921, ii, pl lxxxii). Added key: **A** Newbury Street, **B** Cloth Fair, **C** Middle Street.

left open; in their own way the arcades of the courtyard made out of the monastic chancel imitated the contemporary arcades of the new Royal Exchange (1566–70).

The break-up of monastic precincts in the City of London, from this brief survey, has two 'periods': the mid-16th century era of the brief urban palaces, and the late 16th century fragmentation of the same precincts into smaller housing and often industrial premises, some at least worked by alien immigrants. It may be that the large houses of the first period (1530–1570, though still in evidence in 1616 at St Bartholomew's) represented, in many cases, the opportunity for a combination of wealth and available space to lay out a number of fashionable mansions for the first time, perhaps, since the great houses of the late 13th and early 14th centuries; though all these houses were constrained by the bulk of the major monastic buildings out of which they grew. These houses are worthy of study as expressions of contemporary mores in spatial planning among the leaders of secular society. By studying archaeological remains, documents and plans it is also possible to reconstruct the medieval plans of urban monasteries from the post-Dissolution evidence.

References

Black, W, 1871, *The history of the Leathersellers' Company.*

Britton, F, 1986, *London Delftware.*

Burgon, J W, 1839, *The life and times of Sir Thomas Gresham.*

CCPR = Card calendar to property references in the Journals and Repertories (CLRO).

CLRO = City of London Record Office.

Colvin, H M, 1966, Views of the Old Palace of Westminster. *Architectural History* **9**, 23–184.

Cox, J E, 1876, *Annals of St Helens Bishopsgate.*

Girouard, M, 1983, *Robert Smythson and the Elizabethan country house.*

GL = Guildhall Library, London.

Knowles, D, and Grimes, W F, 1954, *Charterhouse: the medieval foundation in the light of recent discoveries.*

Harben, H A, 1918, *A dictionary of London.*

Kirk, R E G, and Kirk, E F (eds), 1902, *Returns of aliens dwelling in the City and suburbs of London — Part II: 1571–1597.* Huguenot Society Publications **10**.

Lethaby, W R, 1900, The priory of Holy Trinity, Aldgate. *Home Counties Magazine* **2**, 45–53

Masters, B, (ed) 1984, *Chamber accounts of the sixteenth century.* London Record Soc **20**

PRO = Public Record Office.

RCHM, 1925, *London II: West London.* London: HMSO.

RCHM, 1929, *London IV: City of London.* London: HMSO.

Riviere, S, 1985, Excavations at 71–7 Leadenhall Street/32–4 Mitre Street, 1984: Archive Report, Museum of London. Unpublished.

Schofield, J, and Lea, R, in prep. *Holy Trinity Priory, Aldgate.*

Stow = J Stow, *Survey of London* ed C L Kingsford, 3rd ed (1971).

Summerson, J, 1957, Three Elizabethan architects. *Bull J Rylands Lib Manchester* **40**, 209–16.

Sutton, A F, Jacob Verzelini and the City of London. *Glass Technology* **2** No.4, 190–2

VCH, 1908, *Victoria History of the Countries of England.*

Vince, A, and Schofield, J, in prep. The Aldgate Potter.

Webb, E A, 1921, *The records of St Bartholomew's priory and of the church and parish of St Bartholomew the Great, West Smithfield.*

5 Water management in the urban monastery

C J Bond

The discussion which follows provides a counterpart to a paper on water management in rural monasteries (Bond 1989). Given the parallel character of the two papers, it has seemed appropriate to adopt here a broadly similar framework to that of the previous article, while hopefully avoiding duplication. Nonetheless, a few introductory points do, perhaps, warrant repetition.

The definition of urban monasteries is taken here to include houses like Lacock (Wilts) and Eynsham (Oxon), located in places which had significant urban aspirations in the Middle Ages, even if they are now little more than villages. It will also include houses in urban-fringe and suburban locations, such as Osney (Oxon). However, sites like Neath (West Glamorgan), Sandwell (West Midlands) and Kirkstall (West Yorkshire), originally rural but engulfed by post-medieval urban expansion, will not be included. The distinction is not always a clear-cut one, however, and no attempt will be made here to apply a rigid definition.

It was suggested in the 1989 paper that the separate discussion of the water management systems of rural and urban monasteries creates a largely artificial division, since the basic requirements for and uses of water were similar in all monastic establishments. In some respects, however, significant distinctions can be made. Urban situations tend on the whole to be characteristic of certain orders, which fall into two broad groups:–

1. On the one hand there are the old established Benedictine monasteries as Evesham, Pershore and Abingdon, and the early houses of canons which subsequently accepted Augustinian rule, such as Waltham Abbey. Many of these religious houses antedated the towns in which they were situated, and in effect served as pre-urban nuclei, though as a rule their most ambitious water-engineering schemes were only developed later on, subsequent to the urban expansion around them. Alongside this group it is proposed to include certain cathedral chapters such as Exeter, Lichfield and Wells which, though not of monastic constitution, were nonetheless involved in water schemes of such similar character that it makes little sense to ignore them.

2. On the other hand there are the late-comers, in particular the various orders of friars, which did not make their appearance until towns were already well-developed. The increased likelihood of pre-existing constraints upon monastic planning and the competition for space, which affected all urban monasteries to a greater or lesser extent, were particularly significant factors in the development of the friaries and other later houses, which rarely had the room to equip themselves with moats or to develop elaborate ranges of fishponds.

5.1 Water supply

Urban communities of both types found it especially difficult to preserve unpolluted sources of drinking water nearby, and were frequently driven to bring in a piped supply from distant springs. Water conduits have also been recorded on many rural sites, including the Benedictine nunnery of Godstow, the Cluniac priory of Monkton Farleigh, the Cistercian abbeys of Stanley, Valle Crucis and Waverley, the Augustinian houses of Canons Ashby, Haughmond and Warter, and the Bonhommes of Edington. Nonetheless, they are a special feature of urban houses, and demand much fuller exploration here than they were accorded in the earlier discussion of rural monasteries.

Water might be supplied to a religious house in a variety of ways. Founders often chose their site with some care in order to take advantage of natural watercourses or springs. At Wells (Somerset) the springs which rise immediately south-east of the cathedral gave the place its name, and one of the spring outlets, St Andrew's Well, supplied the conduit serving both the cloister and the town in the early 13th century (Rodwell 1980, 14).

Where no surface springs were directly available, the first water supply was normally acquired by sinking wells. At Canterbury (Kent) the famous 12th-century plan (described further below) shows a well in the infirmary cloister, which was presumably the main source of water prior to the introduction of a piped supply, and continued to be maintained as a reserve for use in emergencies. Between it and the infirmary laver was a column with a capital like a great funnel, and an annotation on the plan can be translated: 'When the piped water supply is deficient, water may be raised from this well and, poured into this column, will supply all the offices'. The townspeople would have had access to a second well in the outer cemetery, shown with a counterweighted bucket. St Werburgh's Abbey at Chester was originally reliant upon wells, one of which still exists just outside the slype, and two more of which are shown on an early 17th-century plan (Burne 1962, 38). St Peter's Abbey at Gloucester also drew its earliest supply from a well within the great cloister garth (Fulbrook — Leggatt 1968, 111).

Wells might have provided an adequate supply of drinking water for a while but, as towns expanded, more and more domestic wells were sunk, so that by the 13th century the water table was often permanently lowered and the older wells were no longer sufficiently deep to reach it. Increasing pollution could also be a problem. Some urban monastic communities simply admitted defeat and uprooted themselves in favour of a rural site with easier access to pure running springs: within twenty years of the first foundation of Augustinian canons within the town of Cambridge in 1092, they had moved out to a deserted hermitage at Barnwell where a supply of fresh running water was readily available and where there was more room to extend their buildings (Dickinson 1950, 150; Dickinson 1961, 7). If such a move was to occur, it would normally happen early on in the life of the community before it had expended much capital upon permanent buildings.

More frequently we find religious houses in towns piping in their drinking and washing water from some unpolluted source beyond the bounds of the built-up area. A town with numerous monastic and ecclesiastical institutions, like London, Oxford or Bristol (Fig 5.1), might be the focus of many converging pipe systems. The number of occasions where distant sources of water were piped into monastic precincts is perhaps the most characteristic and most impressive of all the aspects of water management in urban monasteries.

It is not clear when this practice began, though there is an apparently unsubstantiated claim that Westminster Abbey was given a piped supply in the time of Edward the Confessor. Many more reliable examples are documented from the middle of the 12th century onwards. The earliest and best-known instance is at the Benedictine Cathedral Priory of Christ Church, Canterbury, where a complex system of pipes and drains was installed by Prior Wibert some time before 1167 (Willis 1868; Hayes 1977). Contemporary with the Canterbury system is that at Lichfield Cathedral (Staffs), described by Gould (1976). Previously the first known specific record of the Lichfield conduit occurred in 1273–8, though references to the name 'Conduit Street' earlier in the same century had been noted by Thorpe (1951, 161). Gould has shown that Lichfield was bringing in piped water before 1166, and has moreover established an interesting and possibly significant personal link between the two cathedrals in the mid-12th century. Walter Durdent, Bishop of Lichfield from 1148 to 1159, had previously been prior at Canterbury, and Wibert had been his sub-prior and successor as prior there. It seems likely, therefore, that the building of the one piped system may have provided the inspiration for the other.

The later 12th century witnessed the instigation of several similar schemes, particularly in the west midlands at Evesham (Heref & Worcs), Winchcombe (Gloucs) and Gloucester. The documentary evidence suggests a considerable increase in the number of piped water systems during the 13th century, which may in part reflect the expansion of lead-mining in Mendip, Derbyshire, and the Pennines during the same period.

The documentation available falls into several classes:–

(i) Private charters recording grants of springs by a benefactor, which often included rights to build a conduit-head, to lay pipes through other peoples' land and to have access for repairs and maintenance, usually on condition that the monastery restored or paid compensation for any damage caused by its excavations or repairs to the pipe.

(ii) Royal licences for the tapping of springs and laying of pipes, normally enrolled in the Patent Rolls. Matters of particular concern to the Crown, which made such licences necessary, included the laying of pipes along the king's highway and the occasional breaching of town walls to admit the pipes; such operations were permitted on condition that the damage was made good.

(iii) Legal disputes resulting on the one hand from the monastery's failure to repair damage caused by pipe-laying or maintenance, or, on the other hand, the illicit tapping or deliberate breaking of pipes by laymen, such as is recorded at Chester, Daventry and King's Lynn.

(iv) Accounts recording expenditure on the building or repair of conduits less frequently survive, although the fabric rolls of Exeter Cathedral provide one instance from which useful information has been drawn.

(v) Medieval plans: because much of the pipework was invisible beneath the ground, records of its position were necessary in case of future difficulties with the supply. Plans of water systems account for a significant proportion of all known English medieval plans. Their survival has often been a matter of chance, and many more have doubtless been destroyed. The best-known and most complex is the mid-12th century plan of the precinct of Canterbury Cathedral Priory showing the system installed by Prior Wibert (Fig 5.3). This survived only by the good fortune of being bound in with the Eadwin psalter, one of the most notable manuscripts of the Canterbury school, now in Trinity College, Cambridge. A second, contemporary Canterbury plan shows the water system disentangled from the buildings which are irrelevant to it, showing in isolation those buildings receiving water, but showing the ramifications of the pipes more clearly (Willis 1868). Amongst the Harleian manuscripts in the British Library is a mid-13th century copy of an original plan of c 1220 showing the layout of the springs, pipes and settling-tanks at Wormley which supplied Waltham Abbey (Fig 5.2). The London Charterhouse still possesses a great parchment roll dating from the mid-15th century, 3m long and 0.5m wide, made up of four membranes stitched together, depicting the Charterhouse pipe and points where it crosses the supply to other London religious houses (reproduced in Hope 1902, and redrawn here as Fig 5.5). Three of the four skins of a later copy of the Charterhouse plan, 2.67 × 0.58m, also survive (a sketch is reproduced in Hale 1869).

(vi) Post-medieval plans: As many pipe systems remained in use after the Dissolution, they were sometimes depicted on later plans. Continuing use usually resulted in piecemeal changes to the water system, and such maps have to be used with some caution as evidence for the situation in the Middle Ages. With this caveat, however, they are often valuable sources of information. A 'Description of ye vaults, pipes, Sestones and gutters belonging to the Church' was drawn up by James Wilkes, 'waterman to ye Deane and Chapter of Christ's Church, Canterbury', on October 27th 1668; this facilitates the correct location of some of the features misaligned on the 12th-century draw-of particular concern to the Crown, which made such licences necessary included the laying of pipes along the king's highway and the occasional breaching of town walls (see below). Clearly, such operations were

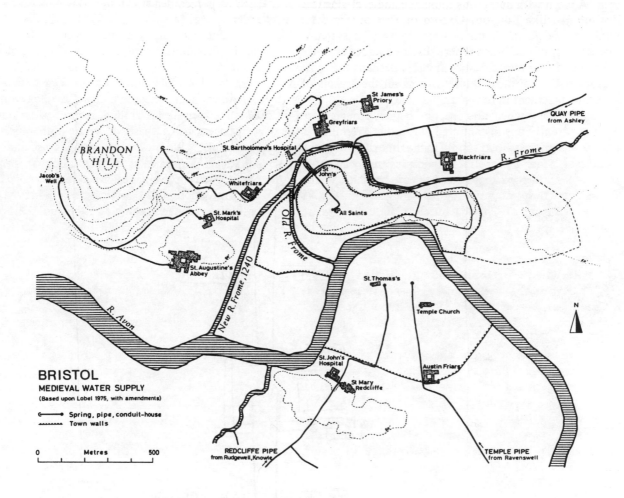

BRISTOL
MEDIEVAL WATER SUPPLY
(Based upon Lobel 1975, with amendments)

⊶——• Spring, pipe, conduit-house
········ Town walls

0   Metres   500

Figure 5.1

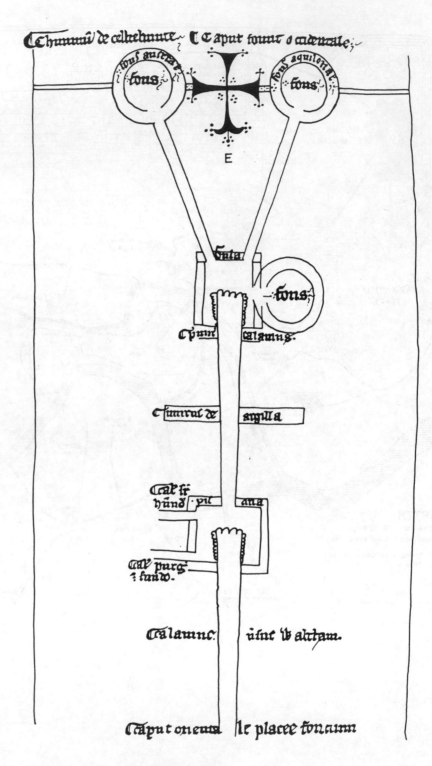

WALTHAM ABBEY

Thirteenth-century plan of pipe from Wormley

Figure 5.2

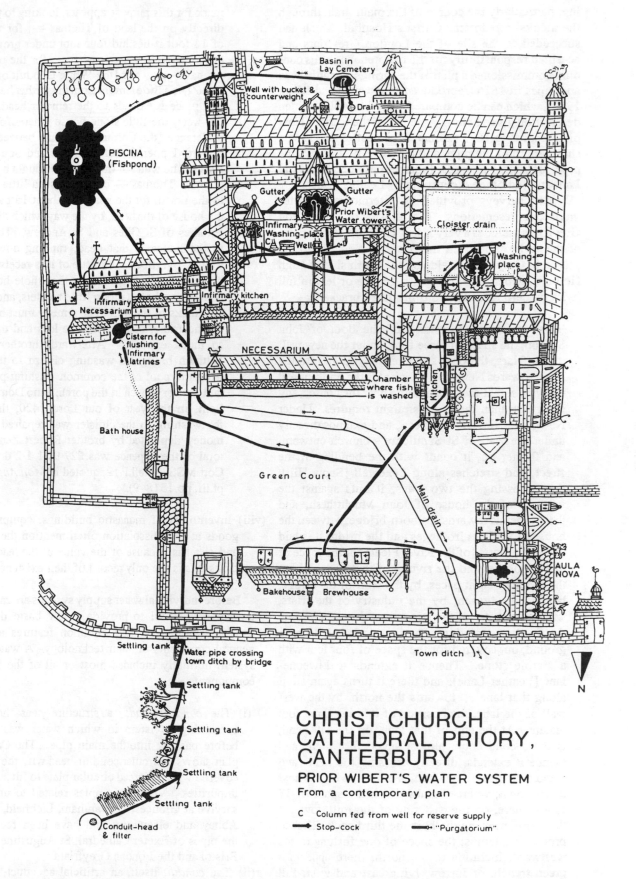

Figure 5.3

CHRIST CHURCH CATHEDRAL PRIORY, CANTERBURY

PRIOR WIBERT'S WATER SYSTEM

From a contemporary plan

C   Column fed from well for reserve supply

→   Stop-cock

•—o   "Purgatorium"

ing, particularly the course of the main drain through the monks' reredorter. Christ's Hospital, which had succeeded to the site of the London Greyfriars and accepted responsibility for the maintenance of its conduit, commissioned a plan of the springs, conduit-head and pipes in 1676 (reproduced in Norman and Mann 1909), which can be compared with the earlier written description given below. An entry in the Christ's Hospital records in 1671 estimates the cost of rerouting a short length of the pipe, and the 1676 plan shows the pipe continuing along Holborn to pass up Gray's Inn Lane instead of the older route by Leather Lane.

(vii) Written surveys provided an alternative to cartographic representations. The register of the London Greyfriars includes a very full description of the course of the entire pipe from the friary at Newgate to the source in Gray's Inn Fields on the north side of High Holborn, which is worth quoting more or less in full [with modern identifications in square brackets]:–

'First, from the threshold of the door of John Sporon, the space of three foot, under the new wall of the friars, the pipe stretches as you go into the street towards Newgate; . . . it holds the north side of the way, sometimes not coming near the houses, any otherwise than the lying straight requires. Under Newgate it lies 12 foot deep, and extends directly under the wall of St Sepulchre's church outward, and farther on, it bends with the bending of the street, and stretches along Lekewell [Snow Hill]; there crossing the two ways, it buts against the window of the house of John Muchtthesh, and there it bends towards Holborn-bridge; between the house of William Irotheges and the bridge it is laid under the water [of the River Fleet] for the space of three foot, beyond the rivulet of that water, about the space of eight paces, by the wall of the bridge, beyond the breach, by the industry of the friars, where the water of the street runs down in a place that is always muddy. The first cock is hid under ground, but covered for the space of four foot with a marble stone. Thence it extends to Liweone-lane [Leather Lane], and there it turns again strait along that lane . . . towards the north, by the west wall of the lane, the position of it being three foot distant. At the end of that lane, on the left hand, is the second cock, almost seven foot high; and thence it extends, directly crossing the fields and hedges, to the mill of Thomas of B—, which is next to the town, where it sinks down the space of 18 foot. There, on the east side of the mill, towards the north, near the ditch, is the third cock. Thence proceeding almost the space of one furlong to the westward, inclining to the north, there appears a green trench, or furrow, lying east and west, full of briers, and winding westwards, almost eight foot wide, dividing the land of John Derkyne, which lies on the south side, from the land of — Basyng, which lies on the north side. In that trench, beginning at the east end 16 paces, not leaps, there from the middle part of the breadth of the trench, where the necessary

mark for this purpose appears, looking to the north, directly on the land of Thomas —, for the space of 14 foot it lies hid four foot under ground. The head which is nearest, whence, for the most part, we have our water [the White Conduit off Chapel Street], is a little remote from the farther head. From that place it extends to the remoter head, towards the west, the little stone house whereof is seen at a distance [the Chimney Conduit between Queen Square, Upper Guildford Street and Southampton Row]. The water of this head is brought beyond the ditch of Thomas — on the west, a little inclining to the north, for the space of about 15 paces from the house of the head, by the way which divides the parishes of St Giles and St Andrew. This water, in the house of that head, running down to the trough, overflows, and little of it is received hence by the trough, but it floods the whole house, and is negligently lost along little rivulets, and through the cracks of the wall. The remedy must be applied by the friars, considering the loss and damage of so much expence. Afterwards brother Thomas Feltham brought a washing cistern to the porch, from the pool of the common washing-place, and laid out very much in the porch, anno Domini 1300. Item, in the year of our Lord 1420, the cistern for washing in the cloister was repaired with the money deposited by brother Robert Zengg. The total of the expence was £27 9s 1 1/2 d. (B.Libr. Cott.MSS, Vitell.F.12, quoted in *Mon.Angl.*, Vol.6, pt.iii, pp.1518–9).'

(viii) Inventories of monastic buildings, equipment and goods at the Dissolution often mention the conduits and cisterns because of the value of the lead. Sometimes this is the only record of their existence.

Before individual water supply systems are catalogued, it may be helpful to provide a few basic definitions and descriptions of their common features and some general comments on their technology. A water supply system normally included most or all of the following components:–

(i) The *conduit-head:* a structure near the springs containing a cistern in which water was gathered before passing into the main pipe. The Canterbury plan shows a circular conduit-head with the exit-pipe covered with a pierced circular plate to filter out gross impurities. Visible examples related to urban sites survive at Gloucester, Grantham, Lichfield, Waltham Abbey and elsewhere, and have been recorded on the pipes of Exeter Cathedral, St Augustine's Abbey, Bristol and the London Greyfriars.

(ii) The *conduit* itself, an artificial aqueduct, gutter or pipe by which water is conveyed from the source to the place where it is used. The Roman engineer Vitruvius describes two basic principles of conduit construction. *Open conduits*, in which the water flowed along an open stone trough or mortared or clay-lined channel, were the more widely used in the Roman world. They had certain drawbacks. They required a reasonably consistent gradient, preferably of not less than 1 in 200, for their flow to be maintained. Consequently, where they were unable to follow the natural contour across broken ground, they required expensive works such as tunnels and bridge-aqueducts. They were more vulnerable to external pollution. On the other hand they could more easily be inspected on a regular basis and more easily cleaned and maintained (Landels 1978, 34–53; *Frontinus-Gesellschaft* 1987, 1988). Open conduits for water-supply are rare on monastic sites, though the rural Cistercian site of Stanley (Wilts) provides a probable example, and the same principle was regularly used for drains and sewers. *Closed conduits* used a system of airtight pipes completely filled throughout with water, and therefore able to slope uphill or downhill at any angle, provided that they did not rise at any point above the level of the intake. They could be laid more readily through the streets of a built-up area and were comparatively secure from external pollution. On the other hand they were vulnerable to bursting due to water pressure if the pipe descended far below either the source or the delivery point, and they were also more liable to become clogged with sediment. Closed conduits were less accessible for inspection and maintenance and much more difficult to repair than open systems, but for medieval urban monasteries their advantages generally outweighed their drawbacks. Vitruvius described the manufacture of lead pipes for closed conduit systems, but warned against the dangers of poisoning from the formation of lead oxide (*cerussa*) in the pipes; he preferred the use of earthenware pipes despite the difficulties of sealing the joints. Nonetheless, lead pipes were almost universally used for monastic conduits, often bedded in clay to prevent leakages, and sometimes encased within stonework for protection and access. Wooden or ceramic pipes are also occasionally found.

(iii) The conduit may pass through *settling-tanks*, another device recommended by Vitruvius. The pipe above each tank is the *feed-pipe*, opening into it above the highest level at which water was required to stand. The sediment is precipitated as the water loses velocity on entering the tank. The *exit-pipe* then draws off the purer water from the upper part of the further end of the tank, and its level in effect controls the level of water in the tank. The mouth of the exit-pipe is often protected in some way to reduce the likelihood of floating debris choking the pipe in its lower course. The exit-pipe from the one settling-tank then becomes the feed-pipe for the next tank below. The mid-12th century Canterbury plan shows no less than five settling-tanks along the course of the conduit between the springs and the city wall, with feed-pipes entering on the western side and exit-pipes leaving at the eastern end. At the supply end of each settling tank is a *purgatorium*, a stop-cock which would allow the tank to be drained to clean it of accumulated sediment by flushing. The last settling-tank is placed against one of the bastions of the city wall, and the

conduit is carried across the city ditch on a bridge-like structure (Willis 1868). The Waltham Abbey plan shows two rectangular settling-tanks with scalloped lines suggesting perforations at the top ends of the exit-pipes. The London Charterhouse plan shows several small square settling-tanks along the upper course of the pipe near the springs and between two larger rectangular cistern-houses. The upper cistern-house, identifiable with the White Conduit in Pentonville, is shown in plan with the reservoir occupying only the northern half: it has a feed-pipe discharging into the cistern through a perforated rose, and there are two exit-pipes, one with a perforated head, the other apparently a waste-pipe to drain off surplus water. The second cistern-house, which is shown in birds-eye view with one wall opened to show the interior, appears to be of red brick with a gabled roof; in this building the reservoir completely fills the interior, with three feed pipes entering it from the north and a single enlarged exit-pipe, again with a perforated head. There is also a small waste-pipe and a plug for draining the cistern for cleansing (Hope 1902). By contrast, at Lichfield the supply seems to have been exceptionally clean. There were no settling-tanks along the entire course of the pipe, and the cistern within the close very rarely needed cleaning (Gould 1976).

(iv) Many pipes had *outlets* or vents at intervals, for various purposes. The London Charterhouse plan includes several features labelled as *suspirals*, which appear to have been conceived as vents to let out trapped air in order to avoid the supposed danger of the pipes being burst by the compression of the air or pressure of water within (Hope 1902, 301fn). The 1676 plan of the London Greyfriars system shows a series of thirteen close-set suspirals along its entire length, and these features are also mentioned in the 17th-century Christ's Hospital records covering the maintenance of the pipe (Norman and Mann 1909, 353–4). On the Lichfield pipe there were plugs where the pipe ran near a stream, and it was thought that the purpose of these was to allow water to be drained off to facilitate repairs (Gould 1976, 76).

(v) In open conduits, chambers with sluice-gates might permit the diversion of part or all of the supply. At Gloucester a sluice-gate in the cistern in the cloister of St Peter's Abbey may have been the control point from which surplus water was permitted to St Oswald's Priory in the later 13th century (Fulbrook-Leggatt 1968, 115). At Wells a stone sluice-box 3m west of the east wall of the Camery controlled the entry to a branch channel of 0.23m × 0.38m leading southwards towards the moat of the bishop's palace (Buckle 1894, 45–6).

(vi) The *conduit-house*, a structure containing a cistern for the storage of water before use. Often this served as a reservoir from which water was distributed to outlets in various parts of the precinct. Prior Wibert's water-tower at Canterbury is the earliest and perhaps most impressive surviving example.

Other technical details which require comment include the considerable length of some supply conduits. Obviously the general practice was to utilise the nearest available source of sufficiently pure water, in order to minimise the expense and practical difficulties of constructing conduits. However, for a variety of reasons, more distant sources sometimes needed to be tapped. The Dominican friars of Boston (Lincs) acquired a royal licence in 1327 to construct a subterranean conduit from Bolingbroke, more than 20km away. This is so exceptional that it must be doubted whether it was ever built; but distances of 3–5km were frequently traversed, for example at Chester, Gloucester, the London Charterhouse, Reading and Waltham.

In view of the length of some conduits, a degree of skill in levelling was necessary in order to ensure that the distribution cistern was lower than the conduit-head at the spring. Burne (1962, 41) has calculated that from the Christleton source acquired by the monks of St Werburgh's Abbey, Chester, in 1282, there was a fall of only 3m over a distance of 3km to the conduit-house in the cloister. This compares with a fall of 7m in 2km in the conduit of the London Greyfriars; even in this latter case, the overall gradient was so slight that the records of Christ's Hospital, which used the same supply after the Dissolution, contain many complaints that the water 'did not come well home' (Martin 1937, 204).

A further point of some interest is the number of occasions where water was piped in from the 'wrong' side of a river. At Oxford many of the religious houses drew water from springs rising on the Corallian hills west of the city, and this had to be piped in across more than one branch of the Thames. Sometimes pipes were laid under the river itself: the Avon at Lacock and the Kennett at Reading seem to have been crossed in this way. On other occasions the pipe seems to have been carried over some convenient pre-existing bridge, as occurred at Worcester. The Canterbury pipe crossed the city ditch by a bridge. Use of bridges made for ease of access for maintenance, but were not always available where needed.

Finally, the application of technological improvements can be detected in some systems. Some of the early closed conduits must undoubtedly have suffered problems from leakage, blockage and bursting, and experience soon showed that better means of access for repairs and maintenance were required. At Wells three manholes have been excavated, spaced 12–13m apart along the course of the 1477 diversion of Bishop Beckington's pipe around Bishop Stillington's Lady Chapel, one of them giving access to a washout valve in the lead pipe which would have allowed the flushing of sediment out of the main (Rodwell 1980, 15). At Exeter the early 13th-century pipe seems to have been laid in a bed of clay and took the most direct route possible to the cathedral. This seems to have proved unsatisfactory, as its mid-14th century replacement took a longer route, making more use of public streets from which direct access could be gained, and the pipe itself was carried within a stone-lined passageway large enough to allow access to all parts of it to permit repairs and maintenance (Fox 1951).

5.2 Provisional catalogue of references to water supply in urban religious houses

The following lists are no more than the products of a preliminary trawl of historical and archaeological references from readily-accessible sources, and they make no pretence of completeness. Much more material undoubtedly awaits collection and synthesis, particularly from local journals and from sources such as the Patent Rolls, where a change of indexing practice after the publication of the calendar for 1317–21 means that items such as aqueducts, conduits and watercourses cannot readily be traced after that date.

5.2.1 Non-Monastic Cathedrals

EXETER, Cathedral

By 1226 water was being brought to Exeter Cathedral from St Sidwell's Well, at the head of the Longbrook Valley. Money for the maintenance and repair of this well was left in the will of John de Doulys in 1267 (Tucker 1858). The original conduit was carried diagonally beneath the city wall at the East Gate and continued down Catherine Street to the close (Morris et al.1932).

In 1346 there was a disagreement between the mayor and citizens of Exeter, the dean and chapter of the Cathedral, and the Benedictine monks of St. Nicholas's Priory over the repair of the conduit from St Sidwell's (Acct. Exeter, 322–3). The settlement of the dispute resulted in the expenditure of over £50 over the following three years on digging a new conduit from the spring known as the Headwell to a new cistern-house in the Cathedral yard. From here watercourses were extended to serve the city and St. Nicholas's Priory, in exchange for annual payments of 8s each (Tucker 1858; Morris et al.1932, 191). The second conduit was longer than its predecessor, crossing the Longbrook stream on two occasions, but making greater use of roads.

The expenses detailed in the account rolls of Walter Haselholt and Thomas Canyng, successive wardens of the Cathedral fabric, over the period 1346–9 include the wages of labourers digging the ditches a rates of 8d-10d per week each, wages of the plumber making the pipes from the Cathedral's own lead, wages of the masons hired to cover the pipes with stones, and costs of stone, lime, firewood, timber, sand, beef tallow and rope. The 1348–9 accounts include two purchases of 158 lbs of tin for the pipes at a cost of 21s 2d with 2d for carriage, perhaps implying that the cathedral's own store of lead had by then become exhausted (Acct. Exeter, 273–4, 276–7, 279–82). There were inevitably a few teething troubles, and the account rolls of 1350–51 and 1352–3 record further expenses for digging, soldering and other repairs, including the wages of a mason hired for one week to repair the wall carrying the pipes at Longbrook (Acct. Exeter, 286, 290–1).

Further repairs to the conduit are recorded in the Cathedral fabric rolls in 1419–20 and again in 1437–9; on the latter occasion there was considerable expenditure on stones for a wall made at

Longbrook for the safe keeping of the pipes (Tucker 1858).

On several occasions parts of the Exeter Cathedral water supply system have been examined archaeologically. In January 1858 the excavation of the railway cutting near St Sidwell's church resulted in the accidental discovery of a very curious structure at the conduit-head. A copious spring was conveyed into a lead stand-pipe soldered into a horizontal lead disc 3m in diameter and about 80mm thick, with a small central aperture. This disc stood upon a round platform, 1.9m in diameter, consisting of two courses of red volcanic Killerton stone laid in five concentric rings around the opening into the base of the standpipe. Each stone was channelled on its underside both segmentally and radially, the purpose apparently being to regulate the flow into the standpipe as well as collecting the water on all sides. The stones were cemented in place, with the lead disc resting flush with the upper surface of the platform, by means of a massive bed of firmly-puddled clay, 1.8m deep and about 6m in diameter. A similar, but slightly smaller, construction was built over a less copious spring close by, with a lead pipe connected to a disc 1.5m in diameter resting upon a stone platform only one course deep but similarly channelled on the underside, all sealed within the same bed of clay. Both pipes originally fed into a cistern at ground level enclosed within a small stone arched building. A third spring 7.6m away was tapped by an ancient square stone well 2.3m deep and linked by a lead pipe with the first spring. No archaeological evidence for the dating of this extraordinary arrangement was recorded, though it was presumed to be ancient. A new conduit-head had been built over the larger spring in 1836 with a brick well-shaft to provide a larger capacity than the original cistern, and this had resulted in the removal of the upper part of the original main standpipe (Tucker 1858).

A section seen in 1984 in King William Street, not far below St Sidwell's, revealed a trench 3.3m deep which appears to have contained a lead pipe (subsequently robbed) upon a bed of red clay. This was probably part of the first aqueduct recorded in 1226, which went out of use when it was replaced by the new line in 1347–9 (*Medieval Archaeol* **28**, 1984, 213–6).

In 1950 the cathedral conduit was encountered *c* 34m west of the city wall, where it was cut by a sewer trench in the shopping centre of Princesshay. Here it was originally built in an open trench dug 3.4m into the natural red clay. The bottom of the trench was 1.7m wide, with sides battered back to a width of 2.7m at the top. The conduit itself was built 1.2m above the floor of the trench, which may imply that the engineers had committed an error in their levelling. The earth filling below the conduit included pottery dating up to the early 14th century, which conforms well with the documented operation of 1346–9; there was no sign here of the earlier conduit of 1226. The conduit itself was 0.7m wide by 1.5m high, built of blocks of trap (the local volcanic stone) dressed on the inner face. It had a vaulted roof constructed in three planes with a flat-based keystone. The floor of the conduit was hollowed slightly to accommodate a 75mm lead pipe. The remainder of the original trench alongside and over

the conduit was filled with redeposited red clay (Fox 1951). The form of construction used for the conduit of 1346–9 in Princesshay represents a distinct improvement over the more basic early 13th-century construction seen at King William Street.

LICHFIELD, Cathedral

An undated charter records that Thomas Bromley gave to the church of Lichfield two springs at Pipe, 2.4km west of the Cathedral, for the conduit then being built, in return for 15s 4d; if Gould's identification of the witnesses is correct, as seems likely, this charter belongs to the period 1140–70. The Pipe Rolls of 1166–7 record that a fine of one mark was imposed upon the cathedral canons for offences in the Forest of Cannock at Pipe, and this is the earliest specific documentation for this place-name, which must surely be derived from the conduit itself. The nature of these offences is unfortunately not specified, but the building of the conduit would inevitably have caused some damage, and if this link can be made, the period of construction can be pinpointed more precisely (Gould 1976, 74). This first pipe seems originally to have entered the close at its highest point near the north-west corner.

A second undated charter records that William Bell of Pipe, in return for 12s, gave to the church another spring at Maple Hayes at Pipe close to the conduit-head already existing; the identity of the witnesses places this charter to within a few years of 1259 (Gould 1976, 74).

In 1280 the Archdeacon of Chester was given permission to tap the main system where it crossed his land at the corner of Shaw Lane, to feed a small extension pipe for his own use (*Magn.Reg.Alb.*, 317, nos. 672–3).

Following the fortification of the close with a defensive stone wall in 1312, the pipe was apparently rerouted to enter by the new West Gate, as four individuals granted permission for the pipe to cross their various lands near this point (Gould 1976, 75–6). It was then led into a stone cistern west of the cathedral, which remained in position until 1786.

In 1489 there was a dispute between the cathedral and Sir Humfrey Stanley, when the door of the conduit-head was broken, and the Chapter appealed to Henry VII to intervene on their behalf (Gould 1976, 76–7).

Leland describes the supply to the cathedral close, 'havynge a castle [conduit-house] ther, from the whiche watar is convayed to the prebendary howses' (Leland, Itin., Vol.ii, p.100).

The medieval conduit-head still remains at Pipe Park, cut into the hillside. It is a rectangular structure with a gabled roof of large corbelled stones, supported internally by a pointed arch of 13th-century character, covering a cistern cut into the solid rock 1.74m long, 1.07m wide and 2.21m deep. Much of the original leadwork was plundered in 1652 and replaced in part with alder pipes; but these were in turn replaced with new leadwork in 1708 (Gould 1976, 77–8). None of the original lead pipes are known to survive, but their replacements continued to supply the Lichfield close with water right up until 1969.

WELLS, Cathedral

As the name implies, Wells Cathedral was amply supplied with water from local springs, and a complex pattern of watercourses also supplied the town (Balch 1925). A stone-vaulted open conduit was built in the early 13th century to carry water from St Andrew's Well through the claustral area out to the market-place of the town. The course of this conduit was partly traced in excavations in the Camery in 1894 (Buckle 1894), and it has been re-examined more recently (Rodwell 1980). The earlier excavations showed that it had clearly undergone at least one major diversion, but its original course was located below St Andrew's Well, entering the Camery below a small niche in its eastern wall. This section had dimensions of 0.53m × 0.97m, and was rubble-walled with a flat floor and cover-stones. 3m west of the Camery wall a sluice controlled the flow into a smaller branch conduit leading towards the moat of the bishop's palace, and 3.66m further on a change in alignment and in the character of the masonry marked the beginning of a later diversion, which can be dated to the later 15th century. The conduit returned to its original course close to the cloister wall, having tapped a further spring on the way, and in this section was 0.76m wide with a vaulted roof.

Within the cloister itself access was provided to the water within a vaulted underground chamber, the so-called 'dipping-place' which, it was suggested by Buckle, was the point from which water was drawn for the cathedral prior to the introduction of the first piped supply, and was perhaps also the laundry-place. The stairway entering the dipping-place was rebuilt in the 16th century, and water continued to be drawn from it into the 19th century (Buckle 1894, 35–6, 45–7). Rodwell (1980, 14) suggests an alternative possibility that the primary function of the dipping-place was as a baptistry.

On 20th September 1451 Bishop Thomas Beckington granted to the burgesses of Wells a portion of the water from St Andrew's Well, 'that they may have a head for a water conduit with reservoirs, vents and other engines above and below ground, for taking and leading a portion of the bishop's water springing within the precinct of his palace of Wells from a spring called Seynt Andrew welle, upon a spot appointed by the said bishop, whereon he has built such head at his own cost sufficient for lead pipes 12 inches in circumference, with dykes, trenches, ponds, cisterns etc., as well within the said precinct as in the public streets of the city, and power to repair the same, break ground and lay pipes, etc., so that the water may flow as far as the high cross in the city market and other places as they shall think fit, making good all damages; provided that the first head and reservoir to take all the said bishop's water be round, of 10 feet diameter within the walls, built of stone, lime or other material at his cost, with one round cistern of lead 5 feet in depth and 4 feet in diameter, and pipes attached on either side of the reservoir or cistern at the cost of the city, half the water to be led towards the city, half to flow to and within divers parts of the palace, and the said head shall have one door and two keys, one to remain with the bishop, the other with the master and burgesses' (Cal.Wells MSS, i, 433). A tall square stone conduit-house with traceried panels was built in the market-place; its appearance is known from an engraving made very shortly before its replacement in 1793 by the present Gothic Revival fountain. Provision was also made for diverting the supply to refill the moat of the bishop's palace on occasions when it had been scoured out, for the opening, inspection and cleansing of the conduit-head at least once every six months, and for the waste water to flow into the bishop's mill stream.

It is likely that the works undertaken in the time of Bishop Beckington reflected an increasingly intensive use of the space outside the cathedral precinct, including the construction of a row of twelve new shops built on the north side of the market-place in 1451–2. Pipes were laid to carry fresh water to the new buildings, but surplus overflow from the springs also appears to have necessitated the construction of further channels more specifically for drainage.

An indenture in Bishop Beckington's Register dated 23rd June 1459 describes the passage of the watercourse recently made by the bishop via 'two gutters or subterranean passages... under the pavement of the street called the 'Marketplace' and the house and garden of Thomas Horewode and the garden of Master John Morton, leading from the said messuages to the stream running from the spring called 'Seynt Andrewis welle' at the back of the house of the said Thomas Horewode'; the Dean and Chapter of the Cathedral were permitted to break up the pavement and ground of the market-place, house and gardens in order to clean, empty, repair or renew the said gutters and passages within a breadth of 8 feet (2.4m) and a depth of 12 feet (3.7m), provided that they restore the ground as soon as possible at their own expense, and compensate the bishop or his tenants for any damage (Reg.Bekynton, i, no.1220, pp.321–2)

A second indenture, dated 1464, records a grant from the bishop to Richard Swan, provost of Wells, lawful possessor of the canonical houses near the outer gate of the bishop's palace, of '...the conduit and watercourse issuing from the ditches called 'le Mote' of the [bishop's] palace and running by the southern end of the bishop's prison ... beyond and over a small stream of water there to the ground of the said canonical houses under the same houses, as the said water is at present carried and runs, and as it used to be carried and to run while the said Master John [Morton] occupied the said houses, which conduit and watercourse the bishop caused to be made with gutters as far as the said small stream in the direction of his mills, in order to draw off the overflow of water which often happens in the said ditches'; accompanying this grant was a licence for Richard and his successors to enter the bishop's land as far as the head of the watercourse to carry out any necessary repairs (Reg.Bekynton, i, no.1619, pp.422–4).

When Bishop Stillington built his Lady Chapel on the eastern side of the cloisters in the late 15th century both the 13th-century open conduit and the lead pipe laid in 1453 to Beckington's new houses had to be diverted into a more southerly alignment to avoid the massive foundations of the new chapel's south transept (Rodwell 1980, 14–16). The excavations of 1894 revealed both the point of departure of Stillington's diversion and its reunion with the older open conduit, recognisable as changes in direction and changes in the type of masonry. The upper part of Stillington's conduit was 0.56m × 0.43m, of squared stones, the lower part similarly built but enlarged to 0.61m × 0.76m (Buckle 1894, 45–7).

5.2.2 Benedictine and Cluniac Houses

CANTERBURY, Christ Church Cathedral Priory

A charter in the names of T(heobald), Archbishop of Canterbury and Walter, Bishop of Rochester, and therefore dated between 1148 and 1162, records a grant to the priory of a source of pure water in a field called The Holmes, c 1.2km to the north-east (Willis 1868, 181, Appendix ii). Water from the springs was conducted to the monastery through a series of five settling-tanks down to the city and precinct walls, and then distributed through a system of pipes, cisterns and drains laid out under the direction of Wibert, who was Prior of Christ Church from 1153 to 1167. The system is shown on two contemporary maps, mentioned above, with the pipe passing through cornfields, vineyards and orchards outside the city walls and crossing the city ditch by a bridge (Fig 5.3)

Some 220m outside the city walls to the north-east, the pipe passed through what was originally the garden of the house of the Archdeacon of Canterbury. In c 1084–5 the Augustinian priory of St Gregory had been founded by Archbishop Lanfranc outside the walls, and its main claustral buildings lay some 130m north-west of the archdeacon's house. In 1227 Archbishop Stephen Langton granted this house and its garden, saving only the course of the conduit through the grounds, to St Gregory's Priory, in order that the canons might enlarge their precinct (Cart.Canterbury St.Gregory, pp.15–16, no.19). In exchange the prior and canons of St Gregory's would give a basket of fruit each year in the second week of September for consumption in the Christ Church refectory; and they promised that the conduit would remain unharmed when they enclosed and planted their orchard and garden there, and that the workmen of Christ Church should have access for repairs when necessary (Cart.Canterbury St Gregory, pp,168–9, Appx.1.5, 1.6).

The arrangements for the distribution of the water within the monastery will be described more fully in a later section.

CHESTER, St Werburgh's Abbey

In September 1278 the monks of Chester acquired a licence to make a conduit from a well called 'Newtones Well' along the high road to their abbey, and to breach the town wall if it proved necessary, on condition that they did no harm to the town, the wall or any person thereby (Cal.Pat.R.,1272–81, 279).

In 1282 this supply was augmented by a further gift, by Philip and Isabel Burnell of Malpas, of a spring in their field at Christleton, 3km east of Chester, a plot of ground around it, and easements for the pipes carrying water to the monastery (Cart.Chester, 224, no.340). This gift is of some interest, since the Burnells had been involved in an acrimonious lawsuit with the abbey in the previous year (Burne 1962, 40). In September 1283

Edward I granted the monks a licence to make a conduit from the Christleton spring and to carry it down to the abbey, provided that they repair all damage thus caused to the lands of the king or other landowners along the course of the conduit and repair any breaches in the town wall (Cal.Pat.R., 1281–92, 75). One landowner, Randle de Merton, forester of Delamere, cut the pipe where it crossed his land, but was forced to make reparations by the king (Burne 1962, 40).

The 'Abbot's Well' at Christleton Bank is now a small muddy pond, with traces of walling in blocks of tooled sandstone around three sides.

DAVENTRY, Priory

A water supply to the small Cluniac priory of Daventry is known from the record of a commission of oyer and terminer set up in 1294 following a complaint by the prior that fourteen named individuals had broken the underground conduit passing through the middle of his ground to the priory, and had carried away his goods and assaulted one of the monks and two of the priory servants (Cal.Pat.R., 1292–1301, 115–6).

DURHAM, Cathedral Priory

Leland quotes 'ex antiquo Codice Dunelmensi', 'Aquae ductus in cellarium derivatus, anno Dom. 1433' (Leland, Itin., Vol.v, 132).

EVESHAM, Abbey

The Chronicle of Evesham Abbey records Abbot Adam (1160–89) building an aqueduct and lavatorium 'with the assistance of many good men' (Chron.Evesham, 100; Bond 1973, 5). The source of the supply is not known.

In 1243, when the temporalities of the abbey were briefly in the hands of the king, Henry III ordered his keeper to repair the abbey's aqueduct if it could be done for 40s. (Cal.Lib.R. ii, 187).

Lead pipes from the conduit were discovered in 1726 (Barnard 1923).

EXETER, St Nicholas's Priory

The cathedral's supply was brought to a conduit-house in the close in 1346, from which a portion was made available by an extension pipe to St Nicholas's Priory. The priory paid the cathedral chapter 8s per annum for the use of the supply (Tucker 1858; Morris et al.1932, 191).

GLOUCESTER, St Peter's Abbey

In the time of Abbot Serlo (1072–1104) a canal called the Fulbroc was dug to bring water from the River Twyver, first to fill the city ditch and then to supply the abbey with water; the grant made by William the Conqueror was confirmed by Henry I, Stephen and Henry II (Hist. Glouc. i, 154–5; ii, 186). As the name implies, this was unfit for drinking and served only to cleanse the drains and drive the mill.

A new piped supply obtained from 'Mattesknoll', 3.7km away on Robins Wood Hill is recorded in two charters preserved in the cathedral library. The first grant is from Philip, son of Philip of Matson to Abbot Reginald

(1163–84), giving 'the fresh water which ...[the abbot and convent] can find on my land ...[and] a stone erection which the said religious men have built beneath Mattesnolle to convey the water collecting there at their pleasure ...I also wish and grant that they may bring together all the rising waters of the well which are on my land at Mattesnolle above their conduit, so that they may better dispatch without any impediment [from me] and my heirs for ever. Moreover, I grant for me and my heirs that the said religious men may bring their watercourse (*aqualicium*) freely through all my land beneath the head of their aqueduct towards Gloucester up to their abbey for ever'. A second charter from William Geraud of Matson, a tenant of the abbey, in *c* 1230, granted 'all that water which ...[the abbot and convent] have found or can find in my land of Mattesknoll, together with a certain piece of land in which is situated the place for gathering of the water and its building, and that the said religious men may dig and ditch in my aforesaid land wheresoever they wish and desire to loosen it at their pleasure at whatoever places and whatsoever time for bringing down and increasing the water, and repairing or setting right the aforesaid place for gathering [the water] as often as necessary' (quoted in Fullbrook-Leggatt 1968, 113–4). A similar grant to the Gloucester Greyfriars (see below) uses the same phrases and is probably contemporary.

The *Historia* of the abbey, recording the death on November 9th 1237 of the sacrist Helias of Hereford, mentions in passing that he made the conduit to the abbey (*Hist. Glouc.* i, 28), presumably as a result of the above grants. The precise course of the conduit is not known, but it is possible that the reservoir discovered in 1888 and still visible within the Great Cloister garth is part of the work of Helias of Hereford (Waller 1889, 48). It clearly antedates the existing cloisters, though by the 14th century it was serving only as a drain, since the waste-pipe of the lavatorium then emptied into it (Heighway 1988, 36).

In 1355 the abbey was involved in a dispute over the springs on Robins Wood Hill, accusing the Greyfriars of interfering with its supply. Edward III sent the Black Prince to hold an enquiry, and an agreement was reached whereby the abbey retained two-thirds of the supply from the hill (Fulbrook-Leggatt 1968, 113–5).

MALMESBURY, Abbey

Abbot William of Colerne (1260–96) laid a conduit to the abbey from the 'water of Niwenton', the Newnton Brook, at a cost of £100. It is recorded that the water first flowed into the lavatorium on Martinmas, 1284 (*Reg.Malm.* ii, 361, 376).

PERSHORE, Abbey

In the 13th century William FitzWarin granted to Pershore Abbey a spring called 'Abblewell' in Wick on the opposite side of the Avon, and gave licence for the monks to repair the conduit conducting water to the abbey where it lay on his lands (P.R.O. Augm.Off.Misc.Bks., lxi, fol.74d, quoted in V.C.H. Worcs. iv, 1924, 171). The precise site of Abblewell is unknown, although there was a mill of the same name close by.

READING, Abbey

A supply of water for drinking and washing was obtained from a spring called the Conduit near Highgrove in Whitley, a little over 3km to the south of the abbey (Hurry 1901, 23).

WESTMINSTER, Abbey

Westminster was possibly the earliest of the London religious houses to have a piped water supply (Norman 1899, 256). A monument near the outfall of the Serpentine in Hyde Park bears the following inscription:

'A supply of water by a conduit from this spot was granted to the Abbey of Westminster, with the manor of Hyde, by King Edward the Confessor. The manor was resumed by the Crown in 1536, but the springs as a head and original fountain of water were preserved to the abbey by charter of Queen Elizabeth in 1560'.

However, no reliable source for the ascription of the grant of the springs and building of the conduit to Edward the Confessor has so far been identified, and there is no other indication of a piped supply to Westminster before the 12th or 13th century.

WINCHCOMBE, Abbey

A spring at Honiwell, on the high ground above Sudeley, was granted to Winchcombe Abbey in *c* 1184–94 by Robert Russel who, together with Robert, the parson of Sudeley, gave permission for the monks to lay the conduit and to have access for its maintenance where it passed through their lands (Winchcombe *Landboc*, i, 237, 242).

On 15th September 1299 John de Sudeley gave the monks full permission to repair the water-pipe from Honiwell at their pleasure, provided that they made good all damage caused by digging in his seed-ground and meadow (Winchcombe *Landboc*, i, 239).

The length of the conduit between Honiwell and the abbey is no more than *c* 2.4km, but it had to descend a steep fall through *c* 100m from the Cotswold edge into the Isbourne valley, and the consequent water pressure must have been considerable (Haigh 1947, 51).

WORCESTER, Cathedral Priory

The cathedral priory apparently first drew its water from the prior's park at Battenhall to the south-east of the city, but this supply proved insufficient. A second attempt was made to tap Hardwick's Spring at Swanpool in St Johns, but finally a more plentiful supply was secured from Henwick Hill. Both the latter sources lay on the opposite bank of the Severn to the priory, and the supply had to be carried in pipes over the town bridge (a short distance further upstream than the present bridge) and then under the streets to the precinct (Noake 1866, 113–4; Richardson 1955, 41). This arrangement was confirmed by Henry IV in 1407 (Habington, Surv.Worcs., ii, 403).

In 1434 the bailiffs and aldermen of Worcester granted to Prior John Fordham (1423–38) and the convent liberty to 'use, enjoy, lay and amend thyer conveyances of water under grownd with thyer pipes as well of wood as lead in the king's high-way and the streete leading before the cotages of the prior and convent in the suburbs of Worcester neere the castle ditch which John Feckenham, shoemaker, held, and which is and are opposite to the towne ditch of Worcester under the castell there extending from thence within the cittie to the priorie gate and land of the prior and convent, . . . provided always that if the prior, convent and thyer successors, shall doe any harme or harme shall happen to be done aboute the amending, lodging, digging, and making of the waterworke, then ye prior and convent shall after reasonable warning given at thyer owne charges repaire what is defective and for ever mentaine the king's highway over the water-worke. And the prior, convent and thyer successors, shall for this graunt pay to the bayliffs and thyer successors a red rose at the feast of ye nativity of S.John ye Baptist.' (Habington, Surv.Worcs. ii, 401; Noake 1866, 111). Henry VI confirmed to the priory its licence to carry its conduit from Henwick over the Severn bridge (Cal.Worc.MSS, 193).

In the time of Prior John Weddesbury (1507–18) a further agreement was reached with the bailiffs and citizens whereby the prior and convent would undertake to mend the pipes whenever they were broken within seven days (Noake 1866, 129).

Habington concludes 'The conduits which before this served the priorie had thyer fountaines between Worcester and Hallow, and from Henwyke and Hilton streete the pipes for conveyance of water had thyer passage over Worcester bridge, and through the cittie to the Priorie, as appeareth by the king's confirmation, 8 Hen.4. The other conduits beiond Sydburie [i.e. the route from the older source at Battenhall] have been neglected and are now almost forgotten.' (Habington, Surv.Worcs.ii, 403). The Henwick supply continued to function up to the Civil War, when the pipes were torn up for their lead. It was recorded that amongst the £8,204 worth of lead and timber removed from the priory buildings and precinct during the Civil War were 2140 yards (1956m) of lead water pipes, and the whole of the conduit houses and the lead cisterns (Prattinton Colln., Soc.of Antiquaries, viii, 405; V.C.H. Worcs.iv, 1924, 396).

5.3   Charterhouses

LONDON, Charterhouse

The London Charterhouse was founded in 1371, but only acquired a regular piped water supply after 1430, when John Feriby and Margery, his wife, were empowered to grant to the Carthusians a spring at Overmead in the manor of Barnersbury in Islington, 3.2km away, with a portion of land 53 perches (266.5m) long and 12 feet (3.7m) wide. The prior was to be permitted to make an underground conduit from this spring through the specified land and along the king's highway to the monastery, paying 12d yearly to John and Margery and their heirs (Hope 1902, 296).

The course of the conduit from Islington is shown in detail on the mid 18th-century parchment preserved at the Charterhouse. At the head was a series of wells and springs with a stone gutter conducting water to the first reservoir. It then passed through several small settling-tanks by means of lead pipes, gradually increasing in volume, to a reservoir which was known after its rebuilding in 1641 as the White Conduit; its site is commemorated by White Conduit Street, Pentonville, London N.1. From this point there was a fall of 19m in 1.6km to the monastery. Below the White Conduit was a second cistern-house, the precise site of which is unknown. The conduit-head of the Knights Hospitallers lay nearby, and the St John's pipe crossed under the Charterhouse pipe immediately below the second cistern-house. The beginning of the conduit of the Augustinian nuns of St Mary's, Clerkenwell, is also shown somewhere to the east. As the Charterhouse pipe continued southwards it passed between two windmill-mounds, the second of which is labelled in a later hand as being levelled into the field. Between the two windmill mounds the Charterhouse pipe crossed at an oblique angle the pipe of the nuns of Clerkenwell, and shortly afterwards the main London-Islington road. The final section of the map towards the Charterhouse precinct itself has few identifiable landmarks. The internal distribution of water within the Charterhouse will be examined in a later section.

The supply remained in use at the end of the 16th century, when Stow records that 'at the gate of this Charter house is a faire water conduit, with two cockes serving the use of the neighbours to their great commoditie' (Stow, Surv.Lond., ii, 83).

SHEEN, Charterhouse

By the strict application of the definition of urban monasteries, Sheen should not appear in this article. However, since the corresponding discussion of rural monasteries was published, Mick Aston has drawn my attention to an article on Sheen containing details of its water system which I had overlooked, and it is of sufficient interest to warrant a brief insert. At the time of the original foundation by Henry V in 1414–15 a conduit from a spring called 'Hillesdenwell' had been granted; but in 1466 Edward IV gave the prior and monks a licence to make a new subterranean conduit from the spring called 'Welwey alias Pickwelleswell', as the original supply had proved inadequate (Cal.Pat.R., 1461–7, 513). It is known that work on new cells was in progress in 1457, and it may have been this increase in accommodation which rendered the Hillesdenwell supply insufficient. A survey of 1649 records that houses on the site 'are very well accommodated with water which is brought and conveyed unto them through several small pipes of lead branched from one great pipe of lead from the stop-cock or conduit head on Richmond Green unto a great cistern of stone placed within the said wall of Shene' (Cloake 1977, 151).

5.3.1   Houses of Regular Canons

BRISTOL, St Augustine's Abbey (Victorine)

The canons of St Augustine's drew their water from one of the two Jacob's Wells in the hollow between Brandon Hill and Belle Vue, where the present Gorse Lane joins Jacob's Wells Road (formerly called Woodwell Lane).

The canons' well, now the property of the Dean and Chapter of Bristol Cathedral, was linked by pipe to the abbey, and also supplied houses in Trinity Street belonging to the canons. A perambulation made by order of Edward III in connection with a charter of 1373 describes bounds running along a 'rivulet called Woodwill's Lake, northwards to the conduit of the Abbot of St Austin's' (Bristol Chart., i, 155). The entrance to the spring-head on the western flank of Brandon Hill is arched and of considerable antiquity. The abbey pipe remained in use well into the 19th century.

GLOUCESTER, St Oswald's Priory (Augustinian)

Some time between 1263 and 1284 St Oswald's Priory was granted the use of the water surplus to the requirements of St Peter's Abbey by an extension from the abbey conduit (Fulbrook-Leggatt 1968, 115).

KENILWORTH, Priory (Augustinian)

In 1251 the prior and convent of Kenilworth were permitted to take water from a well which lay within the court of Edith Lawerthin in the town and lead it by a conduit wherever they wished through the court and buildings of the priory, on condition that they recompense Edith for any loss or damage she incurred as a result (Cal.Pat.R.,1247–58, 93).

LACOCK, Abbey (Augustinian Canonesses)

Water was brought by conduit to Lacock from springs at Bewley Common on Bowden Hill in the time of the second and third abbesses, Beatrice of Kent (1257–c 1280) and Alice (fl.c 1280–87). This undertaking involved protracted negotiations between the abbey and those of its neighbours whose property was crossed by the conduit, particularly Sir William Bluet of Lackham and his tenant Robert de Holta (Lacock Chart. 25, nos.49, 50, 51). A small oblong building with a steeply-pitched roof, the successor to the medieval conduit-head, built shortly after the Dissolution by Sir William Sharington, still stands opposite the church on Bowden Hill. The pipe, which passed under the River Avon, was still in use in the 1940s.

LINCOLN, St Catherine's Priory (Gilbertine)

In November 1306 the prior and convent of St Catherine's outside Lincoln received a licence to lead water from a well in the field of Canewyk to their house by an underground aqueduct (Cal.Pat.R.,1301–7, 482).

LONDON, St Bartholomew's Priory, Smithfield (Augustinian)

Before 1433 St Bartholomew's Priory had an aqueduct bringing in water from its manor at Canonbury. In that year the master and brethren of St Bartholomew's Hospital were allowed half the supply (see below).

The sale of the priory premises after the Dissolution to Sir Richard Rich included 'all that water and watercourse and aqueducts, running from a certain place called the condyte hede of Saint Barthilmewes within the manor of Canbery in the parish of Iseldon, and all lez cesternes and lez pypes of lead, as William Bolton or any other Prior had used held or enjoyed the same' (Norman 1899, 256).

LONDON, St Mary's, Clerkenwell (Augustinian Canonesses)

A house of Augustinan canonesses was founded at Clerkenwell c 1140. It is not clear when it secured its water-supply. The square conduit-head is shown on the Charterhouse plan already described, labelled 'here bigynneth the nonys condite of clerkynwelle'. From here the pipe runs southwards to a small square stone cistern, then deflects south-westwards to a second cistern labelled 'the receyte of clerkynwell condite'. Immediately below this its line is crossed by the Charterhouse pipe itself, and the spot is labelled on the map 'the pipe of clerkynwelle goyng undir oure home pipe'. The continuation of the pipe on to the nunnery was of no interest to the Charterhouse's cartographer, so its lower course is not shown (Hope 1902, 303, 305).

OXFORD, Osney Abbey (Augustinian)

In the time of Abbot Clement (1205–21) the canons of Osney acquired a spring called 'Reve Mores Well' in the field of North Hinksey from Abbot Hugh of Abingdon (1189–1221), with permission to make an aqueduct through Abingdon Abbey's arable lands and meadows on the Berkshire bank of the Thames, subject to the usual conditions of recompense for any damages (Oseney Cart. iv, p.472, no.432).

This grant was subsequently confirmed by Henry, son and heir of Roger of Botley, Abingdon Abbey's tenant (Oseney Cart. iv, p.473, no.433).

An inspeximus and confirmation of charters in favour of the abbot and convent of Osney in 1320 includes '. . . the grant of Henry, son and heir of Roger de Bottel', of the spring on his land in the field of Hengstesy, called Reve Moreswelle, with all the brooks and water-courses flowing to or away from it, without any impediment by the said Henry or his heirs to prevent the said spring or the streams flowing to it or flowing thence by the conduit from the house of Osney; the grant of the said Henry to dig about the said spring and water-courses and clean them; the grant of the said Henry of the right to build a house eighteen feet long and thirteen feet wide over the said spring and to have easements upon his land for repairing the same 'and also' . . . the gift of Hugh, abbot of Abingdon, and the convent thereof, of the spring called Revemorewell, to make an aqueduct to the court of Osney; and the grant in the same charter of power to make the said aqueduct over the land of the said abbot and convent, either arable or pasture' (Cal.Chart.R.,1300–26, 424, 426).

The conduit appears to have run under the westernmost branch of the Thames somewhere south of Hinksey Ferry, crossing King's Mead to pass the next branch of the river below Osney Mill. A conduit-house is said to have stood 'adjoyning to the Fratries and Cloyster walls of the West side of ye Cloyster' (Hurst 1899, 212), and in the 1880s bits of the pipes, lead within stone, from under the river, were still to be seen lying near Osney Mill (Hurst 1899, 58).

TAUNTON, Priory (Augustinian)

When the canons moved to their new site on the edge of Taunton in 1158 they were granted by Bishop Giffard of Winchester the water of 'Syreford', the Sherford Brook, to drive their mill, and the brook was diverted to serve the new precinct.

Competition with the town for the use of this water ultimately led the canons to seek an alternative source, and in 1332 they were permitted to take water from the Blackbrook (Cal.Chart.R., iv, 312–18), which was conducted to the priory by a leat known in later years as Stockwell or·Winter's stream. Subsequently the flow was contained within a 'subterranean leaden aqueduct' which became blocked in 1387 (Bush, in Leach 1984, 104).

WALTHAM, Abbey (Augustinian)

An account of 1220–2 describes the construction of a conduit from Wormley on the Hertfordshire bank of the Lea Valley to Waltham, a distance of nearly 5km (B.Lib. Harl.MS 391, fols.1–5). This was accompanied by a contemporary map, of which a mid-13-century copy survives, showing in highly diagrammatic form the layout of the springs, pipes and settling-tanks (B.Lib. Harl.MS 391, fol.6r; redrawn here as Fig 5.2). The conduit-head at Wormley has been recorded (Bascombe 1973).

5.4 Friaries

BOSTON, Dominicans

In 1327 the Blackfriars of Boston acquired a royal licence to construct a subterranean conduit from Bolingbroke to their house for their own use and for the use of others in the town (Cal.Pat.R.,1327–30, 182). Bolingbroke is 20km away from Boston, and this would have been a phenomenal achievement if it was completed. Three years later Bishop Burghersh granted indulgences to all who helped in construction work (V.C.H. Lincs. ii, 1906, 214).

BRIDGNORTH, Franciscans

The inventory of the Bridgnorth Greyfriars at the suppression in 1538 indicates a very poor house in a severe state of decay, where even the water system had ceased to function: the property included 'a conduit coming from the High Cross which was not seen many years' (Inv. Salop., 378–9; Martin 1937, 210).

BRISTOL, Austin Friars

The Austin Friars, whose house lay just inside the Temple Gate in Temple Backs, in that part of Bristol on the southern side of the Avon, acquired a water source at Ravenswell in Totterdown from Sir John de Gournay, lord of Knowle. The friars also supplied the whole of Temple Fee with an extension of their pipe to a conduit-house a short distance north of Temple Church (Lobel 1975, 9).

Part of the system of tunnels, c 1.5–2m. high by 1m wide, cut through the solid rock to channel the watercourse, still survives in the area south of Temple Meads railway station, and several strong springs still rise within rock-cut chambers at the ends of the tunnels.

BRISTOL, Carmelites

The Whitefriars were settled in the parish of St Augustine north of the River Frome in 1267. The friars located two springs on the north-east and east sides of Brandon Hill, and from this site laid a series of pipes conveying the water to a conduit-house at the friary which also served the surrounding neighbourhood. The inventory compiled by the Suffragan Bishop of Dover for Cromwell in 1538 lists 'diverse gutters, spouts and conduits of lead . . . a goodly laver and conduit coming to it' (Taylor 1906, 97).

Underground passages 1.2m-1.8m high beneath the present line of Park Street give access to the springs and cisterns, and 75mm lead pipes have been recorded from the course in Park Street. The lower part of the course, immediately west of the Friary itself, is still called Pipe Lane.

From their conduit-house the Carmelites granted a feather pipe in the 14th century to the vestry of St John. The conveyance granting this right from the Whitefriars to the parish has attached to it a fragment of silver pipe 25mm long × 12mm bore to show the diameter of the extension pipe. It is about the diameter of a goose quill, hence the term 'feather'. On 1st October 1376 a contract was made between the mayor and commonalty and Hugh White, plumber, for the latter at his own cost to bring water to the Quay Pipe, All Saints Pipe and St John's Pipe, at the yearly rent of £10; if the supply failed for more than six days he was to forfeit the £10; moreover, he was to make new lead pipes every year and to 'lay the same so that they shall endure for ever' (G.R.B. Bristol, i, 114–7). On the dissolution of the Carmelites the entire cost of maintaining the conduit fell upon the churchwardens of St John's, and on more than one occasion the cost of repairs is said to have swallowed up the parish revenues for the whole year.

The line of the St John's extension came down Host Street and Christmas Street to the town wall at St John's Church. The St John's conduit-house originally stood inside the town gate, by the present south-western entrance to the church, facing Broad Street, but was later moved outside the gate to its present position on the Nelson Street side.

The complex course of the whole conduit from its head in Park Street down to St John's Church has been traced and recorded in some detail by the Temple Local History Group in Bristol (Lea-Jones et al.1984).

BRISTOL, Dominicans

The Bristol Blackfriars received a licence to make a conduit in 1232. Their original source was probably at St Mary's Well in Bar Street. In 1391 the friars gave a well called Pennywell at Ashley to the east to the city authorities in exchange for a share in the newly-constructed Quay Pipe from Ashley, and drew a feather pipe off that main (Fig 5.1) (G.R.B. Bristol, ii, 191ff; Lobel 1975).

BRISTOL, Franciscans

The Greyfriars, who had first appeared in Bristol in about 1230, moved to a new site on reclaimed marshland in Lewins Mead ten years later. They acquired a spring in an orchard on the south-east side of Kingsdown by the present Terrell Street from Joan, wife of John de Lidiard, who had been mayor of the city in 1277. This grant, which consisted of 'a rood of land and the spring and conduit on it', was confirmed to the friars by Edward III (Cal.Pat.R.,1370–74, 471; Martin 1937, 219).

In the 14th century three extensions from the Greyfriars' supply appear to have been made, serving (i) St James's Priory, which at an earlier date probably drew its supply from a deep well on St James's Barton, discovered c 1940. Road works in 1932 and bombing in 1941 revealed sections of underground masonry tunnels leading towards the priory; (ii) St Bartholomew's Hospital, also originally supplied by a deep well in Colston Street; and (iii) over the Frome by St John's Bridge and up Broad Street to a conduit head in Corn Street serving the city-centre parish of All Saints (Fig 5.1).

After the Dissolution of the friars in 1538 responsibility for the supply was taken over by All Saints parish. Weare (1893, 32, 36) describes the subterranean passages and arrangements for the storage and outflow of water then existing, extending under Upper Maudlin Street, with the leaden main pipes still in position passing beneath the burial-ground of the Moravian chapel. This course no longer functions; the water is believed to have been diverted into a street sewer near its source in Terrel St in 1935. Earlier, the laying of telephone cables in 1905 encountered an early square manhole with a rectangular settling chamber and trough below and part of a conduit of 50mm lead pipes. The pipes were occasionally intercepted by receivers or settling tanks cut out of natural rock. Rock-cut passages with winding steps to the springs are said to survive.

East of the claustral buildings, parallel with Whitefriars Lane, an enormous conduit aligned from north to south was identified during building operations in 1973; the wider part of the structure ended at the south in a fine freestone arch 1.8m wide by at least 2.3m high, with a narrow chamfered bottom, but it continued southwards in a narrower channel towards Lewin's Mead (Ponsford 1975).

Earlier, during the laying of a water-pipe in Upper Maudlin Street in 1971, the remains of another medieval conduit were discovered, almost 2m high in three branches with slightly pointed vaults, and a freestone doorway (Miles and Ponsford 1971). This is presumed to be part of the extension of the Greyfriars system towards All Saints church.

CAMBRIDGE, Franciscans

The Cambridge Greyfriars laid an aqueduct in 1327 to bring water from a source a little over 2km beyond the Cam to the west, near where the Observatory now stands. The supply led under the former King's Childer Lane. After 1433 the aqueduct was held jointly by the friars and the scholars of King's Hall. After the Dissolution Henry VIII granted the entire supply to Trinity College, and the ornate water fountain in the college quadrangle is still fed by the friars' conduit (RCHM Cambridge ii, 1959, 233).

CHELMSFORD, Dominicans

The original water supply to the Blackfriars of Chelmsford appears to have been an artificial watercourse led off the River Can, which served the kitchen and lavatorium first and then the reredorter, with the foul water being returned to the river. Either because of silting due to the sluggish flow, or because of increasing pollution in the river, this source was superseded. In 1341 the Blackfriars obtained a licence to construct a culvert from a spring in the Town Field, probably to be identified with the Burgesses' Well, which is some 700m to the north-west of the friary on the further side of the River Can (Cal.Pat.R. 1340–3, 227–8; Drury 1974).

Excavations in the kitchen area in 1938 recovered many tapered earthenware water-pipes, and excavations in 1973 showed that the supply of water for flushing the reredorter was reorganised some time after its first construction at beginning of the 14th century (Drury 1974, 78; Drury 1976). It is possible that both of these innovations may be linked with the securing of the new water supply in 1341.

CHESTER, Dominicans

In 1276 the Blackfriars were permitted to build a water conduit through the king's land near the River Dee from a spring near the gallows outside the city, and to open, pierce and reclose the said land, the city wall and the highway where necessary (Cal.Pat.R.,1272–81, 165; Bennett 1952). A well-built sandstone drain excavated in 1979 may have been the main outfall from the conduit (*Medieval Archaeol* **23**, 1979, 249; **24**, 1980, 238).

CHICHESTER, Franciscans

The detailed inventory of the Greyfriars' buildings taken at the Suppression in Oct.1538, describes 'the cloister with a fair laverys and a conduit coming to it'. The leadwork on the buildings, including 'divers gutters and a goodly conduyt leade' is separately listed (Inv. Sussex, 71; Martin 1937, 56).

COVENTRY, Franciscans

At the Dissolution it was reported to Cromwell by Dr John London that the conduit of the Greyfriars at Coventry, the head of which was 3km outside the town, was 'better than that of the town and has a better head', and the corporation was recommended to purchase the friars' supply since much of the city would lack water if they failed to do so (L & P. Henry VIII Vol.13(2), 257, no.674; Martin 1937, 70).

EXETER, Dominicans

In 1244 Peter le Wayner and Isabel his wife granted to the recently-founded house of Blackfriars in Exeter three springs in two unidentified places called Chalvescroft and Puddewyll with nine feet (2.7m) of land in length and breadth around them, and the right to construct an aqueduct and keep it in repair (Little and Easterling 1927, 31).

On 10th February 1440–1 the Mayor of Exeter was negotiating with the friars about a proposal to construct a new aqueduct for the city since, although the city already had its own supply, the supply to the friary was regarded as particularly good. A lead-worker from London attended this discussion, and Friar Robert Cole was paid 13s 4d for his expenses in riding to London about the business of the aqueduct. In 1485 the water conduit 'apud freren-land' was repaired and a door added (Exeter City Muniments, quoted in Little and Easterling 1927, 38–9).

The supplies to the cathedral and city have been examined archaeologically, but the course of the Blackfriars' supply remains unknown.

EXETER, Franciscans

In 1303 the Greyfriars of Exeter moved from a cramped and insanitary site within the city walls to a new location outside the South Gate. The new site proved to be deficient in water, and shortly before 1315 the Bishop of Exeter granted the friars a spring within his house in 'Bolehulstrete'. Queen Isabella then gave the friars licence to make a subterranean conduit from this spring along the middle of the street and so under the South Gate or through the town wall to the new friary, provided that they kept the street, wall and gate in repair from any damage thus caused (Cal.Pat.R.,1313–17, 398).

In 1347 the Greyfriars took further steps to improve their water supply by digging to a greater depth two adjoining springs in the bottom of the city ditch between the East and South Gates, making a well and enclosing it within a low stone wall, and bringing the water from there across the highway in an underground pipe to their convent, which was said to be situated in a dry place to which no water ran (Cal.Pat.R.,1347, 424; Little and Easterling 1927, 19).

GLOUCESTER, Carmelites

In 1341 the Whitefriars of Gloucester acquired from Walter, son of Thomas Toky, a well called 'Gosewhitewell' beyond the East Gate of the city and land around it 8 feet (2.4m) in circumference to make a conduit in the field of Kingsbarton by Gloucester for the supply of water to their house (Cal.Pat.R.,1340–3, 255).

GLOUCESTER, Franciscans

Soon after their foundation in c 1230, the Gloucester Greyfriars were granted by William Geraud the use of a spring at Brerescliffe on Matson Knoll on Robinswood Hill, 3.6km away, with the right 'to repair it when necessary without let or hindrance', subject to the usual proviso, 'Should it happen that I and my heirs and assigns have to suffer damage to the grass and meadow at the hands of the aforesaid friars because of the conduit and renewal of the water aforesaid, the aforesaid friars shall satisfy me ... for the grass and meadow by the view of lawful men' (Fulbrook-Leggatt 1968, 117–8). The benefactor, William Geraud, had made a similar grant to St Peter's Abbey in Gloucester at the same time, and in 1355 there was a serious dispute between the two houses over the use of the source, the abbey asserting that the friars were interfering with its own supply.

Edward III sent the Black Prince to Gloucester to settle the argument. The Patent Rolls record his judgement in 1355, with a licence for St Peter's Abbey to grant to the Greyfriars permission to have 'an underground leaden pipe in the head of the stream of the abbot and convent's conduit at Breresclif in the fields of Mattesdon, of the size of a third part of the pipe of the said conduit, through which water can flow from the head of the conduit through the soil of the abbot and convent' to the friary (Cal.Pat.R., 1354–58, 243).

More detailed specifications of the agreement are recorded in a document of 1357: the friars were granted 'the right to lead the water through a leaden pipe into a pool or reservoir running from the said spring of Breresclyft newly constructed below the said spring, near the pipe of the ... Abbot and Convent [of St Peter's], lying in a line with their pipe or 2 pipes equal in size to the pipe of the friars; and that the said Friars Minor might lawfully have their ... aqueducts on the soil of the said monastery, the said Friars defraying a third of the cost of maintaining and repairing the said pond or reservoir and aqueduct from the head of the spring to the said pond. The friars renounce any right that they may have had or claimed to the water or aqueduct aforesaid, desiring to have the said water from the present new grant of the Abbot and Convent'. (Glos.C.R.O. no.966, 352–3, quoted in Fulbrook-Leggatt 1968, 114–5).

In 1438 the bailiffs of Gloucester acquired three-quarters of the Greyfriars' supply from Robinswood Hill for the use of the town. The town was to lay lead pipes from the conduit-house in the friars' garden to the High Cross and other places in the town at its own expense. The Friars retained responsibility for maintaining the pipe from the hill to the friary, together with 'all middle channels of stone or wood, and the houses, walls, receptacles and other things, both in digging and in other necessaries, from the heads of the springs of the water aforesaid to the said hill'; but the town agreed to provide three-quarters of the cost of necessary repairs (Gloucester Corporation Records, no.1112, quoted in Fulbrook-Leggatt 1968, 115). The High Cross with its water-spouts appears as one of the sketches of notable buildings in the city in Robert Coles's rental of 1455 (Glos.C.R.O., G.D.R. 1311; Stevenson 1890).

References to repairs and upkeep continue till the Dissolution. After the suppression the property of the friars was acquired by Thomas Pury, including 'all the waters and springs, and heads of springs, channels, pipes etc., in the ground of the hill called 'Mattesknoll' or 'Robinhoodes Hill' in Co. Glouc., and also that pipe or conduit of lead stretching under the ground from the said hill to the garden of the Greyfriars in Gloucester, and of the fourth part of the water coming through the said pipe' (Gloucester Corporation Records, no.1287; Fulbrook-Leggatt 1968, 116). The pipes were finally cut by the Royalist army during the siege of Gloucester in 1643.

There are some remains of the works on Robins Wood Hill. A number of streams rising on the north and east sides of the summit were conducted around its flanks to a stone cistern at the Well Cross lower down on the north side of the hill, immediately above the Tuffley

Reservoir. One of the springs, *c* 180m higher up the hill, was protected by a stone spring-house (Walters 1928, 57–8, 61–2, plate xviii; Fulbrook-Leggatt 1968, 112, 116).

GRANTHAM, Franciscans

In 1314 Ralph of Barneby gave the Greyfriars of Grantham a spring of water in the South Field of Gonerby, a little over 1km to the west of the town. Richard Kellaw, Bishop of Durham, authorised the friars to enclose the spring and to bring the water to their house by leaden pipes and to dig the ground in the common pasture to lay and repair the pipes, provided that they restore the ground after the disturbance (Reg.Pal.Dunelm. ii, 1255–6, iv, 385–6). The grant of the friary premises in 1541 to Robert Butcher, gentleman, and David Vincent, one of the king's pages, included the conduit (V.C.H. Lincs., ii, 1906, 218).

The conduit-head, rebuilt in 1579, still survives.

GRIMSBY, Franciscans

In 1313 the Greyfriars of Grimsby acquired a licence to make a subterranean conduit from Holm to their house in Grimsby through the king's land in Grimsby and the land of John Yornborough and Ralph de Skirbeck in Holm (Cal.Pat.R., 1307–13, 597).

HUNTINGDON, Austin Friars

In 1363 the Austin Friars of Huntingdon received licence to make an underground conduit from a spring called 'Caldewell' by the town through the common land of the town, to lay the pipes under the ground where this might most advantageously be done, and to repair the pipes when necessary (Cal.Pat.R.,1361–4, 306).

KINGS LANGLEY, Dominicans

In 1358 King Edward III granted to the Blackfriars the head of a stream in Abbots Langley, with permission to construct an underground conduit to their house (Cal.Pat.R. 1358–61, 34).

KINGS LYNN, Dominicans

William Bardolf granted the Blackfriars a well called 'Brocwell' in Middleton by Lynn. This grant was confirmed in 1293, and they were allowed to lead a watercourse from it to their house (Cal.Pat.R., 1292–1301, 15).

In 1308 there was a commission of oyer and terminer concerning certain persons who had broken the subterranean conduit of the Friars Preachers at Lynn by which water was conveyed from Middleton to Lynn (Cal.Pat.R.,1307–13, 89).

KINGS LYNN, Franciscans

Thomas Bardolf and Robert de Scales granted to the Greyfriars of Kings Lynn a well in North Runcton (4km south-east of the town) called 'Bukenwelle'. This was done without royal licence, but in 1314 the friars were permitted to retain the well and to lead the water into the friary by underground conduit (Cal.Pat.R.,1313–17, 128).

LICHFIELD, Franciscans

In 1301 Henry Campanarius, son of Michael of Lichfield, bellfounder, granted 'for the use and comfort of the friars minors of Lichfield' his springs at Fowlewell or Donniwell near Alreshawe (Aldershall, 2.5km south-west of the city), with permission to erect a conduit head of stone, to enclose the water and to convey it in pipes through his ground to the friary, and to repair the pipes when necessary subject to the usual arrangements for restitution of damage, on condition that the friars should give no part of the water to anyone else without the grantor's consent (*Magn.Reg.Alb.*, pp.252–3, no.528).

The supply proved to be more than was needed by the friars, and later part of it was led to St John's Hospital, while a large conduit was built at the friary gate to serve the town as a whole. Leland records that 'There comith a conducte of watar out of an hill browght in leade to the towne, and hathe 2 castelets in the towne, one in the est waule of this fryers close on the strete syd, anothar about the market place' (Leland, Itin. ii, 100).

Documents connected with the sale of the friars' premises in October 1538 included the 'cundyt of ledd in the cloyster', the 'lytle cundyt standyng at the revestrye dore', and lead cisterns in the kitchen, in the brewhouse and elsewhere (Lett.Supp.Mon, 274–7; Martin 1937, 165–6).

The supply continued in use to the 19th century.

LINCOLN, Dominicans

In 1260 the Blackfriars of Lincoln were licensed to tap springs at 'Gretewell' on land belonging to a cell of St Mary's Abbey, York, in the eastern suburbs of the city and to make a conduit of water along the high road to the friary and to amend and repair it when necessary (Cal.Close R., 1259–61, 37; Cal.Pat.R.,1258–66, 67).

LINCOLN, Franciscans

On 8th April 1535 licence was granted to the warden of the Lincoln Greyfriars to lay his conduit in the common ground of the city where he should think most convenient (Cal.Linc.MSS, 33; V.C.H.Lincs.ii, 1906, 223; Martin 1937, 92).

The friary was undergoing considerable repairs at the time, and this may have been seen as an opportunity for reorganising the water system.

Given the general difficulties of water supply in Lincoln it seems curious that the Greyfriars had not brought in a piped supply before, even though they were in the lower part of the town where wells could be shallower; but no evidence of any earlier piped supply has been found.

The water was derived from a spring near Monks Abbey east of the town, where a small brick intake-house survived till the early 18th century, and from there lead pipes conveyed water to the friary, where the original conduit survived between two buttresses of the existing Greyfriars building (believed by Martin to be the church, but recently reinterpreted by David Stocker as the infirmary hall) at least as late as 1810.

At the Suppression the mayor and aldermen of Lincoln negotiated for the friars' water supply to come into possession of the town, and in 1539 they were successful in acquiring both the Blackfriars' and Greyfriars' conduits. In 1540 the city authorities extended the pipe from the Greyfriars southwards into the Wigford suburb. A new conduit-house was set up in St Mary-le-Wigford churchyard, built largely of stone either from the nearby Whitefriars or from one of the recently-demolished city churches; it is mentioned by Leland (Itin. i, 31). By 1864 the building had become a traffic obstruction, and was moved bodily backwards into the churchyard, where it still stands (White 1980).

LONDON, Dominicans, Site 1: Holborn

The Blackfriars first settled in Holborn in 1221. On October 29th 1259 Henry III gave the prior and friars preachers of London £20 to make their aqueduct (Cal.Lib.R. iv,1251–60, 484), tapping a spring at Clerkenwell. A similar sum was given on January 8th 1261 (Cal.Lib.R. v, 1260–7, 16). In 1279, with the aid of the Archbishop of Canterbury, the Blackfriars sold their Holborn site to the Earl of Lincoln and moved to the recently-slighted site of Baynard's Castle, south-west of St Paul's.

LONDON, Dominicans,

Site 2: Baynard's Castle

An anonymous 14th- or 15th-century lampoon upon the friars entitled 'Pierce the Ploughman's Creed' (quoted in Clapham and Godfrey 1913, 256–7 and Schofield 1984, 72) describes the Blackfriars church and the cloister 'With conduits of clean tin, closed all about' and 'Washing basins wrought of shining latten'. A piped water supply is implied, and possibly the conduit was extended from the Holborn site.

LONDON, Franciscans, Newgate

The Greyfriars had moved to a site on the north side of Newgate from Cornhill in 1228. Their register records that a spring outside the city in what is now Bloomsbury was given to them in the time of Henry III by William, the king's tailor, at the instance of Brother William Basinges, who is said to have supervised the construction of the aqueduct and completed it. The building of the aqueduct was financed by the king, Salekyn of Basing, Sir Henry Frowyke and Sir Henry Basynges (Norman 1899, 348; Kingsford 1915, 158–9; Martin 1937, 185–6). In 1255–6 Henry III granted the friars 14 1/2 marks towards the cost of this aqueduct (Cal.Lib.R. iv, 1251–60, 274).

In the early 14th century a second conduit-head was built by Brother Geoffrey de Camera, who also carried out repairs to the first and to the rest of the pipe (Norman 1899, 348; Kingsford 1915, 158–9; Martin 1937, 185–6). The Greyfriars' register gives a very detailed description of the course of the pipe with both sources, quoted earlier.

At the Dissolution one of the items disposed of was 'the water course of lead to the sayd Fryer house belonging, contayning by esteemation in length 18 acres' (Stow, Surv.Lond., i, 319). The conduit continued to be used into the 18th century by Christ's Hospital, which took over the Greyfriars site.

The plan prepared for Christ's Hospital portraying the water system as it existed in 1676 shows the two conduit-heads. At the further source, half-a-dozen tiny circles are shown, representing the springs feeding it, connected by red lines showing distances between them and the conduit-head. This site, almost certainly to be identified with the head of the extension made by Geoffrey de Camera in the 14th century, is referred to as the 'Chimney or Devil's Conduit' in 1756. In 1893 the remains of this further head, at the rear of 20 Queen Square, were discovered by Dr Philip Norman. A flight of modern steps led down to a medieval arched passage, which descended ten more steps to a subterranean square ashlar-built tank c 3.4m × 3.7m with a barrel-vaulted roof also of medieval appearance (Norman 1899). This structure was demolished in 1911, when a fuller record was made (Norman 1916, 18–26). Its stones were numbered, and it was subsequently re-erected in the grounds of the Metropolitan Water Board in Rosebery Avenue, London E.C.1 (Martin 1937, 203).

The lower conduit-head, labelled as 'White Conduit' on the 1676 plan (and not to be confused with the White Conduit at Pentonville on the Charterhouse system), probably represents the original source given by William the Tailor. It was abandoned in c 1740 due to the encroachment of neighbouring buildings, but its remains were rediscovered by Mann in 1907 beneath the floor of a workshop to the rear of no.13 Chapel Street (now Rugby Street). It consisted of a subterranean rectangular chamber 2.7m × 1.8m, stone-built, with an arched roof, entered from the south. A stone settling-tank occupied the south-western corner of the chamber (Norman and Mann 1909).

NORTHAMPTON, Dominicans

On July 15th 1279 Edward I confirmed a grant by Queen Eleanor of a well called 'Flexwell' in the field of Kingsthorpe on the north side of the town (Cal.Pat.R., 1272–81, 322).

NORTHAMPTON, Franciscans

In 1291 the Greyfriars of Northampton received licence to unite the course of a spring called 'Triwell' at that time running in three directions between the towns of Northampton and Kingsthorpe, and to lead it by subterranean conduit to their house, provided that they indemnify the persons who held land in the field through which the watercourse was to be taken for the damage, which was estimated to be 1 mark if the lands were sown at the time (Cal.Pat.R.,1281–92, 442).

NOTTINGHAM, Franciscans

In 1303 the Greyfriars of Nottingham received licence to make an underground conduit from their spring of 'Athewell' to the friary (Cal.Pat.R. 1301–7, 131).

OXFORD, Dominicans

In 1267 the Oxford Blackfriars were granted a spring at Hinksey, and in 1285 they were given permission to dig in the king's meadows if necessary to repair it (Cal.Pat.R.,1281–92, 165). This was confirmed in 1437 (Cal.Pat.R.,1436–41, 50). The friary premises included 'a very fair conduit' in 1538 (L and P.Henry VIII, xiii (i), p.500, no.1342).

OXFORD, Franciscans

The Oxford Greyfriars also had a lengthy system of lead pipes, first recorded in 1221, which are said to have been paid for by a local magnate at his own expense; they apparently extended 'many miles under the watersheds of the Thames and Cherwell' (Little 1892, 28fn). This must imply the tapping of a spring on the east side of the city on the Headington hills. If this is correct the Greyfriars pipe may well have crossed over that of the Blackfriars pipe coming from the opposite direction.

When Cromwell's commissioners visited Greyfriars in 1538 they reported:- 'They haue taken vppe the pypes of ther condytt lately and haue cast them in sowys to the nombre lxxij, wherof xij be sold for the costes in taking vppe of the pypes, as the warden saith. The residew we haue putt in safe garde. But we haue nott yet weyd them. And ther ys yet in the erthe remaynyng moch of the condytt nott taken vppe' (Little 1891, 117; L and P Henry VIII, xiii (i), p.500, no.1342).

PONTEFRACT, Dominicans

The friars apparently had a conduit supplied from a spring in a small piece of land called Cockliff Turfmore, but it is not known how or when this was acquired (V.C.H. Yorks, iii, 1913, 272).

RICHMOND, Franciscans

Leland mentions that the conduit supplying the Greyfriars was the only one in the town (Itin., iv, 25).

SCARBOROUGH, Dominicans

In 1283 the Scarborough Blackfriars petitioned the king to be allowed to draw water from the spring at Gildhuscliff, but this was refused on the grounds that the spring had already been granted to the Greyfriars of the town (see below) (Yorks.Inq., ii,1897, 9; V.C.H. Yorks.iii, 1913, 277).

SCARBOROUGH, Franciscans

In or shortly before 1283 the burgesses of Scarborough gave a spring at 'Gildhuscliff' outside the town on Falsgrave Moor to Robert of Scarborough, Dean of York, for him to make at his own expense a conduit for the use of the Greyfriars, on condition that the borough should have the joint use of the water when it was constructed. The source was about 3.2km distant from the friary. Robert died in 1290 with the project still uncompleted, but he left the friars 100 marks in his will for this purpose (V.C.H. Yorks.iii, 1913, 275). To pay this legacy his executors had to call in a debt of 78 marks owing from the abbey of Meaux, and the monks of Meaux found that they could only repay the debt by stripping the lead off the roof of their lay brothers' dormitory (Chron. Melsa, ii, 237).

It was nearly thirty years before the friars finally acquired a licence, in 1319, to make an underground conduit to run to the friary from the well granted to them by the town, to lay pipes under the streets and lanes of the town wherever most convenient, and also when necessary to repair the conduit (Cal.Pat.R.,1317–21, 376–7)

Part of the Franciscan water system was discovered in 1976 at the junction of Stepney Road and Scalby Road. It consisted of a stone conduit bedded in clay, the base formed of solid rectangular sandstone blocks hollowed out to form a half-round channel and then capped with thin flags (*Medieval Archaeol* **20**, 1976, 192).

SOUTHAMPTON, Franciscans

Plans for the construction of a water conduit were conceived in 1290, when the friars acquired a licence to enclose within a stone wall the spring of Colewell in the manor of Shirley. The project may not have been commpleted until *c* 1310, when the friars 'out of reverence to Henry, Archdeacon of Dorset, and their goodwill to the community', allowed the burgesses to carry one pipe with a 'key' from the cistern above their lavatorium through to a further cistern outside the friary wall, which they were to construct at their own expense. Any surplus from the town's supply was to be conveyed back into the friary cloisters, presumably for flushing the drains. By the 15th century the friars were no longer able to afford the costs of maintenance, and in 1421 the conduit was purchased by the town authorities, who agreed to build a new cistern-house opposite Holy Rood Church in the main street, from which two pipes of equal capacity were to supply the townspeople and friars respectively. The friars' conduit continued to contribute to the municipal water supply into the present century.

The Colewell spring-head, in what is now Hill Lane, was enclosed in three vaulted chambers. The outermost chamber seems to have been a later addition. From it a short passage led to a second vault where the water was gathered. A low tunnel, *c* 3m long, 0.8m wide and 1.5m high, led off at an angle from this second chamber to the third chamber, *c* 1.8m in diameter, containing the spring itself. The water was then conveyed by a lead pipe to a conduit-house which still stands in Waterhouse Lane off Commercial Road, where other springs were also later collected. From there it was conveyed by pipes on to the friary itself, an overall distance of a little over 3km. Portions of the lead pipe have been found in Havelock Road. From here it came to Above Bar, passing through the Bargate and changing from the west to the east side of the street, heading for the friary on the site of the present Gloucester Square. An extension from the friary served the medieval hospital of God's House.

In 1986 a small excavation was undertaken around the conduit-house in advance of landscaping. Items recorded included a brick tank and lead and cast-iron pipes all derived from the continuing use of the supply in the post-medieval period, but evidence of medieval pipes was also seen (Garner and Lindsey 1987). Excavation in Broad Lane revealed a length of medieval ceramic water pipe still *in situ* (Russell 1987).

STAMFORD, Dominicans

In 1244 Henry III granted the Blackfriars 15 marks out of the farm of the county for making their aqueduct (Cal.Lib.R. ii,1240–45, 250) The supply for the spring was in Northamptonshire, so the pipes must have crossed the River Welland. The conduit is recorded amongst the details of the site on its surrender to Dr London in 1538 (V.C.H. Lincs.ii, 1906, 226–7).

STAMFORD, Franciscans

When the site of the Greyfriars was granted to the Earl of Suffolk in 1541 the principal buildings had already been razed to the ground; but two lead cisterns and a conduit together with a malting-chamber and kiln-house survived (V.C.H.Lincs.ii, 1906, 228–9).

SUDBURY, Dominicans

On August 1st 1380 Simon, Archbishop of Canterbury, and his brother John Chertsey, obtained a licence from King Richard II, by payment of half a mark, permitting them to alienate the the Blackfriars of Sudbury a plot of land 20 feet square at Ballingdon Hall, 1km south-west of the town. The same licence gave the friars permission to build an aqueduct from the spring on this land across the River Stour to their hoseu (Cal.Pat.R.1377–81, 534). There seems to have been considerable local opposition to this project, for on March 10th 1385 the king ordered the public proclamation of his protection for five years to the friars 'who fear hindrance in the construction thereof at the hands of certain rivals, and peril to their men, servants and labourers' (Cal.Pat.R. 1381–5, 537).

5.4.1   Military orders, Hospitals and Churches

BRISTOL, St John's Hospital, Redcliffe

When Robert Berkeley granted the church of St Mary Redcliffe a pipe of water from Rudgewell on Knowle Hill (see below), he also allowed St John's Hospital to have an extension 'of the dimension of a medium-sized thumb' carrying part of the supply to its premises. This charter can be dated within the limits of 1186–1216 by the fact that one of its witnesses was John, Abbot of St Augustine's (Latimer 1901, 173).

In 1320 Henry de Aston, vicar of Bedminster, was absolved of the crime of breaching the pipe carrying water through St Mary's churchyard to St John's Hospital, and the workmen of St John's were permitted to enter St Mary's churchyard to mend the broken pipes without interference from the church authorities (Reg.Drokensford, 145).

BRISTOL, St Mark's Hospital

St Mark's Hospital at Billeswick outside Bristol had a water supply by c 1240, brought from the springs at Jacob's Well, on the west side of Brandon Hill, by a lead pipe. This was larger than the St Augustine's Abbey pipe and ran parallel with it as far as St George's Road, then diverged to the hospital, where it filled a tank on the corner of Unity Street (Lobel 1975, 9).

This foundation was reorganised in the later 13th century as Gaunt's Hospital, and Gaunt's Pipe, taken over by the Corporation after the Dissolution, continued to function to 1888, when it was diverted to serve the public baths in Jacob's Wells Road.

Several lengths of lead pipe from this conduit were unearthed during the construction of the Council House

on College Green in 1938.

BRISTOL, St Mary Redcliffe Church

In about 1190 Robert Berkeley granted the church of St Mary Redcliffe a pipe of water from his spring at 'Rugewell' (Rudgewell) on Knowle Hill, and this was probably the earliest of the many conduits converging upon Bristol (Lobel 1975, 9). The spring is by the site of Gay's Farm in Lower Knowle, near St Barnabas' Church. The conduit-head was formerly protected by a flat stone about 0.6m square. Maintenance of the pipe is recorded in the churchwardens' accounts; in 1558 it was noted there that 'the water was stopped up with two cats that did live in the pipe'. Up until the 1939–45 War representatives of the church vestry annually walked the line of the pipe through Lower Knowle, Bedminster and Victoria Park to maintain their right of way over its course. A length of the pipe was discovered intact in 1984 during sewer construction.

BRISTOL, St.Thomas's Church

From the St Mary Redcliffe pipe a feather pipe was run on to St Thomas's church through the Redcliffe Gate, along Portwall Lane and down St Thomas Street. This is first recorded in the will of John Stoke in 1381. In the 15th century the churchwardens of St Thomas's were paying St Mary Redcliffe 1s *per annum* for the use of the pipe, and on 14th July 1566 they agreed to pay one-third of the cost of repairing the great pipe from Knowle. The conduit-house originally stood in the middle of St Thomas Street, but in 1673 it was removed to Church Lane east of the Seven Stars Inn.

LONDON, Priory of St John of Jerusalem, Clerkenwell

The Knights Hospitallers brought a water supply in lead pipes from springs in the meadows called Commandery Mantells at Barnsbury, in what is now Pentonville.

The 15th-century Charterhouse plan shows the Knights' conduit-head immediately to the east of the second Carthusian cistern-house, with the pipe crossing under the Charterhouse pipe immediately below it.

At the suppression in 1546 the conduits, water-pipes and springs were amongst the possessions of the priory granted to Viscount Lisle.

LONDON, St. Bartholomew's Hospital

In 1433 the Master and Brethren of St Bartholomew's Hospital gave an annuity of 6s 8d to the Prior of St Bartholomew's, Smithfield, on condition that they should have the use of half the supply of pure water from the priory's springs at Canonbury (Norman 1899, 256). Water was led from the cistern in the priory across the king's highway (Duck Lane) and into the hospital. The prisons of Ludgate and Newgate were also served by this supply.

OXFORD, St John's Hospital

The Hospital of St John the Baptist lay outside the East Gate of the city, on the site now occupied by Magdalen College. It is first recorded in 1180, and seems initially to have been a hostel for the entertainment of travellers, but was refounded in 1231 as a hospital for the sick. In 1246 the king permitted the brethren of the hospital to take their water by an aqueduct from a spring called 'Crowell' at the north-east corner of the town ditch (Cal.Close R., 1242–47, 438). The watercourse is shown on Agas's map of 1578, and in part on Loggan's map of 1675, very close to the town ditch.

Recent archaeological work in Magdalen College has revealed a substantial aisled medieval building fronting the River Cherwell, with an ashlar-lined culvert along the inside of the river wall, issuing into the river at its southern end. A flight of steps came down to the culvert from the interior of the building, which seems to negate its most obvious function as a latrine. The spring lies some 400m north-west of this point, and it seems likely that the purpose of the culvert was to channel fresh water from this source, keeping it separate from the river. Its position seems anomalous if the provisional interpretation of the building containing it as the chapel at the east end of the infirmary hall proves to be correct, unless it was employed in the healing process (Durham 1988).

5.5 Distribution and utilisation of water within the monastery

Once water had arrived within the precinct, it was put to a variety of uses, both domestic and industrial. This section will be concerned primarily with the methods by which water was stored and fed through the monastery; the nature of the buildings accommodating specific uses of water will be discussed in the ensuing sections.

The arrangements for the distribution of the water are best-known at Canterbury, from the evidence of the mid-12th century plan (Fig 5.3) and its interpretation by Willis (1868). Entering the precinct from the north-east after passing beneath both the city and precinct walls, the main supply pipe passed east of the granary and beneath the infirmary kitchen on its way to Prior Wibert's water-tower, which still stands in the middle of the south side of the infirmary cloister. This building served two main purposes: it contained the primary cistern at first-floor level from which water could be distributed by gravity feed to all other parts of the precinct, and it also contained a laver where the monks could wash on their way from the dormitory to the choir. The 12th-century plan shows a conical-roofed, stone-built structure of two storeys, with round-headed arcading at both levels, containing an octofoil basin on the upper floor with its feed-pipe and exit-pipe clearly shown. The lower part of the original building remains: it is circular in plan, of dressed stone, entered from the cloister walk to the south, with seven Romanesque arches, five of which remain open on the north and west sides, and added buttresses, partly of brick. It is clearly an addition to the infirmary cloister walk, although within a few years of it in date. The upper storey is later, rubble-built, octagonal, with Gothic windows, its roof rising to a central point. The central cluster of columns survives in much-modified form; it supports a vaulted roof carrying the cistern above, and

originally enclosed the pipes carrying water to and from it.

The exit-pipe from this main water-tower fed into a second laver in front of the refectory, where the monks could wash before meals. This too had an octofoil basin standing on the ground. The feed pipe passed up through a central pillar into a smaller quatrefoil basin at a higher level, with spouts between its lobes which would have poured a continuous flow of water into the lower basin. There must have been a drain to carry off the superfluous water from the lower basin, but the map does not show this. This laver too was originally contained within a projecting circular or polygonal arcaded building. The third laver was a sexfoil basin contained in a similar but smaller structure on the east side of the infirmary cloister, serving the infirmary itself. The main pipe ran on beneath the south aisle of the infirmary hall and across the monks' cemetery to supply the great fishpond, labelled 'piscina' on the plan. The overflow from the fishpond was piped to the prior's tank ('fons') and water-tub ('cupa'), and the waste water from this passed beneath the infirmary reredorter to join the main drain.

A branch pipe leaving the main between the second and third laver passed beneath the church to the lay cemetery, providing another supply-point there ('fons in cimeterio laicorum') which was available to the townspeople. The plan shows no signs of a stopcock at this point, and this was probably dispensed with here because of the dangers of some careless or malicious person leaving it running; instead, water could be dipped by pail from a basin on a stone pedestal. Waste from this basin again passed into the fishpond.

A second branch pipe, leaving the main near the refectory laver, supplied the various domestic offices by means of stand-pipes and stop-cocks: first the kitchen and the chamber where fish were washed, then across the Green Court to the bakehouse and brewhouse, then westwards to a further sexfoil laver which stood beneath the Norman porch of the 'aula nova'. A further branch left this pipe in the middle of the Green Court, passing to the bath-house ('balneatorium'), where there was a standpipe and stopcock, then feeding into the prior's tub ('cupa') by a vertical standpipe, the open end of which is shown curling over the lip of the tub.

The Canterbury system involved several reservoirs or cisterns at successively lower levels, each with their own feed-pipes and exit-pipes.

At the angle of every feed-pipe, where it turned vertically to pour its water into such a tank, the plan shows a short horizontal branch taking off from the angle of the pipe to terminate in a stop-cock close to the nearest drain. These are each labelled 'purgatorium', and their function, like those attached to the settling-tanks, was to flush out sediment from the pipe. Towards the lower end of the system, where the head of water was insufficient to feed any further basins, water was tapped where it was needed by means of short vertical stand-pipes, soldered to the mains underground, the issue of water from their upper ends controlled by a plug, spigot or stop-cock.

The 12th-century plan also shows the gutters, drains and sewers within the precinct. Rainwater dripping from the roof-eaves of the great cloister and the north side of the church was collected in an open gutter around the edge of the garth, linked with a drain passing through the centre. From here the water flowed to a small underground cistern opposite the door of the locutory, the passage leading between the two cloisters. In the main cloister further gutters are shown issuing from the north-east transept. Next the water passed along a gutter following the passage to the infirmary hall, turning sharply right opposite the crypt door to pass south of the infirmary cloister, beneath the sub-vaults of the vestiarium, then turning north under the infirmary hall, joining the drain from the prior's tub. The united drain then served the monks' reredorter ('*necessarium*' on the plan), before crossing the Green Court and leaving the precinct to empty its contents into the town ditch (Willis 1868).

Repairs to part of the ancient drainage system were carried out under Prior Chillenden (1390–1411), who 'repaired and amended the gutter which is conducted along the way which leads from the cloister to the infirmary: first by that way straight to the end of the chapter-house outside; then straight on the outside of the prior's chapel on the south side as far as the sub-prior's chamber; then across the sub-prior's chamber and across the great hall of the infirmary; then along the prior's private chamber; and so by the chamber under the gloriet; then to the head of the third dormitory, and so it turns into an aqueduct in the third dormitory; this gutter, old, wasted and ruined, was now repaired at great expense, and leaded underground for the most part' (Willis 1868, 170–1 and Appendix vi, 188).

Further repairs and alterations were carried out under Prior Goldston (1495–1517), who 'constructed a subterranean aqueduct outside the church, on the south side, and close to it, with bricks and cement, vaulted and firmly constructed, to carry off the inundations of rainwater which, for want of proper channels, were wont to inundate the whole crypt of the Virgin and the adjacent chapels, and greatly hinder the access of the pilgrims . . .'. Prior Goldston's new rain channel passed round the southern and eastern sides of the church, through the cemetery, to the sub-prior's chamber, where it joined the old channel previously repaired by Prior Chillenden (Willis 1868, 170–1).

The other site where the internal plumbing arrangements are known in some detail from contemporary cartographic evidence, and from the interpretation of Hope (1902), is the London Charterhouse. The characteristic Carthusian individual-cell plan demanded special arrangements for water supply and drainage more complex than anything required by the coenobitic orders (Fig 5.4). The course of the conduit to the London Charterhouse from Islington has already been described. The pipe led to a large conduit-house in the centre of the great cloister from which the water was then distributed to the remainder of the precinct. The caption identifies this building by the obsolete and otherwise apparently unrecorded English word 'age', which may derive either from the medieval Latin *alveus* or *augea*, meaning a trough, or from the Old French *auge*, meaning height. The conduit-house is depicted and described as having an octagonal

stone base with a plinth, corbelled out to support a timber-framed octagonal upper stage with windows in its upper half, containing a square lead cistern supplied by the main feed-pipe. The pyramidal roof has a concave profile rising to a sharp peak with a banner and cross finial at the apex. A south-facing door at ground level gave access to the pipes and an east-facing door in the upper storey approached by ladder gave access to the cistern.

Four branch pipes issued from the distributing cistern in the central conduit-house towards the middle of each side of the cloister. Within the cloister garth each pipe passed by a small square tank; the northern service pipe ran parallel with the main supply pipe, and the caption identifies the tank there as a suspiral serving both pipes. The northern, western and eastern service pipes each passed beneath the cloister wall to the line of the gardens behind the cells, and then branched right and left to serve each cell along the range.

The southern pipe initially ran to a lavatorium built into the cloister wall, which consisted of a projecting semi-hexagonal stone base carrying a trough and flanked by piers supporting a stone canopy above, sheltering a cistern with a row of taps.

Two further pipes descended from the cistern of the lavatorium. One ran eastwards to supply the sexton's cell, the laundry and the two cells of the south range nearest the south-east corner. Each was served by a stop-cock, and there was a suspiral between the branches to the last two cells.

The second pipe ran westwards past the sacristy, passing then through a passage to the little cloister west of the church, where it sent off a branch to the prior's cell. Another branch taking off just beyond this served the buttery. Just outside the little cloister a further branch led to a large circular tank in the brewhouse. The main line then turned southwards to a cistern from which two further pipes issued. One continued southwards past a small suspiral, and the caption indicates that it served the Elms and the Hart's Horn, presumably two taverns outside the precinct. The other pipe ran south-eastwards through the gatehouse and past another suspiral to a gabled rectangular building with the somewhat cryptic label 'Egipt', containing a rectangular cistern. This cistern was also fed by yet another pipe leaving the little cloister and passing direct to 'Egipt', its only feature a suspiral close to and linked with that on the pipe from the gatehouse.

From the cistern in the building called 'Egipt' another pipe departed through a small suspiral inside the building and ran on to another rectangular building identified as the 'Windmill', presumably another tavern (Hope 1902, 307–11).

No archaeological investigation of any monastery in any town has yet come close to providing so much information on internal water distribution as that derived from the cartographic evidence just discussed. Nor is this ever likely to happen: in urban situations the prospects of total excavation of any monastic precinct are remote.

However, occasionally some upstanding evidence for features connected with the storage, distribution and use of water does remain.

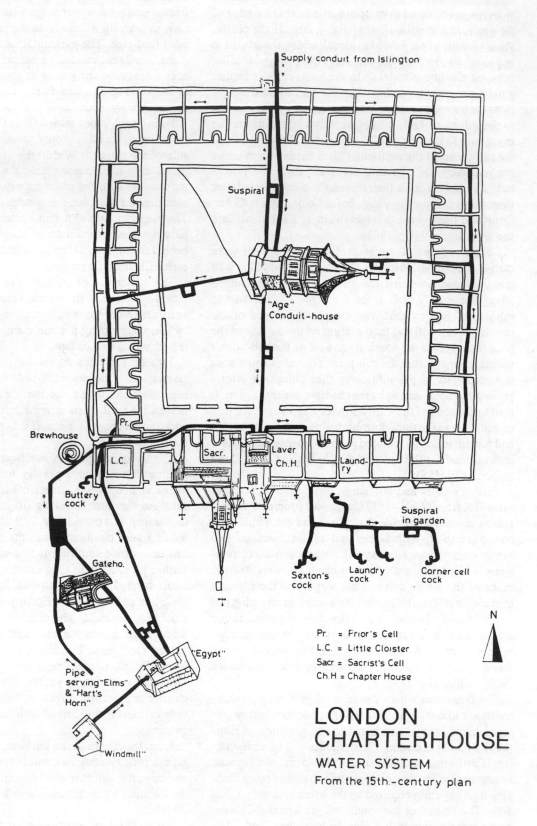

Supply conduit from Islington

Suspiral

"Age"
Conduit-house

Brewhouse

Pr.

L.C.

Sacr.

Laver
Ch.H.

Laundry

Buttery
cock

Suspiral
in garden

Gateho.

Sexton's
cock

Laundry
cock

Corner cell
cock

N

"Egypt"

Pipe
serving "Elms"
& "Hart's
Horn"

Pr. = Prior's Cell
L.C. = Little Cloister
Sacr. = Sacrist's Cell
Ch.H. = Chapter House

"Windmill"

LONDON
CHARTERHOUSE
WATER SYSTEM
From the 15th.-century plan

Figure 5.4

Lavatoria, to be discussed in the following section, are the commonest and most readily-identifiable structures of this type. Others, less distinctive, may not always be recognised for what they are. An example of the problems of interpretation comes from Westminster Abbey, where, towards the end of the last century, Micklethwaite described a narrow stairway within the thickness of the late 14th-century wall separating the refectory from the buttery and parlour. Halfway up the stairway was a landing with a shallow recess in the side wall, in which was set a stone shelf supported by a central mullion. Two round holes 65mm in diameter passing through the shelf, and traces of two more holes in the same line but since broken away, suggested some function connected with the piped water system, and Micklethwaite presented an ingenious reconstruction involving a filtering-tank partly filled with sand or some other suitable material standing on the shelf, two of the holes accommodating the feed-pipe, a third the service-pipe taking clean, filtered water down the stairway to the next point of use (probably the lavatorium recess in the west wall of the cloister immediately north of the parlour), and the fourth hole accommodating a waste overflow which would control the water-level within the tank (Fig 5.5). Initially the waste-pipe seems simply to have discharged onto the floor and down the steps, but it was subsequently channelled down a lead gutter set in a chase on the side of the stairway. The service-pipe followed the same course nearly to the bottom of the stairway, then turned through the wall into the buttery. Here there was a draw-off point, and from a shallow drain below a bronze tap, described as a half-inch full-way bibcock type, was recovered, together with fragments of lead possibly from the cistern itself (Micklethwaite 1892). The identification of the landing recess as the site of a filtering-cistern involved a considerable feat of imagination, but it is entirely consistent both with the evidence on site and with what is known of contemporary technology.

Since many of the components of the supply and storage system within the monastic precinct were above ground level and consisted of leadwork, which has usually been plundered since the Dissolution, the information derived from excavation has been somewhat fragmentary; and waste-pipes and drains figure far more prominently in the archaeological record than supply pipes or cisterns. Nonetheless, many excavations have produced at least a few glimpses and hints of the complex water systems which must have existed.

At Waltham Abbey excavations in the 1970s located some evidence for the piped supply to the lavatorium, and a length of lead pipe was also found cut into the floor of the building interpreted as the brewhouse. A drain passed through the kitchen into the sewer, contemporary with the 12th-century north claustral range (*Medieval Archaeol* **14**, 1970, 166; **16**, 1972, 173; **23**, 1979, 250; Musty 1978).

Excavations on the north range of the cloister on the north side of the church of the Benedictine cathedral priory of St Mary in Coventry in 1965–7 located the kitchen, a detached building linked with the refectory by

a pentice, similar to the arrangement at Christ Church, Canterbury.

Two stone drains capped with sandstone slabs crossed the kitchen court, both leading from the refectory door-way, one of them presumably coming from the lavatorium in the cloister garth. A further substantial stone drain ran from the infirmary towards the main reredorter drain, but appears to pass through it and may be of post-medieval date (Hobley 1970, 97, 98–100).

At St. Augustine's Abbey, Canterbury, open drains from the early kitchen, and more substantial drains from its successor and from the reredorter have been recorded, together with a well-preserved section of terracotta water pipe (*Medieval Archaeol* **28**, 1984, 224; **29**, 1985, 190).

At the Oxford Blackfriars a narrow drain was traced from the main cloister garth through the western range, apparently then turning southwards parallel with the range; a further drain was traced between the kitchen and the scullery, turning round a sharp angle and debouching into a larger open culvert; the line of this culvert continued southwards, passing alongside and beneath some of the domestic buildings beyond the subsidiary cloister to the south; here it was 3m wide, and built of ashlar blocks (Lambrick and Woods 1976, 191–2, 200; Lambrick 1985, 151–3, 157–9). Plant and invertebrate remains from the kitchen drain and the main culvert were consistent with a primary function of carrying away kitchen refuse, and provided important evidence for environmental conditions and the diet of the friars (Robinson 1985, 196–201).

Excavations at the Beverley Blackfriars have revealed a well-built ashlar-lined circular tank at the north-west corner of the refectory, which apparently served as a reservoir storing water which was then fed through lead pipes of 15th-century date serving the west range of the main cloister. One length of pipe turned around the south-west corner of the west range, terminating in the south cloister alley. Outside the west range a substantial southward-flowing open drain served the friars' reredorter before passing beneath the building now known as the Old Friary (possibly the medieval guesthouse) in a vaulted culvert. An extensive network of brick-and stone-lined drains and watercourses of several periods and types of construction has been traced in the great cloister and beneath the west range, feeding into the main sewer, in the little cloister north of the refectory, and in several other locations (inf. M. Foreman).

At St Peter's Abbey, Gloucester, parts of a complex system of culverts have been traced in recent observations (Heighway 1988). A subsidiary culvert 0.25–0.4m deep, discovered at Miller's Green in 1984, possibly took waste water away from the abbey kitchen. Nearby one of the abbey's main drains was found, 0.8m high, walled with oolite and lias and roofed with lias slabs. It is likely that the water of the Fulbrook was led through at least three main conduits within the precinct. Of these, the southernmost is probably the earliest, as it passes beneath the cloister garth, and the northernmost is probably the latest, serving the 14th-century abbot's house and its successor, the 16th-century episcopal palace.

Many tapered earthenware water-pipes dated to

c 1341–50 were found in the kitchen area of the Chelmsford Blackfriars in 1938 (Drury 1974, 78). Two types of mid-15th century earthenware drainpipe have also been recorded from Thetford Priory, one associated with the piscina inserted into the presbytery south aisle, the other with the rebuilt infirmary (Coppack 1973).

The infirmary cloister at Thetford had a cobbled garth with surface drainage running into a round stone-lined cistern in the centre (*Medieval ArchaeolI*,1957, 153). Two drains have been excavated within the cloister garth at Faversham Abbey, together with the lavatorium (*Medieval Archaeol* 9, 1965, 180). At St Neot's Priory an open drain of Collyweston slates led from a building interpreted as the brewhouse towards a large soakaway pit (*Medieval Archaeol* 9, 1965, 180). At the Chester Blackfriars a length of fine sandstone drain has been recorded, running from the friary living-quarters northwestwards via the Watergate towards the River Dee; this was possibly the outfall of the conduit made in 1276 (*Medieval Archaeol* 23, 1979, 249). Few monastic excavations on any scale have failed to produce some evidence of drains removing surface run-off, eaves-drippings or domestic waste.

5.5.1 Lavatoria

Architecturally the most distinctive structures concerned with water utilisation were those providing facilities for washing at the beginning of each day and before meals. Documentary evidence for the building of lavatoria first appears in the 12th century. At Abingdon Abbot Faricius (1100–17) is recorded as rebuilding the main claustral ranges including the lavatorium; and in 1308 his lavatorium was replaced, or perhaps supplemented, by another adjoining the abbey church (Chron.Abingdon, ii). At Battle, Abbot Walter de Luci (1139–71), towards the end of his life, embarked upon the replacement of the original cloister there, which was felt to be unworthy of the abbey. The new cloister was to have 'pavement and columns of marble, polished and smooth; when that was completed, he had plans to construct a place to wash, of the same material and workmanship, and had hired the artisans'. Although Abbot Walter never saw the new lavatorium finished, he earmarked a sum of money for its completion after his death (Chron.Battle, 262–3).

The earliest regular form of lavatorium appears to consist of a free-standing square, circular or polygonal building projecting out into the cloister garth, with piped water rising through a central column to a reservoir above, from which it was distributed by taps to a basin. This type is common on the continent, appearing at influential French monasteries like Cluny, La Charité-sur-Loire and Fontenay as well as Portugese, Spanish and central European houses, and there are some indications that it was also once widespread in Britain. Such a building was described at Durham in 1593: 'Within the Cloyster garth, over against the Frater house dour, was a fair Laver or Counditt for the Monncks to washe ther hands and faces at, being made in forme Round, covered with lead, and all of marble, saving the verie uttermost walls; within the which walls you may walke rownd about the laver

of marble, having many litle cunditts or spouts of brasse, with xxiiij cockes of brass, round about yt, havinge in yt vii faire wyndowes of stone woorke'. A bell hung by the east side of the door of the washing-place to give warning of mealtimes, and there were aumbries for towels on either side of the refectory door (Rites of Durham, 70). Bills of payment for the construction show that this lavatorium was built in 1432–3; the expenses included the purchase of marble from the Eggleston quarry, the carving and carriage of the stone, 22s paid to Thomas the plumber for the leadwork and 9s paid to Laurence, a workman from Newcastle, for making the spouts (Hist.Dunelm., ccccxliii).

The octagonal basin of Eggleston marble still survives. Excavations have suggested that the basin was placed in an earlier building, perhaps of early 13th-century date, circular internally but octagonal outside, with angle buttresses. This was itself the successor to a 12th-century square building containing a circular laver in the south-west angle of the old cloister (Hope 1903).

Godfrey (1952) lists four English examples of the projecting plan dating from the later 12th century. At Battle only slight traces of the foundations survived in the south-west corner of the cloister garth, insufficient to permit the determination of its shape. At Lewes the building was circular with an arcade of double columns with spiral mouldings (Hope 1906; Godfrey 1927, 18); a fragment of the basin itself survives, enough to show that this was ornamented with an arcade with round piers and cushion capitals with vine and grape decoration in the spandrels. At St Nicholas' Priory, Exeter, a dependency of Battle, the lavatorium was also circular and also had an open arcade of nine double shafts of Purbeck marble carried on a dwarf wall (Brakspear 1916, 245, 250). At Much Wenlock the building, dating from c.1180–90, was octagonal and the basin contained within it was richly-carved in 'Wenlock marble', a hard Silurian limestone. Two panels survive, one with two apostles beneath twin arches, the other depicting Christ calling Peter, Andrew, James and John, with their two boats, all under a trefoiled arch; and there are further fragments with anthemion, scroll and shell decoration (for photographs of the Much Wenlock panels and J.C. Thorn's reconstruction of the entire laver, see Zarnecki et al.1984, 200–202). Other examples may have left fragments: part of a basin from Peterborough, and Purbeck marble shafts from Glastonbury very similar to those from the Lewes lavatorium.

The projecting lavatorium generally fell out of favour after the beginning of the 13th century, to be superseded by the long trough type set in a recess, normally in the refectory wall; this version was cheaper to construct and less vulnerable to damage from frost. However, one unusually late example of the polygonal type survives, no longer *in situ*. This is at Sherborne, where a hexagonal lavatorium with buttressed angles, traceried windows, plain parapet and internal ribbed lierne vault was built by Abbot John Mere (1505–35). This originally stood within the cloister, but was removed after the Dissolution by Sir John Horsey and re-erected in Cheap Street outside the east gate of the precinct. The present open-arched west entrance was originally the entry from the north alley of the cloister, and the window mullions and walling below have been removed (Godfrey 1952, 97).

The recessed trough type of lavatorium was normally set in the refectory wall under one or more blind arches, as at Peterborough and Chester. At Lacock the original lavatorium of c 1235 was contained in a lofty arched recess immediately east of the refectory entrance towards the west end of the north cloister walk. When the cloister alley was rebuilt in the 15th century the arch proved too high to be contained within the new roof, and was nearly bisected by one of the springers of the new vault. In its place a projecting trough with a richly-panelled pedestal was built, but this was destroyed after the Dissolution (Brakspear 1900,139).

Alternatively the lavatorium recess may be located in the west wall of the cloister close to the refectory entrance, as at Westminster, Norwich, and the Newcastle Blackfriars. These require little further discussion.

Exceptionally the laver may be set into the garth wall of the cloister alley itself: at Gloucester a splendid fan-vaulted lavatorium survives at the west end of the north walk, dating from c 1400. It contains a broad stone ledge with a trough, which originally contained a lead tank from which water was tapped through spigots. On the facing wall of the cloister walk the recess where towels were hung also survives.

5.6 Brewhouses

Brewhouses were a regular feature of monastic precincts, often being located within the outer court. Brewing equipment frequently figures amongst the furnishings and fittings listed at the time of the Dissolution. For example, John Scudamore, the king's receiver for several west midland and Welsh border counties, recorded the sale of furnaces, lead cisterns, wort vessels, vats and tubs from the Greyfriars and Austin Friars of Stafford and from the Greyfriars of Lichfield (Lett.Supp.Mon., 269, 272, 274).

Large-scale brewing remained almost a monopoly of the greater monastic houses in the early Middle Ages. Although many houses had their own vineyards and orchards and produced their own wine and cider, ale was the normal staple drink. The cellarer usually acted as the master brewer, sometimes with two or three assistants. At Abingdon Abbey, where references to ale occur from the 12th century onwards (Chron.Abingdon, ii, 237–8, 402), the cellarer was responsible for providing ale for the monks at dinner and after compline, and jugs of ale were regularly given to various monastic officials in token of their duties. Malting barley was extensively grown on the abbey's estates, and although it gained considerable profits from the sales of malt the greater proportion was assigned to the cellarer to brew for the abbey's own use (Acct.Obed.Abingdon, 23, 42). References to *bona cervisia* and *debili cervisia* indicate different strengths of ale being produced (Acct.Obed.Abingdon, 16, 44, 53, 62, 75, 77, 87, 91, 105). The original brewhouse and malthouse of Abingdon Abbey almost certainly stood in

the south-west corner of the precinct near the mill and the still-extant checker building.

A brewhouse is also recorded at Bicester Priory (Oxon.); in 1447 the granger accounted for 161 quarters and 4 bushels of malt, used for the brewing of ale for the convent. Here the canons' own production was insufficient for all their needs, however, and ale was being purchased from outside the monastery, both for their own consumption and for the entertainment of guests. Expenses incurred at the burial of Prior Richard Parentyn in 1434 included '24 quarts of ale bought, besides our own brewing, 4s.', while a later account of c 1460–70 records the purchase of 74 gallons of ale bought at 2d a gallon for 8s 6d and a further 93 gallons at 1 1/2 d per gallon (Blomfield 1884).

Corrodies provide a revealing glimpse of the scale of the demand. The standard allowance often stipulated a gallon of good ale a day per person, and sometimes a second gallon of weak ale. When the austere Archbishop Peckham carried out a visitation of Eynsham Abbey (Oxon.) in 1284 he found that the Bishop of Lincoln had provided an unnecessarily liberal pension for the previous abbot, John of Oxford. The archbishop ordered that the former abbot's daily allowance of four gallons of ale must be reduced and made to suffice for the monk assigned to be his companion as well as for himself (Reg.Epist.Peckham, 843–5).

Despite the importance of the brewhouse in the life of the monastery, comparatively few buildings survive or have been excavated. One recent excavation, at Nuneaton Priory in 1981, included a partial examination of the small detached building south of the dormitory, previously identified by Brakspear as the brewhouse. This revealed a small medieval vat in a circular projection at the south-east corner of the building, possibly for steeping barley before it was spread out to germinate (Andrews *et al.* 1981, 61, 64–5). Other possible brewhouses have been noted at Waltham Abbey (Musty 1978) and St Neot's Priory (*Medieval Archaeol* 9, 1965, 179–80).

5.6.1 Reredorters

The course of the natural drainage, the position and direction of flow of local rivers and streams, was a powerful influence upon the planning of any monastic precinct and, more than any other single factor, was responsible for deviations from the standard layout.

An extreme example of adaptation to the natural drainage occurs at Worcester, where the River Severn flowed conveniently below the west front of the Cathedral Priory church. The temptation to take advantage of the river for sewage disposal resulted in a wholesale reorganisation of the entire precinct plan, with the dormitory being built as a detached block west of the church and the reredorter extending over the river bank.

Because natural watercourses often formed estate boundaries, however, they were not always available for direct use, and they also had the disadvantage of often being subject to irregular regimes of flooding and drought. From an early date, therefore, artificial diversions were made by which the water could be more strictly controlled and could be led more precisely where it was needed. The earliest known record of an artificial watercourse being cut for sewage disposal is at Abingdon, where in c.960 the Chronicle records Abbot Æthelwold digging a drain from the reredorter down to the River Ock (Chron.Abingdon ii, 278). On the face of it, such a course would have involved an unnecessarily lengthy and devious cut, and it is difficult to see why it was not aligned to drain directly into the Thames. Many later examples can be recognised from archaeological evidence. For example, at Ponte-fract Priory a stone-lined conduit diverted water from a nearby stream to flush the reredorter (*Medieval Archaeol* **10**, 1966, 184). At Reading Abbey the main reredorter drain must have taken off from the Holy Brook (itself an artificial cut driving the abbey mill) and rejoined the River Kennett (Hurry 1901, 12–13). The reredorter of the Oxford Greyfriars was drained by a culvert taken off the Trill Mill stream (Hassall 1974, 60–61). At Lanthony Priory by Gloucester a stone-lined culvert 0.68m wide × 0.77m deep taken off the Sudbrook, apparently of 13th- or 14th-century date, has recently been explored (Atkin 1988, 14–15).

Even comparatively small communities sometimes undertook substantial engineering schemes of this sort. In 1286 the master and brethren of St John's Hospital, Bridgwater (Somerset), 'being in great need of running water', received licence 'to make a watercourse from the River Parrett, on the south of the great bridge of Bridgwater, by means of a dyke three feet (*c* 1m) broad over their own land and the land of others, and of a depth according to the depth of the river, as far as the said hospital, and thence along the causeway on the north side back to the said river, so as to cleanse the privies of the said hospital, the said dyke to be covered, where necessary, with stones and earth, so as to be level with the adjoining land, and kept in repair by the said hospital' (Cal.Pat.R., 1281–92, 244). This hospital lay in the Eastover suburb on the opposite side of the Parrett to the town, and the channel could have been cut largely through open land.

In built-up areas open sewers could become fairly noxious, hence the provision to cover the Bridgwater example. In 1297 the master and brethren of St Bartho-molew's Hospital, Smithfield, were allowed after inquis-ition 'to cover, on account of its excessive stink, a water-course running through the middle of their hospital and descending to the bridge of Holborn with wood and stone, on condition that the course of the water be not impeded by the covering' (Cal.Pat.R.,1292–1301, 288).

Sometimes there is archaeological evidence of alter-ations to the drainage through the reredorter. At the Chelmsford Blackfriars the reredorter was added to the dormitory range shortly after 1300. Originally it was cleansed by means of water taken off a stream to the north, led through a culvert lined with tile wasters, passing under the wall through a round-headed arch faced in Caen stone and floored with Purbeck marble; the flow of water was controlled by a sluicegate in the culvert. Subsequently the culvert was blocked, a new water-supply was brought in by pipes along the north side of the building (perhaps as a result of the 1341 licence mentioned earlier), and a new sluicegate was built at the outlet (Drury 1974). At

the Austin Friars in Leicester a stagnant ditch bisecting the precinct was linked with the River Soar in the 15th-century, lined with stone and converted to an eastward-flowing drain equipped with a sluice. The southern range of the little cloister straddled it, and a single garderobe discharged into it, the main reredorter probably being further to the east (Mellor and Pearce 1981, 35–7, 41–2).

Where no natural watercourse was available for di-version close at hand, the waste water from the supply conduit plus run-off from roofs and courtyards might be channelled into the main drain. From the evidence of the 12th-century plan this appears to have been the case at Christ Church, Canterbury, where the whole complex of pipes and drains fed ultimately into the great drain which flushed the large 55-seater reredorter building.

The internal arrangements of the reredorter varied according to the position of the building and the course of the drain through it. The commonest arrangement consisted of a single row of seats along one wall or a double row arranged back-to-back over a single central drain. At the Exeter Greyfriars the reredorter lay south of the dormitory and water was conveyed to it by a stone-lined culvert running down the eastern side of the range. The latrine channel was 0.6m wide with a rounded floor built of finely-dressed volcanic ashlar (*Medieval Archaeol* **26**,1982, 177). A similar pattern has been identified at St Mary's Priory, Coventry, where the reredorter block extends eastwards from an almost square dormitory undercroft (Hobley 1970, 98).

At Lacock the original reredorter building of *c* 1235 was a large two-storey block at the north end of the dormitory range, projecting eastwards. Its lower storey comprises a long waggon-vaulted room, perhaps used as a fuel store, occupying two-thirds of its width, with a single ground-level garderobe occupying a recess in the north-east corner perched over the main drain, which passed along inside the length of its northern wall. At first-floor level the building was entered from the south by a door at the end of the central dormitory passage, and there was a row of garderobes occupying the whole of the north wall. In the 14th century the dormitory was extended northwards, incorporating the western half of the reredorter and reducing its accommodation by half; it is not clear whether this alteration resulted in any alternative latrine provision being made (Brakspear 1900, 149).

A more elaborate arrangement appears at Glastonbury, where the flow of water was divided into two parallel channels through the reredorter range, separated by a solid mass of dumped clay revetted in stone, so that the building had no open space at ground floor level. It was entered from the first-floor dormitory, and all the seats were arranged around the walls of the building facing inwards (Peers *et al.* 1934). The Westminster reredorter was also double-sided with drains down both long sides of the building.

Other parts of the abbey often had their own reredorters or privies. At Bermondsey Abbey the infirmary latrines have been investigated, revealing two phases of sewers with a reconstruction after the 12th-century (*Medieval Archaeol* **29**, 1985, 178; **31**, 1987, 132). At the

Carmarthen Greyfriars a building on the south side of the subsidiary cloister, also interpreted as the infirmary, had a small single privy projecting from its outer side with a tank just above which seems to have provided some sort of flushing arrangement (*Medieval Archaeol* 30, 1986, 194–6). Recent excavations at Shrewsbury Abbey have revealed a 14th-century square stone building in the outer court, probably the guesthouse kitchen, with a staircase at the south-east corner which possibly gave access to a garderobe tower. A stone-built drain along the south wall of the building was flushed by a leat taken off the Meole Brook, which also fed the abbey fishponds before eventually discharging into the mill-stream (Baker *et al.*1986; Baker and Cooper 1988).

5.7 Fishponds

The general significance of fisheries and fishponds in the monastic economy has been explored elsewhere recently (Bond 1988), and only a brief summary of matters relating to the fishponds of urban monasteries is given here. However, one or two points made in that earlier paper now require reappraisal in the light of subsequent contributions.

The earliest known references to artificial fishponds in monastic ownership all pertain to urban houses. In the Domesday survey two fishponds are recorded at Bury St Edmunds and another at St Alban's. At the end of the 12th century an interesting conflict is recorded between Abbot Samson and the cellarer and infirmarer of Bury St Edmunds, due to the enlargement of the abbot's pond at Babwell at the expense of neighbouring meadows, pastures, orchards and arable land (Chron. Brakelond, 131). Abbot Adam of Evesham (1160–89) was responsible for the construction of a number of fishponds, probably including the largest of the three ponds at the abbey itself, the other two being added by Abbot Randulf (1214–29) (Bond, 1973, 31–2). It is clear that fishponds were a regular feature of monastic precincts by the end of the 12th century.

However, Currie (1989) has argued persuasively that the role of monasteries in the development of fishponds was less innovatory than had been assumed, and that royal, episcopal and secular landlords were more active in fishpond construction at a comparatively earlier date. Leaving aside the examples quoted above, he shows that many of the earliest recorded monastic ponds were in fact pre-existing ponds given to monastic houses by lay magnates.

The form of urban monastic fishponds tended more frequently to be constrained by space than those in rural situations. Fairly simple layouts involving no more than three ponds appear to be characteristic of Benedictine houses like Evesham, Pershore and Great Malvern, and Augustinian foundations such as Cirencester, Osney and Bristol. Even where remains of such ponds survive, they are not visually very exciting, and have often failed to be recognised; it was not until 1981–2, for example, that the slight earthworks of a single fishpond in the south-eastern part of the Glastonbury Abbey precinct were first identified and surveyed (Burrow 1982). Somewhat more complex groups of small rectangular ponds also occur, for example at Waltham Abbey, where there are two nearly square ponds and two long rectangular ponds in Veresmead with the cropmarks of two or three associated buildings (Huggins 1972), and at Peterborough, where there was a rather similar complex of ponds south of Abbot Godfrey's moated *herbarium* (Harvey 1981, 13, 85). More extensive chains of larger fishponds are uncommon in urban monasteries, and seem to appear only at sites whose urban status is itself marginal. At Eynsham (Oxon) the small town is concentrated around the northern side of the precinct, and a chain of five ponds was laid out along the valley bottom to the south after the extension of the precinct by the purchase of neighbouring properties in 1217 (Bond 1988, 101–3; Bond, forthcoming). An even larger series has been recorded at the Cluniac priory of Daventry, and here too the ponds are on the further side of the precinct from the small town, effectively in open country (R.C.H.M. Northants. iii, 1981, 68–9).

A second point which Currie (1989) has challenged is the suggestion, prompted mainly by the seemingly large extent and elaborate form of monastic fishponds such as Eynsham and Daventry, that these were operating on a commercial basis. There are, in fact, records of sales of fish from at least one monastic pond. At Abingdon two of the four surviving gardener's accounts identify sums received from fish sold, 12s 8d in 1388–9 and 21s 4d in 1412–13 (Acct.Obed.Abingdon, 52, 74). However, these are exceptional, and must be seen in the context of considerable purchases of both fresh-water and marine fish.

Documentation for large-scale commercial exploitation elsewhere is conspicuously lacking, and Currie argues that yields from monastic ponds would not normally have been sufficient for a surplus to be sold. Indeed, far from providing a regular surplus, they did not even supply day-to-day internal needs, and their main function probably now has to be seen as the provision of fresh fish for important guests and for special feasts.

Evidence from the excavation of urban monastic fishponds is not extensive. At Christchurch Priory a garderobe was apparently reused as a fish hatchery (*Medieval Archaeol* 14, 1970, 168). At the Pontefract Blackfriars the fishpond remained in use after the Dissolution (*Medieval Archaeol* 8, 1964, 246). The fullest account comes from the Augustinian priory of Taunton, established on a new site on the edge of the town in 1158. Here it is recorded that the Sherford Brook was diverted to serve the new precinct, and this could have filled ponds and driven the mill. Excavations in 1977–8 revealed water channels linked with a clay-lined pond edged with wooden stakes, dated to the first period of monastic occupation. Both ceramic evidence and radio-carbon dating indicated that the pond had fallen into disuse and had been filled in by the mid-13th century, probably as a result of the replanning of the outer precinct as the buildings of the priory expanded. The only upstanding medieval structure, the so-called 'Priory Barn', was subsequently built over the filled pond, initially as a domestic range and gateway.

Interestingly, in the light of the discussion above, the fish remains amongst the domestic debris used to fill the pond and channels were exclusively of marine species — hake, whiting, conger eel, plaice and haddock (Leach 1984, 111–24, 193–4).

5.8 Water-Mills

The use of water-power to drive corn-mills on monastic estates was well established by the mid-10th century, and it is from the same period that we have the first record of construction of a monastic mill which involved substantial water engineering. The chronicle of Abingdon Abbey describes the mill 'below the *curia*' being built by Abbot Æthelwold who, we are told, diverted part of the Thames into a leat to feed it, and cut the tail-race to rejoin the main river near St Helen's church (Chron. Abingdon i, 480–1, ii, 270, 278–80, 282, 285).

There is every reason to suppose that Æthelwold's mill was on or very near the site of the present Abbey Mill, and that the existing leat and tail-race in essence follow the course cut by Æthelwold in *c* 960. This leat leaves the Thames 0.8km upstream, and the contour of the ground leaves no doubt that it follows a completely artificial course and is not a modified natural backwater (Bond 1979, 69). Today the tail-race rejoins the river after a further 0.3km, still some distance above St Helen's Church. However, air photographs suggest that this branch of the Thames formerly had a slightly more easterly meandering course below Abingdon Bridge, and the old county boundary between Oxfordshire and Berkshire conspicuously diverges from the present stream to follow this abandoned channel along the Oxfordshire bank for a further 0.2km to a point below St Helen's church. If this was the extant main stream at the time Æthelwold's mill was constructed, as seems likely from the fact that the 10th-century county boundary followed it, the abbey chronicle's description of the digging of the tail-race becomes comprehensible. It is not clear when the river moved into its present course. The abbey appears to have been involved in at least two schemes to improve the navigation of the Thames in the 11th and 12th centuries, and one of these may have occasioned the straightening. Alternatively it may not have been the result of any conscious decision; I am grateful to Mrs Ellarose Carden of Mandeville, Louisiana, for her observation, based on knowledge of mills on the Mississippi, that the main stream may itself have been dragged upstream and westwards into a new course by the scouring effect of the tail-race.

Æthelwold had been a contemporary of Dunstan at Glastonbury and it is tempting to speculate that his confidence in water engineering may owe something to his earlier career in the Somerset levels. Also, as one of the key figures in the Benedictine revival, he was in close touch with the ideas and technology of continental monasticism. The building of the Abingdon mill can be seen as part of a conscious attempt to fulfil the ideal specified in Chapter 66 of the Rule of St Benedict of having everything necessary for the abbey, including the mill, within its own precinct.

The Domesday survey records large numbers of mills in monastic ownership, and sometimes indicates significant changes in their provision.

At Waltham Abbey some time between 1066 and 1086 the number of mills was increased from one to three. The account of the construction of the water conduit from Wormley in 1220–2 mentions 'the stream of the lower mill' and 'the stream of the second mill'. It was probably within the period 1066–86 that a second, more elevated water-supply feeding one or both of the new mills was channelled along what is now the Cornmill Brook, parallel to, east of, and *c* 1.5m above the original leat feeding the lower mill. The two mill systems may have worked together for many years, but ultimately the Cornmill Stream completely superseded the lower, western leat system. In 1482 a complaint was made that the abbot was taking a head of water 16 feet (4.9m) broad along the Cornmill Stream, where it should have been only 4 feet (1.2m) broad, thereby damaging the king's river, the old course of the River Lea. In 1528 two mills are recorded for the first time under one roof, conceivably, though not necessarily, implying the abandonment of the lower mill. The lower leat was certainly blocked by *c* 1581, when the Cornmill Stream was briefly adopted as the main navigation channel of the Lea (Huggins 1970, 128).

The races of medieval monastic mills often long outlived the original buildings, and sometimes remained in use into the present century. Two mills were granted to Tewkesbury Abbey at time of its foundation in 1102 (*Mon.Angl.*ii, 65, 81). There are frequent references to two water corn mills belonging to this abbey between 1291 and 1535, and later references suggest that these represented two sets of stones in one building, on the site of the present mill. The Mill Avon at Tewkesbury probably originated as an artificial watercourse, newly-made in the 12th century, to divert part of the Avon from its original course through the mill(V. C. H. Gloucs. viii, 112, 139).

Stream diversions of this nature were often of considerable magnitude. The leat for the Reading Abbey mill, the Holy Brook, takes off from the River Kennett near Theale, more than 8km upstream, and at least the lowest 3km of this stream are straight and wholly artificial. Excavation on the Reading Abbey waterfront in the early 1980s produced evidence for a series of major changes of alignment of both the Kennett and the mill leat. Early in the 12th century the river margins were first consolidated with a dump of clay forming a wattle-revetted causeway. The tail-race and overflow channel of the mill were first cut in this period. Later in the 12th century the front of the clay bank was strengthened with post and plank structures. Early in the 14th century there was a major reorganisation, with the mill tail-race diverted southwards to a new confluence with the Kennett, and a new river-wharf built. Further minor modifications continued to the Dissolution (*Medieval Archaeol* 28, 1984, 208–9).

There is a great deal of documentary evidence relating to mills, because alterations to watercourses often brought their owners into conflict with neighbouring landowners.

The proliferation of mills on the braided channels of the Thames west of Oxford resulted in numerous quarrels. Osney Abbey had at least two corn mills here by 1150; by 1249 it had built a fulling-mill, followed in the mid-14th-century by another two mills on one of the backwaters, and in 1412 there were said to be four newly-built mills in the abbey (V. C. H. Oxon., iv, 330). In consequence, the canons of Osney found themselves involved in a long series of disputes with the crown and the civic authorities, being accused of appropriating the water which should have fed the king's mills at Oxford castle, blocking the channel which should have been used for navigation, and damaging the fisheries and neighbouring meadows (Cal.Inq.Misc. iii, p.20, no.46, p.302, no.806; Oseney Cart. ii, p.470). The mill built in the early 13th century by the abbess of Godstow, and Abingdon Abbey's Botley Mill, built in c 1344, were also both accused of damaging the mills of Oxford castle (Rot.Hundr. ii, 35; Cal.Pat.R. 1343–5, 401).

Another instance comes from Lacock where, although the manor of Lacock itself formed part of the original endowment of the nunnery, the interests of other landowners, particularly the Bluets of Lackham, sometimes stood in the way of the nuns' attempts to develop their property. In 1241 there was a disagreement between Abbess Ela and Roger Bluet concerning a mill and its ponds and a bridge built in the town by the abbess, which was resolved by Roger agreeing to allow the mill to remain as it was, without molestation and without dues, and the abbess agreeing to maintain the bridge and to re-erect it in the event of its collapse (Lacock Chart. p.46, no.168). Less than a quarter of a century later Sir William Bluet of Lackham and Abbess Beatrice found themselves in conflict over the same mill; Bluet had apparently diverted the watercourse away from the mill in the nunnery's close, but agreed to restore it to its rightful course and to grant to the nuns a spring on his land in 'Lachameslie' opposite the mill, with the right to enclose it and make a new watercourse across his land, in exchange for various other pieces of land (Lacock Chart. p.44, no.157; p.47, no.169).

Mills make a correspondingly early appearance in the cartographic record. One of the best-known examples is the mid-15th century map in the Chertsey cartulary which depicts the abbey's meadows below Laleham on the Thames. Close to the abbey site the map shows two undershot mills on either side of a backwater (P R O, E.164/25, f.222r).

By contrast with the rich documentary record, there is comparatively little surviving architectural evidence for urban monastic mills, though one of the mills at Durham retains some 13th to 14th century masonry (Luckhurst 1964, 13–14). Nor is the record of archaeological excavation particularly extensive, though there have been some sightings during redevelopment; for example, substantial sandstone footings of the south wall of the Coventry Priory mill, demolished in 1847, were rediscovered in 1967 (Hobley 1970, 87, Plate 21b).

The earliest and fullest evidence comes from Reading, where considerable portions of the west, south and east walls of the medieval abbey mill formerly survived incorporated into a large 18th and 19th century mill,

which used the same mill-race until its closure in 1959 (V. C. H. Berks.ii, 339–49; Luckhurst, 1964, 12–13). The demolition of the later mill in 1964–5 destroyed some parts of the medieval structure. The portion of the west wall which survives includes a length of rubble masonry 17m long pierced by three arches, designed to carry at least one upper storey. The central four-centred arch spanning the Holy Brook is 4.3m wide, and is made of reused 12th century masonry with a heavy chevron moulding; this arch is set into the infill of a larger earlier pointed arch. It is likely that the medieval mill would originally have contained a single centrally-placed undershot wheel, though after the Dissolution it contained two undershot wheels set side by side. The round-headed ashlar-faced land arch to the north is 2.3m wide, and where the mill encroached onto the south side of the brook is a further small arch. Limited excavation during the redevelopment of the area revealed the footings of the parallel eastern arches, and suggested an original construction date within the 12th-century, with evidence of a considerable fire about a century later (Slade, 1972, 62–79).

5.8.1 Precinct Moats

Monastic houses in towns as well as the countryside sometimes made use of water-filled moats to define the bounds of their precinct, with or without the addition of a wall. At Evesham it is recorded that Abbot Reginald built a fine precinct wall round the abbey and its cemetery, and that he intended to supplement this with a moat, but was dissuaded by the advice of his uncle, Milo, Earl of Hereford, lest the king should then seize the abbey as a fortress (Chron. Evesham, 98).

A moat certainly existed at Abingdon, first recorded in 1369–70. In 1388–9 the gardener's account recorded the expenditure of 22s 10d for 'cleansing the great moat'. The moat also served as a fishpond; a later gardener's account of 1450–1 records 4s.10d spent on weles (wickerwork traps) for taking fish in the convent moat. It survived as a prominent feature in the landscape at least to 1585, when a list of features on the site of the former abbey includes 'The Covent dytche' (Acct.Obed.Abingdon 19, 54, 130, 167; Bond 1979, 60, 69). The outline of a canalised watercourse surrounding three sides of the rectangular precinct, the fourth side fronting the Thames, is clearly shown on the 16th-century map which hangs in the Abingdon guildhall, but no trace remains visible today.

At the Austin Friars at Leicester the watercourse which later served as the main drain may initially have been dug as a precinct ditch enclosing the early friary buildings on the northern side. In its early phases it seems to have been stagnant, revetted with wooden stakes and wattle fencing, and partly culverted. Only later does it appear to have been linked with the river to provide a flow of water through it (Mellor and Pearce 1981, 11–15).

Moats were sometimes used to enclose particular features within the precinct. At Peterborough in 1302 Abbot Godfrey of Crowland made 'a beautiful herbarium' south-west of the claustral buildings, about two acres in extent, 'surrounded . . . with double moats (*stagnis*), with bridges and pear-trees and very lovely plants' (quoted in Harvey 1981, 12–13). At Waltham Abbey a rectangular moat still encloses a large area east of the church which was presumably also originally an orchard or garden.

5.9 Conclusion

Water was a basic necessity to any monastic institution, for drinking, for food preparation and brewing, for washing and laundry, for sewage disposal, for filling moats and fishponds, as a power source, and for a miscellany of other purposes. Fig 5.5 is an attempt to summarise in diagrammatic form some of the standard uses of water within the monastic precinct, and some of the archaeological manifestations which can be expected. Yet, despite the fundamental importance of water management, it has rarely been the primary focus of investigation, either by archaeologists or historians, and has never really attracted the attention it deserves.

This article should be regarded very much as a provisional summary of investigations in progress, and parts of it will undoubtedly soon require revision. Several cautionary notes are necessary. In the interests of the wide view I have drawn freely upon interim reports of some excavations, without always having had the opportunity for discussion with the archaeologists responsible; and it must be recognised, therefore, that statements based upon those interim reports may need to be reappraised when the final reports find their way into print. I would not for one moment claim that my search of the published literature has been exhaustive, and I will undoubtedly have overlooked some significant contributions. Nor would I claim to have first-hand personal knowledge of all the sites discussed here, and this, too, may have led me into errors of fact or interpretation. Nonetheless, despite these admitted shortcomings, it is felt that the gathering together of information in this way is an essential preliminary step before re-evaluation of the existing evidence and further advances in understanding can be made.

Acknowledgements

As with any attempt at synthesis, most of the substance of this paper derives from the labours of others. My greatest debt, therefore, is to all those archaeologists and historians whose published work I have quarried. Most of them are named in the references below, and my apologies are due to anyone whose contribution I have overlooked. Amongst the many individuals who have shared their knowledge with me, I would particularly like to thank Warwick Rodwell for information on Wells, Martin Foreman for information on Beverley, and Mr and Mrs M Leach for introducing me to some of the complexities of Bristol's medieval water supply. My wife, Tina, has read the text, suggested several improvements, and saved me from a number of bizarre spelling errors. Errors which remain are my responsibility alone.

Finally I would like to thank the editors for their patience and tolerance in accepting a manuscript which has not only been delivered late but has also turned out to be several times longer than they, or I, had originally envisaged.

Published Documentary Sources

Acct.Obed.Abingdon, 1892, *Accounts of the Obedientiars of Abingdon Abbey*, (ed) by R E G Kirk. Camden Society, new series, **51**.

Acct. Exeter, 1981, 1983, *The Accounts of the Fabric of Exeter Cathedral, 1279–1326* (ed) by A. M. Erskine. Devon and Cornwall Record Soc. new series, **24** (1981), **26** (1983).

Bristol Chart., 1930, *Bristol Charters, 1155–1373*, (ed) by N Dermott Harding. Bristol Record Society, **1.i, 1.ii, 1.iii**.

Cal.Chart.R., *Calendar of Charter Rolls* London: P.R.O.

Cal.Close R., *Calendar of Close Rolls* London: P.R.O.

Cal.Inq.Misc., *Calendar of Inquisitions Miscellaneous* London: P.R.O.

Cal.Lib.R., *Calendar of Liberate Rolls* London: P.R.O.

Cal.Pat.R., *Calendar of Patent Rolls* London: P.R.O.

Cal.Linc. MSS, 1895 *The Manuscripts of the Corporation of Lincoln*. London: Historical Manuscripts Commission, **37**, 14th Report, appendix, part viii.

Cal.Wells MSS, 1907, 1914, *Calendar of the Manuscripts of the Dean and Chapter of Wells* London: Historical Manuscripts Commission, **12.i** (1907), **12.ii** (1914).

Cal.Worc.MSS, 1895, *Muniments in the Possession of the Dean and Chapter of Worcester* London: Historical Manuscripts Commission, **37**, 14th Report, appendix, part viii

Cart.Canterbury St Gregory, 1956, *Cartulary of the Priory of St Gregory Canterbury*, (ed) by A M Woodcock. Royal Historical Society, Camden 3rd series, **88**.

Cart.Chester, 1920, 1923, *Chartulary of the Abbey of St Werburgh, Chester*, (ed) by J Tait 2 parts, Manchester: Chetham Soc., new ser., **79** (1920), **82** (1923).

Chron.Abingdon, 1858, *Chronicon Monasterii de Abingdon*, (ed) by J Stevenson. London: Rolls Series, **2.i, 2.ii**.

Chron.Battle, 1980, *The Chronicle of Battle Abbey*, (ed) by E Searle. Oxford: Clarendon Press.

Chron.Brakelond, 1949, *The Chronicle of Jocelin of Brakelond*, (ed) by H E Butler. London: Thomas Nelson and Sons.

Chron.Evesham, 1863, *Chronicon Abbatiae de Evesham*, (ed) by W D Macray. London: Rolls Series, **29**.

Chron.Melsa, 1866–68, *Chronicon Monasterii de Melsa*, (ed) by E A Bond. London: Rolls Series, **43.i** (1866) **43.ii** (1867) **43.iii** (1868).

G.R.B. Bristol, 1933, 1938, *The Great Red Book of Bristol*, (ed) by E W W Veale. Text, parts i and ii. Bristol Record Soc. **4** (1933), **8** (1938).

Habington, Surv.Worcs., 1893–5, 1897–9, T Habington, *A Survey of Worcestershire*, (ed) by J Amphlett. 2 vols, Worcs Hist Soc.

Hist. Dunelm, 1839, *Historiae Dunelmensis Scriptores Tres*, (ed) by J Raines. Surtees Society, 9.

Hist. Glouc., 1863, 1865, *Historia et Cartularium Monasterii Sancti Petri Gloucestriae*, (ed) by W H Hart. London: Rolls Series, **33.i** (1863) **33.ii** (1865).

Inv. Salop, 1905, Inventories of the Religious Houses of Shropshire at their Dissolution. *Trans Shropshire Archaeol and Nat Hist Soc*, 3rd ser, **5**, 377–92.

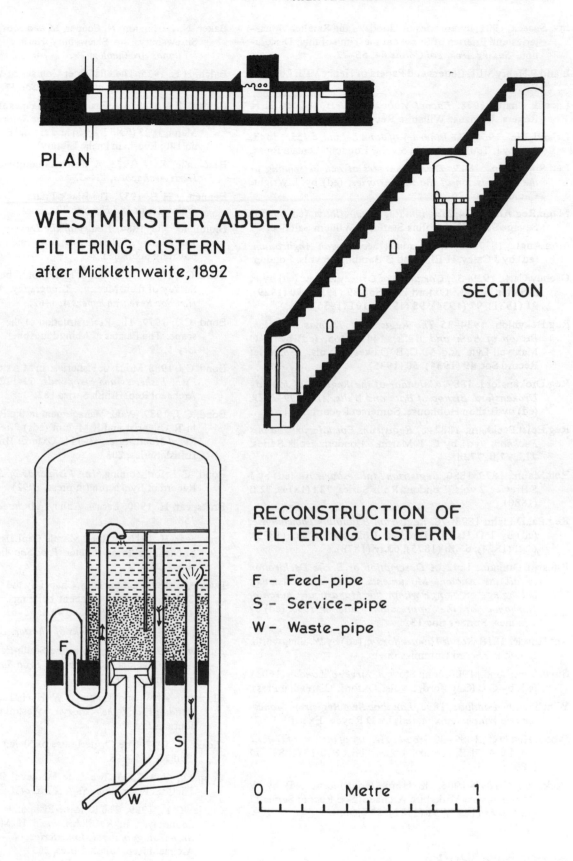

PLAN

WESTMINSTER ABBEY
FILTERING CISTERN
after Micklethwaite, 1892

SECTION

RECONSTRUCTION OF FILTERING CISTERN

F - Feed-pipe
S - Service-pipe
W - Waste-pipe

0   Metre   1

Figure 5.5

Inv. Sussex, 1901, Inventories of Goods of the Smaller Monasteries and Friaries of Sussex at the Time of their Dissolution. *Sussex Archaeol Collns* 44, 55–72.

L and P Henry VIII, Letters and Papers of Henry VIII. London: P.R.O.

Lacock Chart., 1978, *Lacock Abbey Charters*, (ed) by K H Rogers. Devizes: Wiltshire Record Society, 34.

Leland, Itin., 1964, *The Itinerary of John Leland, c.1535–1543*, (ed) by L Toulmin Smith, 5 vols. London: Centaur Press.

Lett.Supp.Mon., 1843, *Three Chapters of Letters relating to the Suppression of the Monasteries*, (ed) by T Wright. Camden Soc., 26.

Magn.Reg.Alb., 1924, *Magnum Registrum Album*, (ed) by H E Savage Staffs Hist Collns Stafford: William Salt Soc.

Mon.Angl., 1817–30, W Dugdale, *Monasticon Anglicanum*, (ed) by J Caley, H Ellis and B Bandinel, 6 vols. London.

Oseney Cart., 1929–36, *Cartulary of Oseney Abbey*, (ed) by H E Salter, 6 vols. Oxford Hist Soc 89 (1929), 90 (1929), 91 (1931), 97 (1934), 98 (1935), 101 (1936).

Reg.Bekynton, 1934–35 *The Register of Thomas Bekynton, Bishop of Bath and Wells*, 1443–1465, (ed) by H C Maxwell-Lyte and M C B Dawes, 2 vols. Somerset Record Soc 49 (1934), 50 (1935).

Reg.Drokensford, 1887, *Calendar of the Register of John de Drokensford, Bishop of Bath and Wells, AD 1309–1329*, (ed) by Bishop Hobhouse, Somerset Record Soc 1.

Reg.Epist.Peckham, 1882–6, *Registrum Epistolarum Joannis Peckham*, (ed) by C T Martin. London: Rolls Series, 77.i, 77.ii, 77.iii.

Reg.Malm., 1879, 1880, *Registrum Malmesburiense*, (ed) by J S Brewer, 2 vols. London: Rolls Series, 72.i (1879), 72.ii (1880).

Reg.Pal.Dunelm 1873–78, *Registrum Palatinum Dunelmense*, (ed) by T D Hardy. London: Rolls Series, 62.i (1873), 62.ii (1874), 63.iii (1875), 63.iv (1878).

Rites of Durham, 1842, *A Description or Breife Declaration of all the Ancient Monuments, Rites and Customes belonginge or beinge within the Monastical Church of Durham before the Suppression, written in 1593*, (ed) by J Raines. Surtees Soc 15.

Rot.Hundr., 1818, *Rotuli Hundredorum*, (ed) by W. Illingworth. London: Record Commissioners.

Stow, Surv.Lond., 1908, John Stow, *A Survey of London* (1603), (ed) by C L Kingsford, 2 vols. Oxford: Clarendon Press.

Winchcombe *Landboc*, 1892, *Landboc Sive Registrum Monasterii de Winchelcumba*, (ed) by D Royce. Exeter.

Wood, Hist.Oxf., 1889–90, *Wood's History of the City of Oxford*, (ed) by A Clark, 2 vols. Oxford Hist Soc 15 (1889), 17 (1890).

Yorks.Inq. 1891–1906, *Yorkshire Inquisitions*, (ed) by W Brown, 4 vols Yorkshire Archaeol Soc Record Series 12 (1891), 23 (1897), 31 (1902), 37 (1906).

Secondary Works

Andrews, D, Cook, A, Quant, V, Thorn, J C and Veasey, E A, 1981, The Archaeology and Topography of Nuneaton Priory. *Trans Birmingham and Warwicks Archaeol Soc* 91, 55–81.

Atkin, M, 1988, Excavations in Gloucester 1987: an Interim Report. *Glevensis* 22, 12–25.

Baker, N and Cooper, M, 1988, Shrewsbury Abbey. *Current Archaeology* 109, 59–62.

Baker, N, Darlington, N, Cooper, M and Moffett, M C, 1986, Shrewsbury, the Shrewsbury Heritage Project. *West Midlands Archaeology* 29, 19–24.

Balch, H E, 1925, The Old Water-Courses of Wells *Reports of Wells Natural Hist and Archaeol Soc* 37, 14–33.

Barnard, E A B, 1923, A Find of Leaden Pipes at Evesham in AD 1726. *Evesham Journal and Four Shires Advertiser*, 3rd March 1923 ('Old Days in and around Evesham' column, no.140; Evesham Public Library).

Bascombe, K N, 1973, A Water Conduit-Head at Wormley *Herts Archaeol* 3, 124–5.

Bennett, J H E, 1952, The Black Friars. *Chester and North Wales Archit and Hist Soc* 39.

Blomfield, J C, 1884, *History of the Deanery of Bicester*, ii: *The History of Bicester, its Town and Priory*. Bicester: privately published.

Bond, C J, 1973, The Estates of Evesham Abbey: a Preliminary Survey of their Medieval Topography. *Vale of Evesham Hist Soc Research Papers* 4, 1–62.

Bond, C J, 1979, The Reconstruction of the Medieval Landscape: The Estates of Abingdon Abbey. *Landscape History* 1, 59–75.

Bond, C J, 1988, Monastic Fisheries. In M Aston (ed) *Medieval Fish, Fisheries and Fishponds*, 69–112. Oxford: Brit Archaeol Rep, British Series 182.

Bond, C J, 1989, Water Management in the Rural Monastery. In R Gilchrist and H Mytum (eds) *The Archaeology of Rural Monasteries*, 83–111. Oxford: Brit Archaeol Rep, British Series, 203.

Bond, C J, forthcoming, *The Fishponds of Eynsham Abbey*. Record of Eynsham 8 (in press, 1992).

Brakspear, H, 1900, Lacock Abbey. *Archaeologia* 57.i 125–158.

Brakspear, H, 1916, Purbeck Marble Capitals and Bases from St Nicholas' Priory, Exeter. *Proc Soc Antiq London*, 2nd series, 28.

Buckle, E, 1894, On the Lady Chapel by the Cloister of Wells Cathedral and the adjacent buildings. *Proc Somerset Archaeol and Nat Hist Soc* 40.ii, 32–63.

Burne, R V H, 1962, *The Monks of Chester*. London: SPCK.

Burrow, I, 1982, Earthworks in the South-Eastern Part of the Abbey Precinct, Glastonbury. *Proc Somerset Archaeol and Nat Hist Soc* 126, 39–42.

Clapham, A W and Godfrey, W H, 1913, *Some Famous Buildings and their Story*. Westminster: Technical Journals Ltd

Cloake, J, 1977, The Charterhouse of Sheen *Surrey Archaeol Coll* 71, 145–198.

Coppack, G, 1973–6, Two Late Medieval Pipe-Drains from Thetford Priory. *Proc Suffolk Inst of Archaeol* 33, 88–90.

Currie, C K, 1989, The Role of Fishponds in the Monastic Economy. In R Gilchrist and H Mytum (eds) *The Archaeology of Rural Monasteries*, 147–172 Oxford: Brit Archaeol Rep, British Series, 203.

Dickinson, J C, 1950, *The Origins of the Austin Canons and their Introduction into England*. London: SPCK.

Dickinson, J C, 1961, *Monastic Life in Medieval England*. London: A and C Black.

Drury, P J, 1974, Chelmsford Dominican Priory: The Excavation of the Reredorter, 1973. *Essex Archaeol and Hist* new ser, 6, 40–81.

Durham, B, 1988, Oxford, Magdalen College. *South Midlands Archaeol* 18, 34–5.

Fox, A, 1951, The Underground Conduits in Exeter, exposed during Reconstruction in 1950. *Trans Devon Assoc* **83**, 172–8.

Frontinus-Gesellschaft, 1987, 1988, *Die Wasserversorgung Antiker Städte*, **2** (1987), **3** (1988) Mainz: Philipp von Zabern.

Fulbrook-Leggatt L E W O, 1968, The Water Supplies of the Abbey of St Peter and the Priory of the Grey Friars, Gloucester, from Robinswood Hill. *Trans Bristol and Gloucester Archaeol Soc.* **87**, 111–8.

Garner, M F and Lindsey, R, 1987, Southampton, Conduit House. In M Hughes (ed), *Archaeology and Historic Buildings in Hampshire: Annual Report for 1986*, 24–5. Hampshire County Planning Dept.

Godfrey, W H, 1927, *The Priory of St Pancras, Lewes.*

Godfrey, W H, 1952, English Cloister Lavatories as Independent Structures. *Archaeol J* **106**, Supplement (1949), 91–7.

Gould, J, 1976, The Twelfth-Century Water-Supply to Lichfield Close. *Antiq J* **56.i**, 73–79.

Haigh, G, 1947, *The History of Winchcombe Abbey*. London: Skeffington.

Hale, Archdeacon, 1869, The Carthusian Monastery of London. *Trans London and Middlesex Archaeol Soc.* **3.10**, 309–331.

Harvey, J, 1981, *Medieval Gardens*. London: B T Batsford Ltd.

Hassall, T G, 1974, The Greyfriars, in Excavations at Oxford, 1973–4, 6th Interim Report. *Oxoniensia* **39**, 53–61.

Hayes, J, 1977, Prior Wibert's Waterworks *Canterbury Cathedral Chronicle.* **71**.

Heighway, C, 1988, Archaeology in the Precinct of Gloucester Cathedral. *Glevensis* **22**, 29–37.

Hobley, B, 1970, Excavations at the Cathedral and Benedictine Priory of St Mary, Coventry. *Trans Birmingham and Warwicks Archaeol Soc* **84**, 45–139.

Hope, W H St J , 1885–97, Notes on the Benedictine Abbey of St Peter at Gloucester. *Records of Gloucester Cathedral*, **3**.

Hope, W H St J, 1902, The London Charterhouse and its Old Water Supply. *Archaeologia* **58.i**, 293–312.

Hope, W H St J, 1903, Recent Discoveries in the Cloister of Durham Abbey. *Archaeologia* **58.ii**.

Hope, W H St J, 1906, The Cluniac Priory of Saint Pancras at Lewes *Sussex Archaeol Col* **49**.

Huggins, P J, 1970, Excavation of a Medieval Bridge at Waltham Abbey, Essex, in 1968 *Medieval Archaeol* **14**, 126–147.

Huggins, P J, 1972, Monastic Grange and Outer Close Excavations, Waltham Abbey, Essex, 1970–72 *Trans Essex Archaeol Soc* 3rd ser, **4**, 30–127.

Hurry, J B, 1901, *Reading Abbey*. London: Eliot Stock.

Hurst, H, 1899, *Oxford Topography* Oxford Historical Soc **39**.

Kingsford, C L, 1915, The Grey Friars of London *British Soc. of Franciscan Studies* **6**.

Lambrick, G, 1985, Further Excavations on the Second Site of the Dominican Priory, Oxford. *Oxoniensia* **50**, 131–208.

Lambrick, G, and Woods, H, 1976, Excavations on the Second Site of the Dominican Priory, Oxford. *Oxoniensia* **41**, 168–231.

Landels, J G, 1978, *Engineering in the Ancient World* Berkeley and Los Angeles: University of California Press.

Latimer, J, 1901, The Hospital of St John, Bristol *Trans Bristol and Gloucester Archaeol Soc.* **24** 172–8.

Lea-Jones, J *et al.*, 1984, *An Account of St John's Conduit — Bristol's Medieval Water System* Bristol: Temple Local History Group.

Leach, P (ed), 1984, *The Archaeology of Taunton: Excavations and Field Work to 1980*. Western Archaeological Trust, Excavation Monograph **8**.

Little, A G, 1891, *The Grey Friars in Oxford*. Oxford Historical Soc **20**.

Little, A G, and Easterling, R C, 1927, *The Franciscans and Dominicans of Exeter*. Exeter: History of Exeter Research Group, Monograph **3**.

Lobel, M D, 1975, Bristol, In M D Lobel and W H Johns (eds) *The Atlas of Historic Towns* **2**. Baltimore: Johns Hopkins University Press.

Luckhurst, D, 1964, *Monastic Watermills: A Study of the Mills within English Monastic Precincts*. Society for Protection of Ancient Buildings, Wind and Watermill Section, Booklet **8**.

Martin, A R, 1937, *Franciscan Architecture in England* Manchester: University Press.

Medieval Archaeol, various dates, Interim Reports in *Medieval Archaeology*.

Mellor, J E, and Pearce, T, 1981, *The Austin Friars, Leicester*. CBA Research Report **35**.

Micklethwaite, J T, 1892, On a Filtering Cistern of the Fourteenth Century at Westminster Abbey. *Archaeologia* **53**, 161–170.

Miles, D, and Ponsford, M W, 1971, Bristol, Upper Maudlin Street, ST.58687344 *CBA XII/XIII Archaeol Rev* **6**, 40.

Morris, P, Thorneycroft, W, and Brown, T, 1932, A Report on the Underground Passages in Exeter by the Exeter Excavation Committee. *Proc Devon Archaeol Exploration Soc* **1**, 191–201.

Musty, A E S, 1978, Exploratory Excavation within the Monastic Precinct, Waltham Abbey, 1972. *Essex Archaeol Hist* **10**, 121–173.

Noake, J, 1866, *The Monastery and Cathedral of Worcester* . London: Longman and Co.

Norman, P, 1899, On an Ancient Conduit-Head in Queen Square, Bloomsbury. *Archaeologia* **56**, 251–266.

Norman, P, 1916, Recent Discoveries of Medieval Remains in London. *Archaeologia* **67**, 1–26.

Norman, P, and Mann, E A, 1909, On the White Conduit, Chapel Street, Bloomsbury, and its Connexion with the Grey Friars' Water System. *Archaeologia* **61**, 347–356.

Peers, C R, Clapham, A W, and Horne, Prior, 1934, Glastonbury Abbey Excavations, 1934, *Proc Somerset Archaeol Nat Hist Soc* **80** 30–35.

Ponsford, M, 1975, *Excavations at Greyfriars, Bristol*. Bristol: City Museum.

R. C. H. M., various dates, Royal Commission on Historical Monuments, County

Inventories

Richardson, L, 1955, The Geology of Worcester *Trans of Worcester Naturalists' Field Club* **11.i**, 29–67.

Robinson, M, 1985, Plant and Invertebrate Remains from the Priory Drains. In Lambrick, 1985, 196–201.

Rodwell, W, 1980, *Wells Cathedral: Excavations and Discoveries* Wells. Friends of Wells Cathedral, revised edn.

Russell, A D, 1987, Southampton High Street, In M Hughes (ed), *Archaeology and Historic Buildings in Hampshire: Annual Report for 1986*, 25. Hampshire County Planning Dept.

Schofield, J, 1984, *The Building of London from the Conquest to the Great Fire.* London: British Museum Publications.

Slade, C F, 1972, Excavation at Reading Abbey, 1964–1967, *Berks Archaeol J* **66**, 65–116.

Stevenson, W H, (ed) 1890, *Rental of all the Houses of Gloucester, by Robert Cole.*

Taylor, C S, 1906, The Religious Houses of Bristol and their Dissolution. *Trans of Bristol and Gloucester Archaeol Soc* **29.1**, 7–126.

Thorpe, H, 1951, *Lichfield: a Study of its Growth and Function.* Staffordshire Hist Collns, 139–211.

Tucker, C, 1858, Discovery of an Ancient Conduit at St Sidwell's, Exeter. *Archaeol J* **15**, 313–7.

V.C.H., various dates, *The Victoria History of the Counties of England.*

Waller, F W, 1889, Note on Norman Work in Gloucester Cathedral. *Trans of Bristol and Gloucester Archaeol Soc* **13. 1**, 48.

Walters, R C S, 1928, *The Ancient Wells, Springs and Holy Wells of Gloucestershire* Bristol. St Stephen's Press.

Weare, G E, 1893, *Collectanea relating to the Bristol Friars Minors and their Convent.*

White, A , 1980, *St Mary's Conduit, Lincoln.* Lincolnshire Museums Information Sheets, Archaeology Series, **19**.

Willis, R, 1868, The Architectural History of the Conventual Buildings of the Monastery of Christ Church in Canterbury *Archaeologia Cantiana* **7**, 1–206.

Zarnecki, G, Holt, J, and Holland, T, 1984, *English Romanesque Art, 1066–1200.* London. Arts Council of Great Britain.

6 The archaeology of urban monasteries in Britain

L A S Butler

In order to present an adequate survey of urban religious houses, it is necessary first to define one's terms of reference and then to lay out the avenues by which one will approach the subject. The definition of urbanism adopted here includes both the legally defined towns possessing borough status (640 in England) and the *de facto* market towns of organic growth which only acquired borough status at the close of the Middle Ages (probably another 100 in England). The term 'religious house' is equally broad: any house devoted to the practice of a common religious observance, whether abbey, priory, nunnery, friary, large hospital or college. This embraces any community which valued a regular liturgical observance so highly that they possessed their own church or chapel, or else sought the exclusive or predominant use of a parish church for that purpose.

The three avenues are time, space and circumstance. These will initially be traversed separately, which may lead to a little duplication, but the paths will be brought together when their influence is assessed. Before exploring these paths it should be stressed that the genesis of this paper lies in my own work on friaries (Butler 1984) and on urban monasteries (Butler 1987). To avoid undue repetition some of the arguments, supporting evidence and references given in those two papers will be assumed in this article and not explicitly stated. The easiest approach route is that of time.

6.1 The passage of time

In England between the mission of St Augustine and the death of Alfred (597–900) there were founded 25 houses of monks and nuns which may be considered as urban (if only eventually). Between the death of Alfred and the death of Edward the Confessor (900–1065) a further 15 houses were founded and most of the earlier ones revived under Edgar and archbishop Dunstan. A total of 40 urban monasteries including 6 nunneries survived the Norman Conquest and a similar number of secular colleges continued beyond the Conquest. The advent of the Normans brought a rapid increase in the number of foundations over the next two centuries with 200 urban monasteries for men, 20 nunneries and 50 urban colleges of canons. In other words there were more than three times as many urban foundations in the first two Norman centuries as there had been in the previous four Anglo-Saxon centuries. The impact of the Normans in Wales is even more striking: urbanism was a phenomenon unknown until the invaders entered south Wales. At eight of their new towns Benedictine monasteries were founded to provide a nucleus of religious provision deliberately kept under Norman control, while at one further town (Haverfordwest) an Augustinian priory was established. In Scotland also the rise of urbanism was a 12th-century characteristic, and abbeys or priories were planted at ten towns.

The next major change to the pattern of religious foundations was the arrival of the friars. The pioneer bands of Franciscans and Dominicans arrived in the early 1220s, establishing houses with great rapidity though greeted with equally great suspicion by the established urban Benedictines. 'O sorrow, O worse than sorrow, a tiresome plague! The Franciscans have arrived in England': so wrote Florence of Worcester (Thorpe 1848). The Franciscan 'plague' reached Worcester in about 1227. By 1250 the Franciscans had 40 houses in England, 1 in Wales and 4 in Scotland; the Dominicans had 20 houses in England, 3 in Wales and 2 in Scotland. The early Carmelites sought rural retreats, appropriate to their origins as hermits on Mount Carmel in the Holy Land. The Augustinian friars settled at Clare in Suffolk in 1248/9 as their first foundation. Running in parallel with this rapid growth was the provision of urban hospitals, with some 300 founded before the Black Death in Britain, 20 being of considerable size and wealth. Each town with a vigorous economic life would be able to support three or more hospitals. Like the friars they can be seen as an obvious barometer of urban status.

After the Black Death the picture changes. Growth in terms of new foundations was succeeded by stagnation. Some alien houses were suppressed or lost their monastic character. A few new houses were founded: the Cistercian abbey of St Mary Graces east of the Tower of London in 1350, and four Carthusian houses, in London (1371), Hull (1377), Coventry (1381) and Perth (1429). Again it was the friaries and the hospitals which showed the most active growth. The Franciscans rose to a maximum of 78, the Dominicans to 69, the Carmelites to 43 and the Augustinians to 40; the houses of the latter two orders were not all urban and where they were they often took over the revenues and the site of the suppressed order of the Friars of the Sack. The urban hospitals suffered a loss of about 150 houses immediately after the Black Death but in the succeeding two centuries recovered to reach a total of 350 houses. A new phenomenon of the secular college was characteristic of the later middle ages; about 60 of these were urban; there were also academic halls and colleges in Oxford and Cambridge, St Andrews and Aberdeen. Colleges of chantry priests or Bederns were established in those cathedral towns where, as at Lincoln, Wells or York, the liturgy was provided by secular canons not Benedictine monks.

The Reformation swept most of these institutions away.

It was a dramatic clearance over a 15 year period in England and Wales, but an insidious attrition extending over 60 years in Scotland. Only a handful of hospitals and a rump of colleges survived in the two kingdoms governed by James VI and I. To summarise, this rise and fall covers the ten centuries in which a maximum of 300 abbeys and priories, 230 friaries, 350 hospitals and 150 colleges were in existence. The major monasteries are normally of early foundation and are related to different stages of urban growth. They may predate it, they may accompany it, they may stimulate it or they may attempt to ignore it. The friaries and the hospitals are predominantly the product of mature urbanism. The colleges are a late medieval phenomenon, flourishing in a period of presumed urban decline.

6.2   The need for space

The second major avenue is that of space. Where were the religious houses located in relation to the town and what light does this throw upon the development of the town? Of the early Anglo-Saxon foundations St Augustine's at Canterbury and St Albans lie outside the Roman city suggesting continuity with a cemetery memorial chapel, while Christchurch at Canterbury and Old Minster at Winchester lie within the Roman walls, suggesting vacant ground ripe for occupation as at the 'rural' Bradwell in Essex, Reculver in Kent or Holyhead on Anglesey. Of the later Anglo-Saxon foundations St Oswald's at Gloucester lies just outside the city defences while its close neighbour, the abbey of St Peter, stands within the north-west quadrant of the Roman walls. However the great majority of the abbeys seem to have been established as rural foundations whose very presence attracted the elements of urbanism to them. Such towns are Abingdon, Evesham, Winchcombe, Amesbury, Malmesbury, Peterborough, Shaftesbury and Tewkesbury. The *bury* place-name indicating a defensive capacity whether monastic or urban; at Abbotsbury and St Edmundsbury the monastery's possession of the town is clearly expressed. Most of the urban secular colleges were either located at former Roman towns (Chester, Cirencester, Dorchester, Dover, Exeter, Leicester, Lincoln, London, Wroxeter and York) or at Anglo-Saxon burhs (Bedford, Derby, Hereford, Shrewsbury, Stafford, Tamworth, Thetford and Warwick). Some colleges served a bishopric (Crediton, Durham, Lichfield and Wells) and some assisted a sub-diocese (Ripon, Beverley and Southwell); in such cases the combination seems to have led to the growth of the town rather than *vice versa* as was urged under the Normans.

These three categories of places whether intentionally chosen as urban, or accidentally chosen as urban and becoming urban through subsequent economic activity are just as marked after the Conquest as before it. Those intentionally chosen as urban must include the two richest of the new Norman Benedictine houses: Reading was a foundation by Henry I in 1103 on an abandoned monastic site, while St Mary's York was established by a band of monks fleeing from the rural solitude of Lastingham amid the north Yorkshire moors. Those chosen because of strong earlier traditions and not because of an urban location include the Benedictine Leominster and the Cluniac Much Wenlock. Houses which soon provided the economic impetus behind urban growth, having initially chosen rural sites, include the Benedictine Battle and Selby, the Augustinian Guisborough and Worksop and the rare female house of Nuneaton (Andrews *et al.* 1981). All these houses first established their own requirements of lay-out and space, and then promoted urban growth outside their gates, just as their predecessors at Evesham and Peterborough had done a century earlier. By contrast the founders of St Mary's at York had accepted a site outside the west walls of the Roman city close to the minster church of St Olave; in very similar fashion the Augustinian houses of St Botolph's at Colchester and St Mary's (*de pratis*, in the fields) at Leicester stood outside the Roman walls. It was rare that such new foundations could be fitted within an existing defence system, as happened at Holy Trinity within the Aldgate at London; all the other priory foundations lay outside London's city walls. Usually the peripheral site was chosen, as is illustrated by the Gilbertine priory of St Andrew and the Benedictine nunnery of Clementhorpe, both south-east of York's defences yet close to the castle.

This link between castle and monastery is best seen in the Cluniac houses, choosing valley floor sites at Castle Acre, Lewes, Pontefract and St Clears. These provided space to expand, water supplies for drainage and to drive industrial machinery as well as peace from the bustle of the town, while still obtaining a strong defence from the castle and an economic foothold in the baronial town. Other aspects of Cluniac siting are considered below. Further away from the town were often situated the nunneries, deliberately placed in the fields: Derby in the King's Mead, Northampton's De la Prè ('in the fields'), St Mary de Prè outside St Albans and Godstow beyond Port Meadow at Oxford. By contrast the early hospitals had to be sited where the poor and infirm congregated or where the travellers came, namely at the town gates, on the suburban approaches or at the edge of the artisan quarters. This is evident at Canterbury, Hereford, Lincoln and Winchester; one must assume a similar location for many sites known only from documentary reference but this assumption would need to be tested by detailed archaeological fieldwork.

In the later Middle Ages space was at a premium, particularly when the friars reached Britain in the early 13th century. In some towns they had at first to be content with rejected premises, such as a confiscated synagogue in London or a decayed hospital in Thetford. Elsewhere they could insinuate themselves into the fabric of the town by occupying the poorest land just within the gates or by accepting a more spacious plot on an approach road just outside the gates. From the fingerhold of a half-tenement the friars could hope to build up their properties piecemeal in exactly the same way that many Oxbridge colleges were to do in the 14th and 15th centuries (Salter 1960, 1969). In both cases it was more to satisfy the aspirations of the wealthy donors than to meet the needs of the scholars or friars. The expansion of Norwich

Blackfriars is an instructive example of this acquisitive process (Tillyard 1983). Professor Dobson (1984) has shown similar processes at work in York, greatly aided there by royal and baronial patronage. Similar patronage was a necessary part of late Cistercian and Carthusian foundation. The Cistercians were planted by Edward III on a former Black Death burial ground just east of the Tower of London (see below); the Carthusians were all on suburban sites: north of London by Sir Walter Manney, north of Hull by the merchant Michael de la Pole, north of Perth by James I and south-east of Coventry by William lord Zouche. The needs of space and solitude dictated these choices which nevertheless ensured a highly visible presence among the merchants, the wayfarers and the burgesses tilling their fields or using the common grazing grounds.

The Reformation brought a variety of fates: conversion to other purposes, piecemeal attrition or total destruction. The most sympathetic conversion was from a Benedictine abbey to a cathedral community of dean and chapter; this kept the church intact, many of the cloister buildings in use and a greater part of the outer precinct still standing. The separate households of the monastic office-holders were changed to become the married quarters of the individual canons with a similar hierarchy of esteem. This is well illustrated at the old cathedrals (Canterbury, Winchester, Worcester, Rochester, Durham, Ely and Norwich, and to a lesser extent at the Augustinian Carlisle). It is paralleled by the survivals at the new post-Dissolution cathedrals formerly Benedictine (Chester St Werburgh, Gloucester, Peterborough, Westminster) and to a lesser extent at two Augustinian houses (Bristol, Oxford St Frideswide's). Elsewhere the church might survive in part or, more rarely, as a whole to serve as a parish church: Great Malvern, Tewkesbury and Selby show near complete examples; Waltham, Bridlington and Malmesbury retain the abbreviated parochial naves to take three examples from the fifty urban survivals. The gradual alteration and cannibalisation of buildings can be shown in many houses — well disentangled for Gloucester Black Friars by Knowles (1924; see also Morley 1979) and for Holy Trinity Aldgate by Schofield (forthcoming, and this volume). The suburban houses were often put to domestic or farm use, as at Hereford Black Friars by the Coningsbys, Sopwell near St Albans by the Dacres, and Godstow near Oxford by Dr. Owen, the king's physician. The great Cluniac houses seldom survived. The destruction of Lewes has been graphically described (Wright 1843, 180–1) and Pontefract priory was dismantled to make a 'New Hall' for Gilbert (Talbot), the seventh earl of Shrewsbury. The entire site of the one Premonstratensian urban house, Alnwick, lies in open parkland created by the Percies, dukes of Northumberland (Hope 1887). The position in Scotland regarding survival and re-use is similar with Culross, Dunfermline and Paisley still partially in use, with Arbroath, Kelso, Newburgh and Jedburgh in ruin, and with parts of the Franciscan friaries at Edinburgh and Elgin rebuilt for religious or charitable purposes.

6.3 The patterns of circumstance

The third avenue is that of circumstance: not so much the individual circumstances of an abbot's initiatives or a baron's vows which resulted in the foundation of an abbey or college, but rather the more general purpose and intention for which a monastery was established and what it might hope to achieve. In the first two centuries of Latin monasticism in Britain the themes might be regarded as providing a missionary base and in parallel a retreat for study and contemplation. The urban location was chosen only in so far as it assisted the missionary message, as at Canterbury, Rochester, London and York. In the 10th-century monastic revival the main theme was praise and intercession; only for those colleges which intended to provide practical service to the community was an urban location desirable. For the committed Benedictines an urban site was secondary in that it enabled the monks to enter a market economy and yet did not undermine their seclusion within the convent. To found a town was a practical and visible way of converting their wealth and donations for the benefit of the community. To found churches to cater for the spiritual needs of the townsfolk, as Abbot Wulsin is credited as doing at St Albans (c.950) would assist pastoral care (Riley 1867, 22). The town also stimulated crop sales and served the practical needs of pilgrims visiting the holy resting places of the saints (nearly all the Anglo-Saxon saints lay within the Benedictine abbeys; a few were within the newly-defended burhs such as Bedford, Chester and Derby: Biddle 1986, 7–11).

The developments after the Norman Conquest encouraged diversity but did not undermine the urban focus of monasticism. The variations were widest in the administrative models adopted by the reformed orders of monks, nuns and canons. They shared a common ethos; only the Cistercians cut themselves off from the town and only the Carthusians cut themselves off completely from society. Both these stances were modified after the Black Death; indeed earlier the Cistercians did have urban houses in Scotland and a cell at Scarborough, the east coast port for their north Yorkshire abbeys.

However the Cluniac houses may be taken as the best example of circumstance. Ostensibly they were founded to serve God through praise and prayers for the souls of the dead. The baron gave lands and privileges to gain peace of mind in this world and salvation in the life hereafter. Along with intangible salvation went tangible benefits from placing a monastery near his castle. There was the visual linking between military strength and spiritual beauty. The baron gained confessors, and clerks with expertise in book-keeping, in legal knowledge, in agricultural practice and in medical skill. He would gain in industrial enterprise and would foster artistic patronage. The monks would assist in the foundation of a town, market and fair at the castle gates, as at Tutbury, Lewes, Castle Acre or Pontefract. Flourishing commercial activity was as much in the monastic interests as it was to the baron's advantage. Both were partners in the urban foundation, and both were dependent upon its success. Additionally the Cluniacs benefitted from the castle's physical protection and from the baron's support in the king's council. A similar interplay and interdependence can be traced in many other monasteries, nunneries and colleges.

The circumstances after the Black Death do not alter dramatically. Instead there is a narrowed focus on particular aspects: the relief of sickness, poverty and senility or on the promotion of preaching, learning and spirituality. This may seem a cavalier way to treat the various developments among the friars, hospitals, academic and secular colleges, but the liturgy was no longer an end in itself except for the colleges of vicars choral and of chantry priests. Good works displaced efficacious prayers; the performance of good works was more necessary and more beneficially visible in the towns. Additionally an increasing concern for an educated priesthood, an informed laity and a measue of relevance to that education made the life of seclusion in prayer and the life of opulence resulting from sound estate management seem equally unpalatable. This motive lay behind the new colleges founded by bishop Alcock, Lady Margaret Beaufort and arinal Wolsey, who in each case used revenues from suppressed monasteries and also took the actual premises for their foundations (Jesus College, Cambridge: 1496, using St Radegund's nunnery; St John's College, Cambridge: 1509–11, using the Augustinian hospital of St John; Cardinal College, Oxford: 1525, using St Frideswide's priory). The same motive lay behind the grander scheme for new clergy training colleges founded by Henry VIII at Burton-on-Trent and Thornton in Lincolnshire, using revenues from the former abbeys, but neither college survived beyond his death in 1547. In Oxford the Cistercian St Bernard's college was transformed by Sir Thomas White into St John's college. At Cambridge two of the empty friaries eventually became the premises of new colleges (Emmanuel 1584, using the Dominican house; Sidney Sussex 1595, using the Franciscan house). In Scotland Queen Mary sought in 1561 to use the vacated friary buildings 'for schools, colleges and other uses for the common weal and service'.

6.4　The material evidence

Having laid out the three avenues by which to approach the subject, the next stage is to convert the theoretical approach, largely document derived, into the practical consideration of the material evidence. The first route is that of time. It is tempting to accept at face value the starting and finishing dates of the monasteries, as provided by documents, and to trim (or stretch) the material accordingly to obtain a fit. Although the finishing date may be soundly based as the end of conventual life it may not be the end of domestic life. There may be no sharp divide in the abbot's lodging or in the guesthouse between the monastic occupiers and the gentry successors. Equally the starting date may mark the formal initiative but how soon was building started (and what was on the site already)? The soundness of the archaeological dates derived from the material evidence must

be examined, whether they depend upon the changing architectural forms of moulding and sculpture, upon the dendrochronological dates gained from earth-fast posts of wharves or bridges and the planking of roads or drains, upon the accidental loss of coins (in a community devoted to individual poverty) or the deliberate concealment of hoards. Can the inscriptions on bronze flagons, on marble tombs or on ceramic floor tiles be accepted at face value and are they contemporary with the buildings in which they are found? Should the archaeologist instead place far greater reliance upon archaeomagnetic dates from hearths or destruction fires, on radiocarbon dates from human bone and on TL dating from non-residual pottery?

It is likely that the choice of site for archaeological attention should be dictated by its potential for containing deep deposits and datable waterlogged material (Carver 1987, 16). Otherwise the chief attraction should be the brevity of its monastic sequence, either an early abandonment or a late foundation as in many of the friaries (25 founded after 1330). Alternatively, though approached in parallel fashion, there should be a clearly maintained distinction between historical sources and archaeological material. Each type of evidence has inherent difficulties in its interpretation and the scholar should always be aware of them. The degree of selectiveness and the importance of the sample size applies equally to the written word and to the discarded artefact. Through both of these sources the element of time is gauged.

6.5　The organisation of space

The monastery is the epitome of efficient organisation of space — a time-and-motion study captured in stone. It contains exclusive zones for prayer, for study, for eating, for sleeping and for storage. There are zones for total silence and contemplative retreat in the cloister, zones for modified silence and greater accessibility in the inner court and in the infirmary court, and zones for wider, yet still controlled, access and movement in the outer court. These zones can also be split between communal and individual households, guest reception and pilgrim circulation. Within a monastic precinct wall there will be many social gradations which change their composition through the course of time, mainly breaking down the emphasis on the communal daily routine and on the celibate exclusion of the opposite sex. It is necessary for the student of urban monasteries to be aware of these differences and to perceive the consequent changes through the surviving architecture and the revealed archaeology. He or she also needs to realise the considerable impact that urban monasteries had on the rural society and economy. The field surveys around Evesham (Bond 1973) and Abingdon (Bond 1979) need to be set alongside the documentary-based surveys as at Westminster (Harvey 1977), Peterborough (King 1973) and Ramsey (Raftis 1957).

To obtain a full plan uncluttered by later post-dissolution disturbances, the rural monasteries offer the greater hope of success, but to understand the compression, the modification in detail and the compromises with the ideal blueprint, the urban monastery has much to offer. Here the distinction needs to be made between a monastery like Evesham or Pershore which is spaciously planned and then creates or promotes the town sited at its gates and, on the other hand, St Botolph's at Colchester or the cathedral priory at Norwich which grew alongside an existing settlement or within a developing city. In this respect the excavation of St Gregory's priory and the associated St John's hospital at Canterbury may prove to be more instructive in the efficient use of space than the unconstrained Faversham. The peripheral monasteries like St Andrew's and Clementhorpe outside York which cling like leeches to the city's limbs might show how limits on space caused modifications to, or even total absence of, those buildings deemed necessary to the communal life on rural sites.

The friaries provide the best examples of this use of urban space. Their churches are pared down to the ritual minimum of a choir (and occasionally transept chapels or choir aisle chapels needed for the burial of benefactors); the nave is designed for its role of a preaching hall with slender columns and spacious windows to maximise visibility and audibility. Their cloisters are compressed by combining cloister walk and ground floor storage within each range and by placing the communal dormitory, refectory and library on the full width of the upper floor in each of the three ranges, thereby separating in function the lower floor from its upper floor. A second 'little cloister' is fitted in wherever space allows. An orchard is included in the more generously laid out urban sites; shops for rent may be crowded along a street frontage. A gatehouse controlled access to the brothers' precinct. Gilyard-Beer (1958, 44) considered that the friars 'often had to be content with inconvenient and restricted sites that gave them little scope for regularity in setting out their buildings'. Yet the cloister plan is universal: nowhere is it abandoned, any more than the Carthusians abandon the great cloister on urban sites. However it cannot be shown to be always primary; its construction may well be delayed until sufficient property and surface area had been obtained. The initial lay-out may not be of one unified space — the ideal cloister — but a gradual development of many spaces; first a lodging house, then a chapel, next a kitchen and a dormitory, then a library and chapter-house. Only when the full complement of living and working spaces had been assembled was it possible to re-arrange the site in order to provide the required cloister-based plan. This seems to be the sequence indicated in some documents; it would be instructive to have the physical proof from excavation.

Parallel to this question is the prehistory of the friary site: is it possible to determine what occupied the site before the friars came? Was it orchards, tannery yards, a town rubbish dump or a swamp (Broad Marsh at Nottingham)? The friars chose to live in the slums among the poor to whom their message of salvation was initially directed. The Austin Friars at Leicester (Mellor and Pearce 1981) has shown evidence of the ill-drained conditions on that site. Yet the friars were always eager to move within the protection of the town walls, even though their riches were spiritual not material. They preferred a restricted internal site to the greater space and potential for expansion on a suburban roadside; the external site was more usually accepted by the hospitals. It is necessary to pay as much attention to a friary site before its foundation for the light it throws upon urban development. Equally there is a need to understand its post-dissolution history and property descent to appreciate its after-life and excavation potential (e.g. Worcester: Carver (ed) 1980, 269–279).

6.6 Research design or rescue opportunism

The third avenue to examine is circumstance. On only two occasions in the last hundred years can one identify a research design for monastic archaeology. The first was devised by Sir William St John Hope who between 1880 and 1915 systematically tackled an example of every type of site, whether of personnel (monks, canons, friars or nuns) or of administrative order (Benedictine, Cluniac, Carthusian, Cistercian, Augustinian, Gilbertine, Premonstratensian or Carmelite). His work, together with that of Brakspear, Bilson and Clapham, marks a golden leisured age, but he did little at urban sites: Alnwick priory (Hope 1887), London Charterhouse (Hope 1902, 1925) and Old Sarum cathedral, excavated from 1910 to 1915 (Hope, Hawley and Montgomerie 1916), St Augustine's Canterbury, published by Hope (1915, 1916) and the London friaries reconstructed by Clapham (1913). The next phase was the Office of Works clearances, a few of which might optimistically be called urban excavations: St Botolph's at Colchester (RCHM 1922, 48–50), Thetford Cluniac priory (Robertson-Mackay 1957), Bury St Edmunds (Whittingham 1971) and St Augustine's at Canterbury (Saunders 1978). Some wartime opportunities were taken, as at London Charterhouse (Grimes and Knowles 1954). The second research programme was initiated under Stuart Rigold and John Hurst, hoping to fill some of the lacunae in medieval monastic planning: the Trinitarian house at Thelsford, the great hospital at Ospringe (Smith 1979; see also Rigold and Dunning 1958, and Rigold 1964), the Templar preceptory at South Witham, the forest hermitage at Grafton Regis, the Benedictine house later granted to the Franciscans nuns at Denny (Christie and Coad 1980) and the Cistercian abbey hastily transferred to the Gilbertines at Haverholme. None was urban and only two excavations have been published. This reluctance to hasten into print maybe one factor which caused Cherry to comment that 'relatively little work has been done on monastic sites' (Longworth and Cherry 1986, 185). Another factor was the absence of large scale excavations apart from Bordesley abbey and Norton priory. The continuous monitoring of developments in the outer courts of Waltham Abbey has provided a useful counterbalance to the usual emphasis upon the church and cloister ranges. The effort once expended on monastic excavation and clearance is now absorbed into urban rescue archaeology in which the houses of the friars or of the nuns are but one element in the complexity of social landscapes and economic hierarchies.

On the broader interpretation of archaeology the Easter conferences of the British Archaeological Association held since 1975 have been a stimulus to architectural research and synthesis, treading in the footsteps of Willis (1845, 1846, 1863, 1869) a century earlier, or of Atkinson (1933) more recently. The major monastic cathedrals of Canterbury, Winchester, Worcester, Gloucester, Ely and Durham and the two great abbeys of Glastonbury and Tewkesbury have been the subject of the first seven monographs, but only three papers have tackled the domestic ranges or the below-ground evidence (Carver 1980; Markusen 1980; Radford 1981).

In view of such modest results from excavation one might well regard research as a mirage, promising much yet producing little. There is always the hope that modern techniques of excavation and analysis can be applied to an uncluttered urban site with good stratification and uncontaminated artefacts. Such sites should still exist. One could suggest Evesham, St Albans and Richmond St Martin's among the Benedictines, Holm Cultram 'Abbey Town' among the Cistercians, Much Wenlock among the Cluniacs, Walsingham among the Augustinians or Winchelsea (Dominican, Franciscan) and Dunwich (Franciscan) among the friars, the last-named under threat from coastal erosion. A review of this type could well be chanelled through the Monastic Sites Index and is a prerequisite for further site evaluation, even though the open ground may conceal a heavily robbed structure. Published work from Faversham (Philp 1968), Battle (Hare 1987), Much Wenlock (Woods 1986) and Canterbury St Augustines (Sherlock and Woods 1988) shows the reality: the first a hurried overview, the second a selective analysis of a single range, and the others a mèlange of unpredicted opportunities. Such major sites need to be assessed for what they actually contribute as new information on plan development, but more particularly for what evidence they provide upon social separation and change, diet and disease, market catchments and distant trade, religious economy and artistic patronage. The plan development may be far better obtained from an open but ruined rural site like Castle Acre or Haughmond; the minutiae of social change may be better seen from Cogges or Polsloe. Economic analysis and the other research desiderata need to be seen through many relationships. If one took Faversham as an example, one would need to look at the house in relation to the other Cluniac houses in England and France, in relation to other local houses of a similar income (based on 1535 figures), and in relation to other neighbouring religious establishments in Kent. Furthermore one should look at the economy of Faversham abbey in relation to Faversham town and in comparison with the trade of nearby Medway ports and of the more distant Cinque ports. Is such an examination a counsel of perfection? The sympathetic and perceptive handling of the pottery from Kirkstall abbey (Moorhouse and Slowikowski 1987, 102–111, Figs 58–63) suggests that it is possible. The research strategies for religious houses prepared by the C.B.A. (Thomas 1983, 9–14), by the Urban Research Committee (Butler 1987, 167–176) and by the Society for Medieval Archaeology (Hinton 1987, 4–5) have each indicated possible targets for action. There are many features in common within these three strategy documents but an order of priority must be tempered by the need to grasp every suitable and available opportunity.

The rescue reality is that all monastic sites have a high public profile; they are easily identifiable in a documentary sense even if they are sometimes elusive in their physical reality. In common with castles and churches they have a good potential for SMR compilation in that complete coverage can be attained. Any threat to an urban plot which includes 'friary (site of)' or 'monastic cell (remains of)' must either be countered by protection or be answered by excavation. Fifteen such urban threats arise each year in Britain (Clarke 1984, 85–8; 20 in 1987). Excavations or watching briefs may be fortunate and provide a recognisable length of masonry or area of flooring that can be identified as part of the standard corpus of monastic plans, just as on Roman military sites a short length of barrack block can be located within the equally standard corpus of fortress plans. There may be a monastic bonus of burials, perhaps with chalices, shroud pins and textiles, together with a few choice pathological anomalies among the arthritic limbs. If the excavator is unlucky, the back-yard or garden under threat has no distinguishing features about the masonry and no particularly interesting specimens among the bones, seeds, pots or metalwork. If work is done on too small a scale, then no monastic plan can be recovered. Yet is part of a friary better than no information at all? The work on the White Friars at Ludlow (Klein and Roe 1988) shows the advantage of a modest excavation. Similarly work on part of a hospital, such as St Mary at Strood (Harrison 1969), St Bartholomew at Bristol (Price 1979) or St John at Cirencester (Leech and McWhirr 1983), is useful in a little-studied field. The danger of arguing from imperfect samples is always present, particularly when urban monastic sites are so prone to fragmentation of later ownership and consequent fragmentation of modern site development, as at Leicester Austin Friars (Mellor and Pearce 1981), Hartlepool Grey Friars (Daniels 1986) or at Bristol Grey Friars (Ponsford 1975). In other cases the difficulties in understanding the whole site may be caused by the limiting practicalities of where to dump the spoil, of how much shoring can be afforded or of what buildings surviving on the site need to be preserved and not undermined. Urban excavation seldom offers perfect conditions: the successes of the excavation at the Cistercian abbey of St Mary Graces has to be measured against the destroyed or inaccessible areas on the Royal Mint site (Mills 1985; Grainger et al. 1988). The recent work at St Mary's nunnery at Clerkenwell has been fragmented by the piecemeal nature of new office developments. Similar difficulties attended the excavation of Carmarthen Grey Friars (James 1992) and three Scottish friaries (Stones 1989).

6.7 Conclusion

Having excavated the site for whatever reasons — impeccable research design or unavoidable local antiquarian pressure — how do you publish the site and for whom do you publish it? Ideally there should be a monograph for each monastery, as at Bordesley (Rahtz and Hirst 1976; Hirst, Walsh and Wright 1983). It may be that a thematic fascicule is the answer: one hospital in a medieval town is excavated and the others within it investigated non-destructively; one friary dug and the others in the city evaluated (for example, Simon Ward's 1990 monograph on Chester). It is best to have the site excavation and the material evidence presented in parallel, as at St Helen-on-the-Walls, York (Magilton 1980; Dawes and Magilton 1980) rather than separated too widely in time and nature of publication. It will be interesting to see the solution adopted by the Scottish Burghs Survey for their monastic surveys and excavations; it will be most useful to assess their rationale. A good example of evaluation work has concentrated upon ten selected Danish towns (e.g. Roskilde: Nielsen and Schiorring 1982) and shown the value of site assessment and finds location. It can be set alongside the predominantly architectural approach followed in the historic towns analysis as at Stamford (RCHM 1977) or Beverley (Miller 1982). No survey volume has yet taken a national view of urban monastic sites though the material to do so could easily be assembled. Until it is gathered together (as in the Monuments Protection Programme of English Heritage) then the danger is that monastic excavation will continue to be prompted more by local pressure and considerations than by a national overview. Yet if excavation is perceived as answering primarily the local questions and as supporting local identity, then such an outcome is inevitable.

The rescue reality is that urban monastic sites will continue to be studied and excavated because they offer the hope of precisely datable time-spans and recognisable communities of men or women, fit or frail. It is essential that their full potential as economic indicators and social spatial samples should be understood and appreciated. The detailed physical evidence of context and matrix must not swamp and submerge the valuable contribution of monasteries, colleges and hospitals to the urban landscape throughout the medieval centuries. Only if all aspects can be brought together will such sites achieve their considerable potential.

References

Addyman, P V, and Black, V, (eds) 1984, *Archaeological Papers from York presented to M W Barley*. York. York Archaeological Trust.

Andrews, D *et al*, 1981, The archaeology and topography of Nuneaton Priory, *Trans Birmingham Warwickshire Archaeol Soc* 91, 55–88.

Atkinson, T D, 1933, *The Architectural History of the Benedictine Monastery of St Etheldreda at Ely*. Cambridge: University Press.

Biddle, M, 1986, Archaeology, architecture and the cult of saints in Anglo-Saxon England. In L Butler and R Morris (eds), *The Anglo-Saxon Church*, London: CBA, Research Report 60, 1–31.

Bond, C J, 1973, The estates of Evesham Abbey: a preliminary survey of their medieval topography. *Vale of Evesham Hist Soc Research Paper*, 4, 1–61.

Bond, C J, 1979, The estates of Abingdon Abbey, *Landscape History* 1, 59–75.

Butler, L A S, 1984, The houses of the Mendicant Orders in Britain: recent archaeological work. In Addyman and Black (eds), 123–36.

Butler, L A S, 1987, Medieval urban religious houses. In Schofield and Leech (eds), 167–76.

Carver, M O H (ed), 1980, Medieval Worcester: an archaeological framework. *Trans Worcester Archaeol Soc*. **3**, 7.

Carver, M O H, 1980, Early Medieval Durham: the archaeological evidence *Medieval Art and Architecture at Durham Cathedral*. Brit Archaeol Assoc Conference Transactions for 1977, 11–19.

Carver, M O H, 1987, The nature of urban deposits. In Schofield and Leech (eds), 9–26.

Christie, P M, and Coad, J G, 1980, Excavations at Denny Abbey. *Archaeol J*, **137**, 138–279.

Clapham, A W, 1913, The friars as builders — Blackfriars and Whitefriars, London. In A W Clapham, and W H Godfrey, (eds), *Some Famous Buildings and their story*, 241–67. Westminster: Technical Jounals Ltd.

Clarke, H, 1984, *The Archaeology of Medieval England*. London: British Museum Publications.

Daniels, R, 1986, The Excavation of the Church of the Franciscans, Hartlepool. *Archaeol J*, **143**, 260–304.

Dawes, J D, and Magilton, J R, 1980, *The Cemetery of St Helen-on-the-Walls, Aldwark*. London: CBA for YAT (Fascicule AY 12/1).

Dobson, R B, 1984, Mendicant ideal and practice in late medieval York. In Addyman and Black (eds), 109–122.

Gilyard-Beer, R, 1958, *Abbeys.An introduction to the Religious Houses of England and Wales*. London: HMSO.

Grainger, I *et al*, 1988, Excavations at the Royal Mint Site 1986–1988. *London Archaeol*, **5**.16, 429–36.

Hare, J N, 1986, *Battle Abbey.The eastern range and the excavations of 1978–80*. HBMC Archaeological Report No. 2. London: HBMC.

Harrison, A C, 1969, Excavations on the site of St Mary's Hospital, Strood. *Archaeol Cantiana* 84, 139–60.

Harvey, B, 1977, *Westminster Abbey and its estates in the Middle Ages*. Oxford: Clarendon Press.

Hinton, D A, (ed), 1987, Archaeology and the Middle Ages. Recommendations by the Society for Medieval Archaeology to the Historic Buildings and Monuments Commission for England. *Medieval Archaeol*, 31, 1–12.

Hirst, S, Walsh, D A, and Wright, S, 1983, *Bordesley Abbey II*. Brit Archaeol Rep, **111**. Oxford: BAR.

Hope, W St J, 1887, On the Premonstratensian abbey of St Mary at Alnwick, Northumberland, *Archaeol J*, **44**, 337–346.

Hope, W St, J, 1902, London Charterhouse and its old water supply. *Archaeologia* 58.i, 293–312.

Hope, W St J, 1915, Recent discoveries in the abbey church of St Austin at Canterbury. *Archaeologia* 66, 377–400.

Hope, W St J, 1916, Recent discoveries in the abbey church of St Austin at Canterbury. *Archaeol Cantiana* 32, 1–26.

Hope, W St J, Hawley, W, and Montgomerie, D H, 1916, Report on excavations at Old Sarum in 1915. *Soc Proc Antiq London* **28**, 174–183, 184.

Hope, W St J, 1925, *The history of the London Charterhouse from its foundation until the suppression of the monastery*. London.

James, T, 1992, *Carmarthen Greyfriars 1983–1990: the structural report. Carmarthen*: Dyfed Archaeol Trust.

King, E, 1973, *Peterborough Abbey, 1086–1310*. Cambridge: University Press.

Klein, P, and Roe, A, 1988, *The Carmelite Friary, Corve Street, Ludlow:its History and Excavation*. Historic Ludlow. Research Paper **6**. Birmingham: BUFAU.

Knowles, D, and Grimes, W F, 1954, *The London Charterhouse:the medieval foundation in the light of recent discoveries*. London: Longmans, Green.

Knowles, W H, 1932, The Black Friars of Gloucester. *Trans Bristol Gloucester Archaeol Soc* **54**, 167–201.

Leech, R H, and McWhirr, A D, 1983, Excavations at St John's Hospital, Cirencester, 1971 and 1976. *Trans Bristol Gloucester Archaeol Soc* **100**, 191–209.

Longworth, I H, and Cherry, J, 1986, *Archaeology in Britain since 1945*. London: British Museum Publications.

Magilton, J R, 1980, *The Church of St Helen-on-the-Walls, Aldwark*. London: CBA for YAT (Fascicule AY 10/1).

Markuson, K W, 1980, Recent Investigations in the East Range of the Cathedral Monastery, Durham. *Medieval Art and Architecture at Durham Cathedral* Brit, 37–48 Archaeol Assoc Conference Trans for 1977.

Mellor, J E, and Pearce, T, 1981, *The Austin Friars, Leicester*. London: CBA Research Report **35**.

Miller, K, 1982, *Beverley.An archaeological and architectural study*. London: HMSO.

Mills, S, 1985, The Royal Mint: First Results, *London Archaeol*, **5.3**, 69–77.

Moorhouse, S, and Slowikowski, A, 1988, The pottery, *In* S Moorhouse and S Wrathmell (eds), *Kirkstall Abbey. The 1950–64 excavations: a reassessment*, 59–116. Wakefield: West Yorkshire Archaeology Service.

Morley, B M, 1979, *Gloucester Blackfriars*. London: HMSO.

Nielsen, I, and Schiorring, O, 1982, Medieval Roskilde — an urban-archaeological survey. *Danish Archaeol* **1**, 133–144.

Philp, B J, 1968, *Excavations at Faversham 1965*. Dover: Kent Archaeol Monographs, **1**.

Ponsford, M W, 1975, *The Grey Friars in Bristol*. Bristol: City Museum.

Price, R, 1979, *Excavations at StBartholomew's Hospital, Bristol*: Bristol City Museum.

Radford, C A R, 1981, Glastonbury Abbey before 1184. Interim Report on the Excavations, 1908–64. *Medieval Art and Architecture at Wells and Glastonbury*, 110–134. Brit Archaeol Assoc Conference Trans for 1978.

Raftis, J, 1957, *The estates of Ramsey Abbey: a study in economic growth and organisation*. Toronto: Pontifical Institute of Medieval Studies.

Rahtz, P A, and Hirst, S, 1976, *Bordesley Abbey, Redditch:excavations 1969–1973*. Brit Archaeol Rep, **23**. Oxford: BAR.

RCHME, 1922, *An Inventory of the Historical Monuments in Essex.III, North-East*. London: HMSO.

RCHME, 1977, *The Town of Stamford*. London: HMSO.

Rigold, S E, 1964, Two Kentish Hospitals re-examined. St Mary, Ospringe and Saints Stephen and Thomas, New Romney. *Archaeol Cantiana* **79**, 31–69 (see also *ibid*, **80**, 29).

Rigold, S E, and Dunning, G C, 1958, *Maison Dieu, Ospringe, Kent*. London: HMSO.

Riley, H T (ed), 1867, *Chronica Monasterii S Albani. Gesta Abbatorum I*. London: Rolls Series **28** iv.

Robertson-Mackay, R, 1957, Recent excavations at the Cluniac Priory of St Mary, Thetford. *Medieval Archaeol* **1**, 96–103.

Salter, H E, 1960, *The Survey of Oxford I*. Oxford Hist Soc **14**.

Salter, H E, 1969, *The Survey of Oxford II*. Oxford Hist Soc **20**.

Saunders, A D, 1978, Excavations in the Church of St Augustine's Abbey, Canterbury 1955–1958. *Medieval Archaeol* **22**, 25–63.

Schofield, J, 1989, Holy Trinity Aldgate, *Dissolution and Resurrection.Monasteries in Britain 1540–1640*, In L Butler (ed) (publication forthcoming).

Schofield, J, and Leech, R (eds), 1987, *Urban Archaeology in Britain*. London: CBA Research Report **61**.

Sherlock, D, and Woods, H, 1988, *St Augustine's Abbey. Report on Excavations 1960–78*. Maidstone: Kent Archaeol Soc Monographs **4**.

Smith, G H, 1979, The Excavation of the Hospital of St Mary of Ospringe, commonly called 'Maison Dieu', *Archaeol Cantiana* **95**, 81–184.

Stones, J A, (ed) 1989, *Three Scottish Carmelite Friaries: Excavations at Aberdeen, Linlithgow and Perth 1980–86*. Soc. Edinbrugh: Soc Antiq Scot Monograph **6**.

Thomas, C, 1983, *Research objectives in British Archaeology*. London: CBA

Thorpe, B, 1848 (ed), *Florentii Wigorniensis monachi Chronicon ex Chronicii II*. London: English Hist Soc **13** ii.

Tillyard, M, 1983, The acquisition by the Norwich Blackfriars of the site for their church c. 1310–1325. In M Tillyard, S Kelly and E Rutledge (eds), *Men of Property.An analysis of the Norwich Enrolled Deeds*. Norwich.

Ward, S W, 1990, Excavations at Chester: *The lesser medieval religious houses*. Chester: City Council, Department of Leisure Services.

Whittingham, A B, 1971, *Bury St Edmunds Abbey*. London: HMSO. (revision of *Archaeol J*, **108** (1951), 168–187).

Willis, R, 1845, *The Architectural History of Canterbury Cathedral*. London: Longman.

Willis, R, 1846, *The Architectural History of Winchester Cathedral*. London: Proc Roy Archaeol Inst.

Willis, R, 1863, The architectural history of Worcester cathedral and monastery. *Archaeol J*, **20**, 83–132.

Willis, R, 1869, *An architectural history of the conventual buildings of the Monastery of Christ Church in Canterbury*. London: Longman.

Wright, T, 1843, *Letters relating to the Suppression of the Monasteries*. Camden Soc **26**.

Woods, H, 1987, Excavations at Wenlock Priory, 1981–6. *Brit Archaeol Assoc* **140**, 36–75.

7   The potential for studies of medieval tiles

J Stopford

7.1   Introduction

This paper aims to show how a detailed study of a particular artefact type — in this case medieval tiles — can contribute to more general discussions of medieval society and economy.

One of the advantages of medieval tiles is that they have survived in considerable numbers. Many can still be seen in the floors of present day cathedrals and churches, while decorated tiles, which have long been of interest to antiquarian collectors, are well represented in museum and private collections. The Ministry of Works' clearance of Guardianship monuments in the early part of this century uncovered large areas of pavements at some sites, and recent excavations continue this process of recovery. Much of the work done on this relatively large sample has concentrated on the art historical aspects of decorated tiles. The tiles do, however, also have a considerable archaeological value partly because of their good survival, particularly on monastic sites, but also because the wide variety of manufacturing and decorative techniques used in their production allows them to be characterised very closely. This means that the products of different workshops can be identified. Where workshops can be dated, variations between them may indicate changes in the organisation of the medieval industry.

This approach depends upon making comparisons between groups of tiles thought to represent different workshops. A rigorous and standardised methodology is essential to ensure that the tile groups used in these comparisons are identified as accurately as possible. The foundations for such a methodology have been set out in Eames' work on the tiles in the British Museum collection (1980) and in the guidelines prepared by the Census for Medieval Tiles (Drury and Eames 1979, Appendix I, 32–3). Problems remain, however, particularly in the level of details required in recording, and in the use of methods which encourage close comparison between tiles.

These problems are best illustrated by the widespread lack of a clear distinction between tiles of the same design and tiles made with the same stamp. The pattern, or design, on most decorated tiles is made using a wooden stamp. This has a mirror image of the design carved on it in relief, and is used to make an impression of the design on the red clay body fabric of the tile. The impression is usually filled with white clay. The whole of the upper surface is then glazed and the tile is fired. On the finished tile the glaze looks a different colour over the light, white clay than it does over the dark, red clay, giving a two-coloured effect. Large numbers of tiles can be made with the same stamp, and the impression made on each of them will be close to identical. Where tiles are found in good condition, the impression made by the stamp

can often be individually identified. This suggests close links in their production. Tiles from different sites made using the same stamps might, for example, be thought to be the products of the same workshop. Where stamps become damaged or cracked with use, the sequence of tile manufacture is also apparent. However in order to draw such conclusions, the identification of stamps has to be clearly distinguished from the identification of the same design. Designs were copied very widely. Common designs, such as the fleur-de-lis or de Clare arms, are found on numerous sites all over the country. In reduced drawings different versions of the same design may appear very similar, but this does not mean that they were made with the same stamps. This important distinction between stamps and designs has not been fully appreciated in discussions of the organisation of the tile industry.

7.2   Recording the tiles from Bordesley Abbey

Excavations at the Cistercian monastery of Bordesley, near Redditch in Hereford and Worcester (see Fig 7.1), have uncovered several metres of well stratified material in the Abbey church. Decorated floor tiles were found *in situ* on four different floor levels, covering a period from the early 13th century to the Dissolution in 1538/9. The floors can be dated independently, with varying degrees of precision, by architectural developments. The Bordesley tiles are of particular interest because of the chronology provided by the succession of floors. Although only small numbers of tiles remained actually *in situ* from each floor, the sequence they provide for the assemblage as a whole presents an unparalleled opportunity to study changes in the tile industry as it related to this site and others in the area.

To make the most of the opportunity provided by this sequence it was necessary to devise a methodology which would adequately record the large numbers of tiles onto a computer database. An assessment was made to see which recordable characteristics would successfully distinguish between groups of tiles. Fifty nine characteristics were recorded for each *in situ* tile, and frequency charts printed out for each characteristic. Useful characteristics, retained in the database, were those showing similarities between tiles found *in situ* in the same floor, and differences between tiles found *in situ* on different floors. This approach was based on the assumption that tiles from the same floor were more likely to have been made together, while those on floors of different dates were more likely to have been made separately. The approach proved satisfactory using the Bordesley assemblage, although allowances had to be

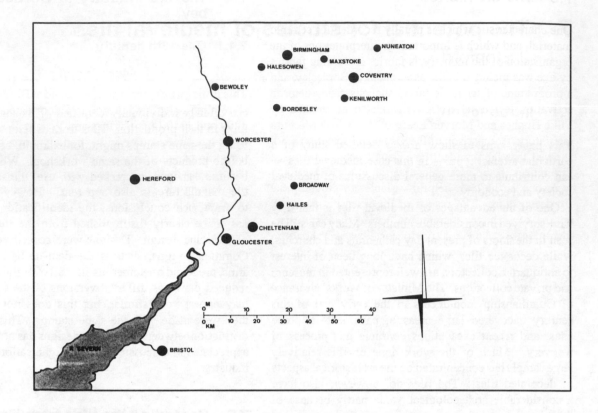

Figure 7.1 Location of sites mentioned in the text.

made for some re-use of material, particularly in the last phase of the site.

The results of this assessment showed that features which can contribute to a close characterisation of the material include the design; the stamp; the decorative technique including the depth of slip or inlay where relevant; the glaze; tile dimensions including both upper and lower surfaces and depth; the standard of manufacture; the degree of wear; the fabric type; the degree of oxidisation of the fabric; keys cut into the lower surface; and nail holes in the upper surface. It is essential to use clearly defined, repeatable methods to record these characteristics. Dimensions, for example, are not comparable unless it is clear exactly what is being measured and that the same thing is being measured each time. In the same way, non-quantifiable characteristics, such as measures of quality, have to be standardised. To achieve this visual comparison charts were used wherever possible.[1]

The object of recording the tiles was to assign them to groups which would accurately distinguish between those made at different times or in different ways. The tiles in each of these groups are thought sufficiently similar to one another for their manufacture to have been subject to the same organisational constraints. They would, for example, not only have been made either by the same person, people or within the same industry, but also have been manufactured using similar processes. A group of people working together might significantly change their methods of manufacture at different times. In that case

the tiles which were the products of the various forms of organisation adopted would belong to separate groups, even though the people making them were the same. The groups formed along these lines have been designated 'production groups' (PG). Fourteen production groups were identified among the tiles from Bordesley.

Comparison between production groups can show variations in the structure and organisation of the tile industry. Itinerant tilers, for example, would have produced tiles for a number of sites in turn, using the same stamps and manufacturing techniques, but using different fabric sources for each site. Industries might be organised on an in-house basis supplying a particular estate, or more commercially, supplying a number of sites in order to make a profit. Variations or changes in the way industries were organised should reflect the role of the occupants of monastic or royal buildings in the local economy. Relative standards of workmanship, the introduction of new and perhaps personalised motifs, the re-use of old tiles, can all show fluctuations in the ideas, aspirations and fortunes of these communities at different times. Once different industries have been characterised in this way, and a chronology established, it should be possible to see how the industry changed through the period at a more general level.

---

[1] This methodology has now been published (Stopford 1990b).

7.3 The tile fabrics

One characteristic which is usually recorded for ceramic material, and which is important in interpretations of the organisation of the industry, is fabric. Recording fabrics by eye was included in the assessment at Bordesley, and a programme of scientific fabric analysis, using neutron activation techniques (NAA), was also undertaken by Mike Hughes and Morven Leese of the British Museum laboratory. Comparison of the visual and scientific work showed that fabrics identified visually only recognised differences in the assemblage at the crudest level, and were one of the least helpful variables in grouping the Bordesley tiles. The results of the scientific analyses, on the other hand, were useful. The fabric clusters identified by neutron activation analysis are shown in Fig 7.2, with a breakdown by production group of the tiles from Bordesley in Fig 7.3. Table 7.1 shows the fabric cluster allocations of comparative material which belongs to production group 2 but which comes from sites other than Bordesley Abbey church. The interpretation of the production groups and fabric clusters are discussed in greater detail below. For a more detailed discussion of the neutron activation analysis of the tile fabrics see Stopford, Hughes and Leese (1991). The results published in that article include statistical work on the effects of dilution but the conclusions with regard the production groups remain unchanged. In general the central or core clusters of 1, 2, 3 and 7 in Fig 7.2 are interpreted as fabrics in the close vicinity of Bordesley because fragments of kiln furniture, which were re-used in one of the hearths on the mill site at Bordesley, only occur in these clusters. This material is unlikely to have been transported more than a few miles. This interpretation may be supported by the allocation of PG13 tiles to the same clusters. Of all the tile groups these laboriously handmade commemorative pieces are thought most likely to have been made at Bordesley.

Clusters 5 and 13, on the left of Fig 7.2, are also thought to represent an origin in the locality of Bordesley. They are associated with the earliest production group at Bordesley (PG8) and with tiles of production group 2 made for St. Stephen's chapel, which lies next to the main west gate of the Bordesley Abbey precinct. Clusters 6 and 8 may represent fabric sources in the vicinity of Coventry because three tiles from excavations at Charterhouse, Coventry, were assigned to cluster 6, and the only production group which is strongly represented in clusters 6 and 8 is also found in Coventry. Finally, clusters 11 and 12 on the right hand side of Fig 7.2 are interpreted as fabric sources to the south and west of Bordesley, perhaps in Worcestershire or along the Severn valley.

7.4 The tile industry at Bordesley Abbey

7.4.1 The 13th century

Production group 8

This is the earliest group of tiles found at Bordesley. They were almost all found *in situ*, in a floor dated to between 1200 and 1250 (Astill, Hirst and Wright 1984). All the tiles were large, square and extremely worn, but it seems that only one design was used (Fig 7.4). The tiles were decorated using a thin layer of white clay, but the process of applying this slip may not be quite the same as that used on the later stamped and slipped tiles at Bordesley. However, the high degree of wear these tiles had received makes it impossible to be certain about this. The first half of the 13th century is nonetheless a very early date for slip decorated tiles, and the use of the technique on the tiles of PG8 seems to be the beginning of a strong and quite possibly locally developed tradition. Neither this design, nor anything similar to it, has been found on any other sites. As shown in Fig 7.3, all four examples of PG8 were assigned to NAA cluster 5.

Production group 2 (Fig 7.6, 7.7)

The next group dates from 1260/80 to 1300 at Bordesley Abbey, and includes tiles of 17 different designs. These tiles are stamped and slipped in the usual way, and are much smaller than the earlier examples. The stamps of several of the designs were used to make tiles at other sites in the area, including Hailes Abbey in Gloucestershire, and Kenilworth and Maxstoke Priories in Warwickshire. The use of the same stamps and other manufacturing techniques suggests that all these tiles are the product of one workshop. The supply of several sites with large quantities of fairly utilitarian tiles also suggests that the industry was both commercial and successful. It could, however, either have operated from one place, distributing tiles to each of the various sites, or the tiles could have been produced at each site by itinerant workers. If the fabrics of all the tiles were similar it would suggest that they were made in one place; if the fabrics differed it would suggest they were made at each site in turn. Unfortunately, the results of neutron activation analysis for PG2 tiles are less distinct than for any other well defined tile group. Examples from Bordesley (including the tiles from St. Stephen's chapel) are found in clusters 5 and 13 on the far left of the diagram, and also in clusters 1, 2, 3, and 7. All these clusters are interpreted as representing clay sources in the close vicinity of the site. However, the tiles from Hailes, Kenilworth and Maxstoke avoid the Bordesley clusters but co-vary with each other. There is one example in cluster 2 but the rest are peripheral to the core, in clusters 4, 6 and 8. The fabrics associated with clusters 6 and 8 are thought to come from the Coventry area.

It is impossible to say whether production was carried out at each site in turn, or whether the tiles were produced at a settled base. It seems likely that a variety of fabric sources were used by this apparently successful commercial industry, which may have been in operation

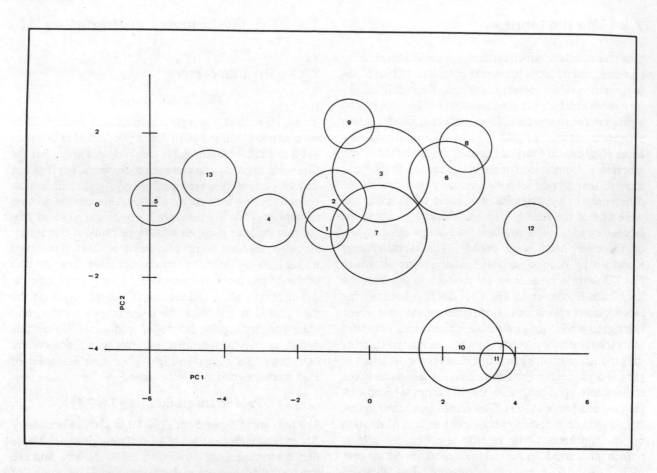

Figure 7.2 NAA clusters using the first two principal components, scaled and logged. The radius of the circles is proportional to their spread.

NAA	KILN	PRODUCTION GROUPS													
		8	2	3	12	4	6	5	1	11	9	14	7	10	13
1			5	6			5		1		1				3
2	8		3			3	2								1
3	1		2	3			1			1					1
4	4				4	1	1				2				1
6									10	5				1	
7			3	2					2		3				
8									18		1				
9									1	1					
10									2						
11												4		1	
12													3		
13			1				1				1				
5		4							1		1				

Figure 7.3 Number of tiles and kiln furniture samples from Bordesley in each NAA fabric cluster (column headed NAA)

No of tiles	Site	Cluster
1	St Stephen's	2
1	Kenilworth	2
1	Hailes	4
1	Kenilworth	4
2	Maxstoke	4
2	Hailes	6
1	Kenilworth	6
4	Hailes	8
1	St Stephen's	9
1	St Stephen's	13
3	St Stephen's	5

Table 7.1 The NAA results for tiles of Production Group 2 from sites other than Bordesley.

Figure 7.4 Production Group 8, Design 64. Scale 1:3

for a number of years. At Bordesley links with PG6, discussed below, suggest it continued in production up to the turn of the century. Some differences in the assemblage of tiles from each of the sites, such as the glaze, the number of tiles scored and split into triangles, and the replacement of old stamps with new versions, also suggests that there was a chronological progression in their manufacture.

Production group 6 (Fig 7.8, 7.9)

A group of tiles with heraldic designs were found in a piece of patching of the 1260/80 floor at Bordesley. This patching is dated by excavation to between 1300 and 1330, but work on the heraldry suggests that a date near the turn of the century is most likely (Stopford 1990a, 79–97). The tiles are so similar to those of PG2 in every aspect of manufacture (apart from design) that it seems very likely they were made by the same tilers. Neutron activation of the clays confirms this, putting these tiles in exactly the same clusters as the Bordesley Abbey examples of PG2. Unlike other PG2 tiles, however, the heraldic examples are not found on other sites in the area. From about 1275 Hailes Abbey was supplied with tiles from other sources. Tiles with heraldic designs were used to pave the newly built extension to the east end of the church at Hailes but their manufacture is quite different from anything at Bordesley, particularly in the 'stabbed' keying of the tile bases (Eames 1980, I, 202).

Three other groups of tiles from Bordesley are less closely dated than those discussed so far, but also belong in the thirteenth century.

Production group 3 (Fig 7.10)

Fabric analysis of tiles of PG3 assigns them to the same NAA core clusters as tiles of PG2 from Bordesley Abbey, and *in situ* examples suggest that the two groups were

Figure 7.5 Frame tile designs from Halesowen (BMD858–60) and Chertsey (BMD867–8). Scale 1:3. After Eames (1980, II)

DN8   DN17   DN21

DN24   DN25

DN41

DN43   DN45   DN51

Figure 7.6 Designs associated with Production Group 2. Scale 1:3

DN42 DN55

DN108

DN59 DN54

DN151

DN159 DN183

Figure 7.7 Designs associated with Production Group 2. Scale 1:3

contemporary, dating from 1260/80. The designs used also have parallels in both groups. However the same stamps were not used and other differences in their manufacture, including the size of the tiles, the depth of the white clay, and the quality of their production, suggest that they were not produced by the same workshops. Tiles of PG3 have been found only at Bordesley. The small scale of this industry might suggest that this was the work of only one tiler. It is possible that the industry was not producing enough, quickly enough, to cope with the growing demand demonstrated by the wide distribution of PG2.

Production groups 4 and 12 (Figs 7.11, 7.12)

Production group 4 represents a different manufacturing tradition to the other 13th century tiles from Bordesley. They are inlaid with a layer of plastic white clay between 2 and 5mm deep. A high proportion of the group are seconds or wasters. Some of their designs are also found on PG 12 tiles. When used on PG12 tiles, however, the decoration is in the traditional method among Bordesley tiles; — i.e. using a thin layer of liquid slip. It is impossible to be positive whether the same stamps were used in both groups, but in the case of design 30 (top left of Fig 7.11 and the top right of Fig 7.12) it probably was. Some of the slip decorated versions of these tiles were sealed in contexts dating to between 1260 and 1300.

The inlay technique, and many of the designs used in

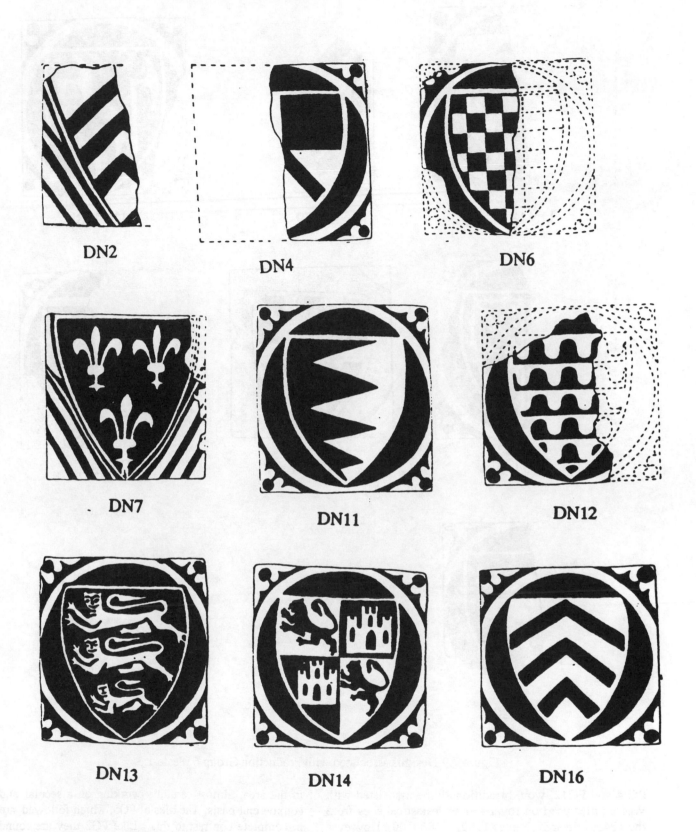

Figure 7.8 Designs associated with Production Group 6. Scale 1:3

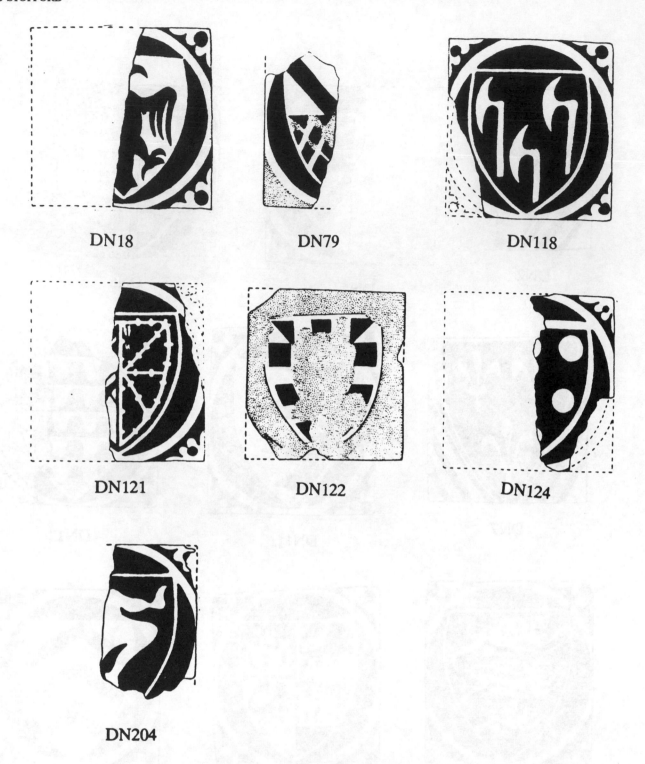

DN18   DN79   DN118

DN121   DN122   DN124

DN204

Figure 7.9 Designs associated with Production Group 6. Scale 1:3

PG 4 and PG12, would traditionally be associated with Wessex tiles used on royal and ecclesiastical sites from the 1240s onwards (Eames 1980, I, 186–200). How ever none of the Bordesley examples have the scooped keys with which Wessex tiles are also associated. The large number of seconds suggests that this was a local attempt to produce tiles using an unfamiliar but more prestigious technique.

There is, then, little change in the techniques used to produce tiles in the west midlands over the best part of the 13th century. By far the most substantial of the identified industries was PG2, which supplied tiles to several sites in the area, almost certainly working on a secular and commercial basis. The tiles of PG5, which followed, are in complete contrast to this. Like PG2 they are found on a number of sites, including Bordesley, Hailes and Halesowen Abbeys. However, while the designs and techniques used in their manufacture were imported from outside the area, production seems most likely to have operated under monastic control.

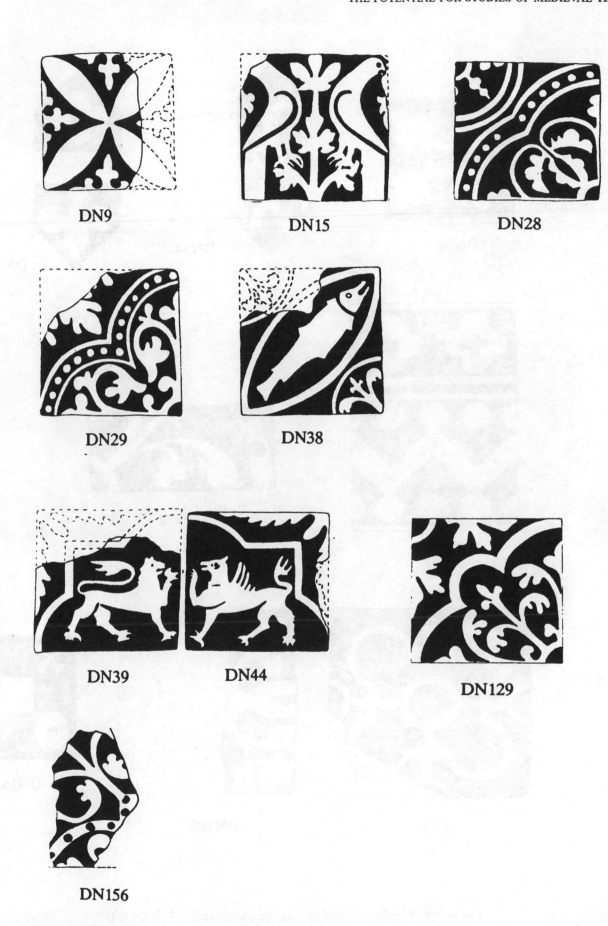

Figure 7.10 Designs associated with Production Group 3. Scale 1:3

Figure 7.11 Designs associated with Production Group 4. Scale 1:3

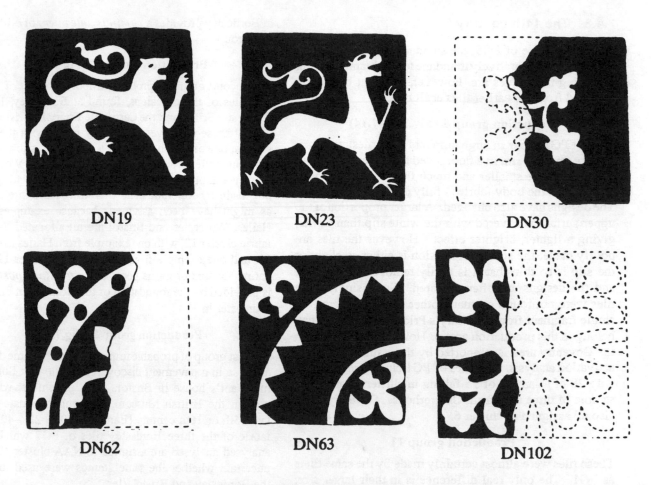

DN19   DN23   DN30

DN62   DN63   DN102

Figure 7.12 Tiles of Production Group 12

7.4.2 The turn of the century

Production group 5

This series of tiles is best known from Chertsey Abbey in Surrey, and includes the famous series of roundels depicting the story of Tristram and Isolde (Gardner and Eames 1954, 24–42; Eames 1980, I, 141–71). The extremely fine detail of these high quality tiles and the use of different sections of the designs in different combinations led Eames to suggest that they were made using metal moulds rather than the usual wooden stamps (1980, I, 154). Some of the Tristram moulds were used in the west midlands in the 1290s, and production seems to have continued into the 14th century (Eames 1980, I, 141–71). The inspiration for these elaborate designs is likely to have come from illuminated manuscripts (Chatwin 1936, 5), perhaps suggesting direct monastic involvement in the organisation of their production.

Apart from the Tristram roundels, which were re-used at Halesowen, the designs found at each site tend to be very similar to each other, but not exactly the same. Differences between the frame tiles at Chertsey and Halesowen are, for example, shown in Fig 7.5. Eames notes that the frame tiles at Hailes are very similar to the Chertsey ones but slightly more elaborate and not identical in any detail (1980, I, 155–6). Different versions of the same designs from this series are found at the three sites in several instances. The roundels at Chertsey and Halesowen are the only clear case where the same stamps were used. It is possible that each site was making, or

having made, their own versions of these high quality designs.

Variations in manufacturing techniques at the different sites support the idea that the work was done by different tilers. Eames has illustrated the way the inscriptions on various tiles in the series were manufactured (Eames 1980, I, 157 Fig 8; 160 Fig 9). At Hailes the inscriptions were made using individual letter stamps or moulds, while at Halesowen the inscription was divided into two moulds or stamps for each quarter of the frame. These tiles are extremely elaborate, and can be seen as the height of medieval achievement in floor tile artistry and technical skill. Production must have been very costly and time consuming. It seems unlikely that they were made by independent commercial tilers as suggested for the tiles of PG2. If production were organised by the monasteries themselves the cost of raw materials and labour would be absorbed by the estate, and facilities such as metal working would be readily available. It should be noted, however, that five fragments of tiles of this type are reported from Coventry (Eames 1980, I, 166).

Only one design of this group has been found in excavations at Bordesley Abbey church and St Stephen's chapel at Bordesley. All the complete examples are extremely worn so that a comparison of stamps with examples from other sites is not possible. Fabric analysis has only been carried out on two PG5 tiles from Hailes, and one from Bordesley. The Bordesley tile falls in cluster 2, while both the Hailes examples fall in cluster 10.

7.4.3 The 14th century

With the demise of PG5, the standard of tile production returns to a comparatively mundane level. Manufacturing and firing techniques are, however, different both from PG5 and from the earlier tiles at Bordesley.

Production group 1 (Fig 7.13, 7.14)

Tiles of PG1 occur in large numbers at Bordesley Abbey and are found *in situ* in a floor dated to between 1330 and 1400. They are smaller and much thinner than previous groups, and the body fabric is fully oxidised in all cases. The designs have also changed. A larger proportion of the upper surface is covered with the white slip than earlier, giving a lighter, brighter effect. However the tiles are poorly made; the stamp impression is either so slight or the slip is so thin that it is easily removed by mistake, and the designs are often smeared. Surprisingly these tiles were not found on many other sites in the area. A single fragment from St. Mary's Priory in Coventry may belong to this production group. However, production in the Coventry area is supported by the results of neutron activation analysis. The tiles of PG1 cluster very tightly, with 28 of a sample of 35 falling in clusters 6 and 8. A sample of three tiles from Charterhouse, Coventry, were also all assigned to cluster 6.

Production group 11

These tiles were almost certainly made by the same tilers as PG1. The only real difference is in their larger size. Fabric analysis supports a close association between the two groups, with 6 of the 7 tiles sampled sharing the same fabric clusters as PG1. One tile of PG11 has a heraldic design showing the arms of Edward III after 1340. This is consistent with the date suggested by *in situ* examples of PG1.

Production group 9

This was by far the most unsatisfactory of the production groups. The tiles of this group are poorly distinguished from those of either PG1 or PG10.

7.4.4 The later 14th or 15th century

In the 15th century the situation changes. Small numbers of tiles, probably not made in the vicinity of Bordesley, or Coventry, are found on the site for the first time. They belong to three different production groups.

Production group 14 (Fig 7.15)

The tiles of PG14 have a distinctive appearance, with a very smooth upper surface, and glaze which fires to a deep reddish purple and cream. It is difficult to tell whether they were stamped in the usual way or not. Examples of these tiles have been found on several other sites in the old county of Worcestershire. No kiln site has been found but Vince has identified the fabric as the same as one of the Lower Severn pottery groups (Eames 1980, I, 250–1; Vince 1977, 257–305). Neutron activation analysis allocates the four examples from Bordesley to cluster 11. The earliest occurrence of a PG14 tile in a sealed context

at Bordesley provides a *terminus ante quem* of *c* 1470 for this group.

Production group 10 (Fig 7.16)

The second group of probable imports consist of a very few tiles of three designs, found at Bordesley, Hailes, Worcester Friary and the Carmelite Friary in Bristol. The tiles at these sites were definitely made with the same stamps, one of which develops a crack in it, showing that the Hailes tiles were made before the ones at Worcester. However fabric analysis suggests that these tiles were not made by itinerant tilers travelling from site to site, as might have been assumed, because examples from Hailes, Worcester and Bristol are all allocated to NAA fabric cluster 12, with one example from Hailes in cluster 10, and one example from Bordesley in cluster 11. The dating for this group is poor, but a *terminus post quem* is provided by the foundation of the Dominican Friary in Worcester in 1347.

Production group 7 (Fig 7.17)

The last group of probable imports are of the same designs as those in a pavement discovered on the first floor of a merchant's house in Bristol. This pavement, which is now in the British Museum, is thought to date to the late 15th or 16th century (Eames 1980, I, 239–47). The fabric of the three Bordesley tiles of PG7 which were analysed analysed are assigned to NAA cluster 12. It is uncertain whether the same stamps were used to make the Bordesley and Bristol tiles.

The assignment of the likely imports to NAA clusters 11 and 12 supports the idea that they were not made in the close vicinity of Bordesley, like the 13th century tile groups. Their known associations are to the south and west of Bordesley, in Worcestershire and the Severn valley. The similarity of the PG14 tile fabrics to a pottery group found in the area of the Lower Severn suggests that NAA cluster 11 lies in that area. NAA cluster 10 is, however, a mixed group.

Production group 13 (Fig 7.18)

Finally, and in contrast to these imported groups, there are some tiles from the last phases at Bordesley which appear to come from the same, local, clay sources as the early PG2 and PG6. These tiles are elaborately decorated by hand rather than with any kind of stamp or mould — quite unlike anything seen previously. They would have been very time consuming to produce, and are unlikely to have been made commercially. They were probably tomb markers, altar surrounds or commemorative plaques of some kind, and may represent the work of a member of the monastic community. In this case the local clay source is what would be expected.

7.5 Conclusions

A complex series of changes in the west midland tile industry can, then, be seen over the 300 year period. First there is the development of a local tradition of slip decorated tiles which flourished as a commercial

Figure 7.13 Tiles of Production Group 1

Figure 7.14 Tiles of Production Group 1

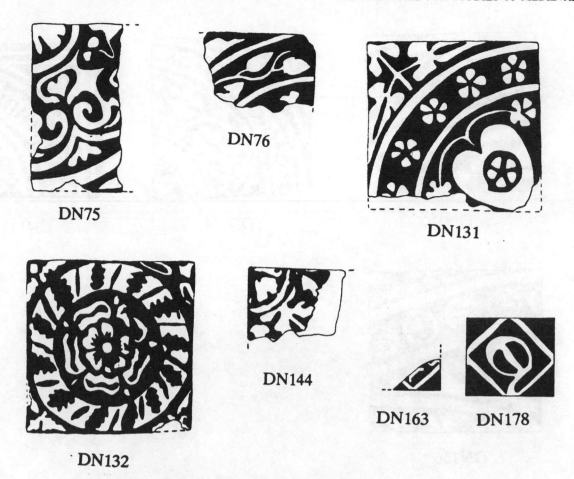

DN75

DN76

DN131

DN132

DN144

DN163   DN178

Figure 7.15 Tiles of Production Group 14

DN219

DN220

Figure 7.16 Tiles of Production Group 10

DN105   DN134   DN135

DN136

Figure 7.17 Tiles of Production Group 17

Figure 7.18 Tiles of Production Group 13

industry in the later 13th century. This seems to have been overwhelmed by the extremely high status Chertsey type tiles, produced using new and complicated techniques, around the turn of the century. The smaller, lighter, fully oxidised tiles of the 14th century suggest the revival of the commercial industry, perhaps now based in the Coventry area. In the later 14th and/or 15th century tiles may have been imported from areas to the south and west of Bordesley. These tiles seem to have been distributed over much greater distances than tiles of any earlier group.

Within this sequence it is clear that different industries were organised in different ways. In some instances production seems to have been organised from within the monasteries, using the extensive facilities and raw materials available to them. In other cases the industry seems to have been operated by the tilers, on a commercial basis. It is possible that these changes have chronological significance. Further work, including a study of kiln sites, will try to set them in a wider social and economic context. As it stands, however, the sequence demonstrates the value of neutron activation techniques in fabric analysis, and shows the necessity for recording tiles in a rigorous and standardised way.

Acknowledgements

I am grateful for the support of the Directors of Bordesley Abbey excavations, particularly Dr S Wright and Dr G Astill. I am also grateful to Dr J Cherry, of the Department of Medieval and later Antiquities, British Museum, for instigating the programme of neutron activation analysis, and to Dr M Hughes and Dr M Leese, of the British Museum Laboratory, for carrying out the work.

References

Astill, G, Hirst, S, and Wright, S, 1984, *Bordesley Abbey Interim Report* (unpublished).

Chatwin, P, 1936, The medieval patterned tiles of Warwickshire. *Trans of the Brimingham Archaeol Soc* 60, 1–41.

Drury, P J, Eames, E S, 1979, The recording and publication of medieval floor tiles for the Census. *Proceedings of the Cambridge seminar for the Census of Medieval Tiles*, Appendix 1, 31–2 (unpublished).

Eames, E S, 1980, *Catalogue of lead-glazed earthenware tiles in the Department of Medieval and Later Antiquities*, 2 vols. British Museum.

Gardner, J S, and Eames, E S, 1954, A tile kiln at Chertsey Abbey. *British Archaeol Assoc* 27, 24–42.

Hirst, S M, Walsh, D, and Wright, S M, 1983, *Bordesley Abbey II; Second report on excavations at Bordesley Abbey, Redditch, Hereford-Worcestershire*. British Archaeol Rep 111, Oxford: BAR.

Hughes, M, Cherry, J, Freestone, I C, and Leese, M, 1982, Neutron activation analysis and petrology of medieval English decorated floor tiles from the Midlands. In I C Freestone, C Johns and T Potter (eds). *Current Research in Ceramics: Thin Section Studies*, 113–22. British Museum Occasional Paper 32.

Leese, M N, Hughes, M J, and Cherry, J, 1986, A scientific study of north midlands medieval tile production. *Oxford Archaeol* 5.3, November, 355–370.

Leese, M N, Hughes, M J, Stopford, J, 1989, The chemical composition of tiles from Bordesley Abbey: a case study in data treatment. In S Rahtz and J Richards, (eds), CAA89 Conference Proceedings, British Archaeol Rep. Oxford: BAR.

Stopford, J, 1990a, *Changes in the structure of medieval industry: an approach to the study of floor tiles*. Unpublished PhD thesis, University of Reading.

Stopford, J, 1990b, *Recording medieval floor tiles*, London: CBA Practical Handbook

Stopford, J, Hughes, M J, and Leese, M N, 1991, A scientific study of medieval tiles from Bordesley Abbey, near Redditch (Hereford and Worcester). *Oxford Archaeol* 10.3, November, 349–60.

Vince, A G, 1977, The medieval and post medieval ceramic industry of the Malvern region: the study of a ware and its distribution. In D P S Peacock, (eds), *Pottery and Early Commerce*, 257–305. London: Academic Press.

8 Bone assemblages from monastic sites: many questions but few data

T P O'Connor

An osteologist colleague once remarked that if certain archaeologists were asked to construct a typology of the motor car, they would produce a detailed stylistic analysis of the dashboard, and would never think of looking under the bonnet to see what powered the thing. On this analogy, it is an interesting question as to what powered medieval monastic houses, in particular the urban houses. It must be stressed that this short paper is presented by a bone specialist who is not an historian, and appropriate indulgence must therefore be begged for any sweeping generalisations, and for venturing a little beyond urban monastic houses into the medieval countryside.

There are several reasons for wanting to study the bones from medieval monastic houses. The houses represent discrete and distinctive economic units functioning within the highly complex medieval economy. Unlike a medieval street, an abbey or priory had clearly defined areas devoted to different activities, and this segregation of activity areas was generally maintained throughout the period of use of a particular building or group of buildings. There is thus every reason to think that an excavated monastic site would show clear patterning in the distribution of all categories of artefact and occupation debris, including bones. Furthermore, some houses are quite well documented, allowing us to conduct a study of the bones against a background of existing knowledge. This does not necessarily mean that we can equate events in the bone record with specific historical events: the connection is one of analogy rather than homology.

An apposite example of what the documentary sources can provide is given in Kershaw's account of the economy and functioning of Bolton priory in the years around the beginning of the 14th century (Kershaw 1973). It is an instructive illustration of some of the questions posed by the historical narrative. Bolton was a moderately prosperous house with substantial land holdings. Although the monastic community was not large — about 20 canons and lay-brothers — the full household, including guests, paupers, corrodians and the like, probably numbered around 200 (Whitaker 1878, 469). The accounts give a detailed record of the livestock held on priory and demesne lands, but it is the records of livestock slaughtered for the meat larder which are of more direct relevance to the interpretation of bone debris. Over the years 1304–1319, the average numbers of domestic livestock slaughtered for the larder in each year were 91 cattle, 119 sheep and 78 pigs (Kershaw 1973, 152), representing a total of the order of 13.5 tonnes of meat. Taking the estimate of 200 for the household, and making no allowance for fast days or for dietary differences between the various sections of the household, this gives a plausible average of about 180gm of red meat per man day, which at least suggests

that the estimates of household size are roughly in accord with the provisioning data.

These simple averages conceal wide fluctuations, however, and the annual 'bone output' of the priory would have varied dramatically. Between 1315 and 1317, for example, disease (the usual 'murrain') reduced sheep flocks held on priory and demesne lands by about two-thirds, leading to a shortage of mutton for the larder in the following year. In order to stock the larder, virtually the whole of the priory's herd of 120 pigs was slaughtered, leaving only six sows and one heroic boar from which to breed. The surviving pigs evidently set about their task with a will, as the herd was back up to 58 pigs within two years. The purpose of this example is to make the point that a rubbish pit of early 14th century date could have 'captured' the debris of 1315–16, with many sheep and few pigs, or of 1316–17, in which the proportions were quite reversed. More probably, the excavated pit fill would contain a little of each year and more besides, thus reflecting the overall picture represented by the averages quoted above but losing the very short-term fluctuations. The existence of such detailed accounts can thus serve to set into perspective the interpretation of variations within the recovered bone assemblages, and underlines the need to examine material from a wide range of features at a particular site, rather than relying on a single drain or group of pits to give a 'representative' sample.

The accounts also show the complexity of trade and subsistence farming within the ambit of a single house. A relative decline in the abundance of cattle in the bone assemblages could have many explanations. At Bolton priory, the use of pigs to replace sheep in the larder during 1316X17 must be set against the fact that in that year only 18 cows were slaughtered for the larder whilst 47 were sold on for cash (Kershaw 1973, 97). Clearly, even though meat was in short supply, cattle were too valuable as a trade commodity for them to be slaughtered to fill an immediate need. At Llanthony priory, Gwent, in 1279, the supply of cattle for the larder was suddenly much reduced, not by disease or market prices, but by the seizure and impounding of stock from two of the prior's manors as the result of a land dispute (Davies 1940, 91; 184: also Evans 1986, 54). These are not events which one could expect to identify in the archaeological record, but their description in monastic records is important as an historic context.

Excavations on monastic sites thus offer an opportunity to examine bone assemblages which can be attributed to clearly-defined activity areas, and which can be interpreted against an often detailed historical background. Urban monastic houses offer the further opportunity of comparing the subsistence pattern of the institution with that of the town around it, and thus of seeing to what extent the monastic house depended on its granges or manors to supply food, or whether monastic subsistence was closely tied into the urban market.

This paper does not set out to give a comprehensive review of bone assemblages from published monastic sites. Such a survey would occupy relatively few pages, however, as it is remarkable how little bone debris has been recovered from even quite major monastic sites. The extensive excavation at Guildford priory (Poulton and Alexander 1984) produced only 119 fragments of bone, much of it apparently from pre-priory occupation. Similarly, excavations at the large Augustinian priory at Clontuskert, Co. Galway (Fanning 1976), produced a small and fragmentary assemblage deemed to deserve only a short paragraph by way of report. One of the few Cluniac houses in England — Pontefract priory — was excavated during the course of 1957–1959, and might have shed interesting light on the diet of this order. Regrettably the site yielded only 300 or so fragments of bone (Ryder 1961). Excavations at Westminster abbey in 1975 gave useful samples of fish bones, but the few hundred other bone fragments warranted only a short and rather dismal report (Black 1976).

Perhaps it could be argued that the excavators of monastic sites are structure-oriented, and tend to overlook bones during their eager pursuit of walls. This hypothesis does not bear close scrutiny, however. From 1978 onwards, the Augustinian priory at Llanthony was the subject of a programme of excavation and consolidation work undertaken by a director well aware of the information potentially available from bone assemblages (and regularly reminded of the same by the present author). Many different areas of the priory were investigated, and yet the published results show that only a few hundred fragments were recovered (O'Connor 1981; 1986).

There are a few exceptions to this tale of woe. The Austin Friars site in Leicester gave a substantial assemblage of nearly 12,000 fragments, though some of this is post-Dissolution (Thawley 1981). Another large assemblage was recovered from Kirkstall abbey, West Yorkshire, from late 15th to early 16th century deposits in the supposed area of the meat kitchen. Though highly informative about a short period of use of one part of the site, this deposit may not be representative of the full range of meat consumption at the abbey. When the opportunity arose to excavate the Gilbertine St Andrew's priory, in York, recovery of bone fragments was given a high priority. A range of sieving techniques was employed to recover assemblages of known and controlled fragment-size bias from a wide range of types of deposit (O'Connor 1988). Analysis of this material shows, that even given an intensive, targetted sieving operation, the archive of bone fragments recovered is quite modest in scale when compared with the extent of the excavation and the quantities of sediment processed (O'Connor 1991). Only a few contexts yielded substantial assemblages: a slow accumulation in the area of the cemetery; Dissolution period dumping around the *frater* and kitchen; and a floor deposit in the cloister ambulatory. Even the fills of refuse pits and a well

contemporary with the period of priory occupation gave relatively small numbers of bones. Work on bones from the Dominican friary in Beverley, North Humberside, has given a hand-collected assemblage of over 5000 fragments and abundant fish bones from wet-sieving (Gilchrist 1989). Again, this is hardly a large amount of material from an extensive excavation on which bone recovery was given a high priority, and, as with Austin Friars and St Andrews priory, the Dissolution period accounts for a substantial proportion of the bones.

Levitan (1989) has discussed bone assemblages from two monastic sites in Exeter. Excavations in 1976–8 on the site of the Benedictine nunnery of St Katherine, Polsloe, produced a total of over 10,000 fragments of bone, of which about 70% can be dated to 1500–1530. A detailed study of the spatial distribution of bones of the main taxa shows considerable differences between the assemblages recovered from different parts of the monastic complex, and considerable variation through time in any one area. For example, the evidence suggests that carcasses were jointed and boned-out in the kitchens, producing deposits with a high proportion of large cattle bones in the adjacent external area. There may be some analogy here with the 'meat kitchen' deposit at Kirkstall abbey. Excavations at St Nicholas priory, Exeter, another Benedictine house, gave an assemblage of nearly 5000 bones, but these were from mid-16th century fills of robber trenches. Interesting though Levitan's account of this material is, it tells us little about the priory, even though the robber trenches probably included a large element of residual pre-Dissolution material.

From the few urban houses which have given useful assemblages we can see that cattle bones generally predominate in a simple analysis of fragment numbers, though not to the extreme extent seen at Kirkstall abbey (Table 8.1). Although direct comparison of the results obtained by different workers must be approached with caution, and notwithstanding the inadequacies of the published results from Pontefract and Kirkstall, considerable variation in the occurrence of the bones of the major domesticates is apparent. At St Andrew's priory, York, there is an apparent difference between assemblages from 13th and early 16th century deposits, the later material showing a lower proportion of cattle bones and a correspondingly higher proportion of pig and domestic birds. This observation should not be taken at face value, however, as the early 16th century data are mostly derived from a single deposit in the vicinity of the kitchen, whilst the earlier data were obtained from bones from a variety of features around the site. Similarly, the Dominican friary at Beverley shows a marked difference in the character of the bone debris from 13th century deposits overlying a timber building north of the North Range, compared with bones from the stone buildings which were constructed upon these same deposits (a supposed 'little cloister'). The later material shows a much higher proportion of domestic bird bones, again in an area interpreted as being close to the *frater* and kitchens. Exactly the reverse trend is seen in samples of bones from within the kitchens at St Katherine's priory, Polsloe (Exeter), where the proportion of cattle bones is markedly higher in 15–16th century groups than in earlier deposits (Levitan 1989, 170). The small assemblage from Pontefract priory is most intriguing, as it shows an unusually low proportion of cattle bones, and an unusual age distribution of cattle and sheep. In other published urban monastic assemblages, the cattle and sheep bones are usually predominantly those of adults, whilst the Pontefract material included '. . . a fair proportion. . .' of both species killed when less than two years old (Ryder 1961, 107).

To return for a moment to the numbers of carcasses taken into the Bolton priory larder during 1304–19, the average annual numbers of cattle, sheep and pigs given above are broadly consistent with the relative proportions seen in Table 8.1. Some very approximate conversion of numbers of carcasses to numbers of bones in an excavated assemblage can be made by examining a series of excavated assemblages and determining the approximate number of fragments by which each identifiable individual animal is typically represented. The very large and well-preserved series from 9–11th century levels at 16–22 Coppergate, York, gave typical 'fragments per individual' values of 65 for cattle, 40 for sheep, and 25 for pigs. Applying these values to the numbers of carcasses given for the Bolton priory larder gives relative proportions of 47% cattle, 38% sheep and 15% pigs. It must be stressed that this is a very approximate means of comparison, but the results are generally in accord with the relative proportions seen at excavated monastic sites.

Moving away from the domestic mammals, the Leicester Austin Friars site shows a relatively high proportion of goose bones; about as many as of domestic fowl. This contrasts sharply with the material from Beverley where, in deposits of the 'little cloister', domestic fowl bones outnumbered those of domestic goose by a ratio of about 22 to one. The early 16th century data from St Andrew's, York, gives a ratio of about 4.6 fowl bones to one goose. The relative lack of geese at Beverley is surprising. The countryside around the town is for the most part low-lying and wet, and suitable land for the keeping of geese must surely have been plentiful.

Fish were a vital part of the monastic diet, more so, probably, than in the secular medieval diet, given a greater adherence to fast days. Rural monastic houses maintained fish ponds, and ensured other means of supply as well. Llanthony priory maintained fish ponds, held fishing rights to the River Honddu beside which the priory stands, and negotiated fishery rights to Llangorse Lake (Evans 1986, 55: Roberts 1847, 32). The Bolton priory accounts describe the purchasing of fish stores (*warnesture*) on a large scale, the mainstay being herrings. These were probably mostly bought as salted herrings, and the priory seems to have been purchasing some 10,000 to 20,000 herrings per annum (Kershaw 1973, 150–1). If this figure seems excessive, simple calculations reduce it to a reasonable two herrings per man-week, assuming a household of 200 people. There is a danger that poor recovery of bones, and naive interpretation of data, may seriously understate the consumption of fish at monastic sites. In discussing the fish from Austin Friars, Leicester, Thawley (1981, microfiche report 9–10)

notes the predominance of marine taxa in the recovered assemblage, without direct comment on the absence of herring. She further observes that the marine fish exploited were generally of a larger size than would be typical today. As the Austin Friars assemblage was hand-collected during excavation, neither conclusion can be given credence. In the absence of sieving, herring bones and those of most freshwater taxa will have been lost, and only the larger individuals of the larger species will be represented. Where deposits have been extensively sieved, as at St Andrew's priory, York, and the Dominican friary, Beverley, the importance of herring in the monastic diet is confirmed, and appreciable exploitation of freshwater fish is also apparent. Indeed, in 1497, a fishing net which belonged to the prior of St Andrew's, and was used for fishing in the River Foss near the priory, was siezed, declared illegal, and burned (Raine 1941, 132).

The matter of the sources of supply of the urban houses is still an open question. Levitan (1989, 171) argues that St Katherine's priory, Polsloe (Exeter), was buying in whole or halved carcasses and undertaking secondary butchery on site. There are some indications from York and Beverley that at least some meat may have been purchased as dressed carcasses rather than as live animals. Late 13th-century assemblages from the Dominican friary, Beverley, appear to show a marked absence of cattle metapodials and skull bones, compared with the more heavily meat-bearing parts of the carcass. The implication is that at least some of the beef supplied to the friary arrived as dressed carcasses, the heads and feet having been removed at the site of slaughter and primary butchery. Similarly, early 16th century deposits at St Andrew's priory, York, gave assemblages of sheep bones deficient in metapodials and phalanges. The danger with this interpretation is that characteristics of supply may be confused with those of deposition. The sheep may have walked into the precincts of St Andrew's priory and there been slaughtered and butchered, but the feet came to be deposited separately from the rest of the carcass. On this scenario, it is an intriguing possibility that the sheeps' feet were removed from the priory precincts whilst still attached to skins being sold on to a fellmonger. The accumulation of sheeps' feet at a late 17th century fellmongers in York has been reported at length (O'Connor 1984a), and a similar depletion of metapodials and phalanges was noted amongst sheep bones in 17th-century pits elsewhere in the city (O'Connor 1984b).

The early 16th century deposits at St Andrew's priory gave assemblages which closely resemble other late-and post-medieval groups from York, and which contrast with earlier medieval assemblages. In particular, the 15th and 16th centuries seem to have seen an increase in the relative abundance and diversity of bird and fish taxa in occupation debris, and the exploitation of newly-weaned cattle for veal. These characteristics have been noted in assemblages from secular occupation at 1–5 Aldwark (O'Connor 1984b) and in currently unpublished assemblages from a late medieval building complex at 2, Coffee Yard and from the Vicars Choral collegiate building at the Bedern, as well as from deposits in the

Table 8.1 Relative abundance percent of major taxa from five monastic sites, based on fragment counts. Data for Kirkstall abbey and Pontefract priory are from Ryder (1961), data for Beverley Dominican friary are from Gilchrist (1989) and data for Austin Friars are from Thawley (1981). Data from different sites should not be closely compared because of differences in the standard of recovery and level of identification during recorded. The data given for St Andrew's priory are derived from material recovered by sieving on a 12mm mesh, and this has probably raised the relative proportions of sheep and fowl bones a little in comparison with the other assemblages, which are all hand-collected. The 'meat kitchen' at Kirkstall abbey also produced 2% deer and Pontefract priory yielded 5% deer. N = number of specimens on which the percentages are based. Because of rounding of percentages, some do not total to 100.

	cattle	sheep		pig	fowl	goose	N
St Andrew's priory, York							
Post-dissolution dumps	45	37	12	5	1		905
Late use of priory	40	32	18	9	2		749
Early use of priory	60	30	9	1	1		949
Dominican friary, Beverley							
'little cloister'	20	31	20	28	1		710
13th century deposits	50	26	19	3	1		538
Kirkstall abbey							
'meat kitchen'	90	5	3	not given			
Pontefract priory	30	45	20	c 300			
Austin Friars, Leicester	56	28	10	4	3		7008

area of the frater at St Andrew's priory. The implication of this is that the priory, the Bedern, and the rest of the city had substantially shared sources of supply, at least by the 15–16th centuries.

To draw this brief overview to a close, several observations must be made. The first is that there are precious few published bone assemblages from urban monastic houses, and therefore progress in this area will require the collection of new data rather than the re-evaluation of published results. The second point is that excavations on monastic sites in general seem to produce remarkably little material. It is as if the meticulous order of the monastic life extended to the disposal of refuse, and in this respect the urban establishments are at variance with the general run of urban medieval settlement. There is clearly much information to be gained, however, which is relevant to the interpretation of individual deposits within a site and to wider questions of meat supply and exploitation. In order to gain such information, the recovery of bones from monastic sites must be maximised, by taking every opportunity to excavate fully any deposits in which bone fragments are clearly present, and by wet-sieving large samples in order to recover the full range of identifiable elements. On many medieval sites, bones are over-abundant, and there may even be pressure to reduce the quantity which is recovered. This is not the case with monastic sites, and if we wish to examine the complex provisioning of the urban houses on the basis of hard evidence, it is essential that a high priority be given to the recovery of as substantial an archive of bone assemblages as possible.

Acknowledgements

I am grateful to Richard Kemp for bringing a number of published sources to my attention, to Roberta Gilchrist for references and unpublished data, and to Harry Kenward for comments on an earlier draft.

References

Black, G, 1976, Excavations in the sub-vault of the misericorde of Westminster abbey, February to May 1975. *Trans London Middlesex Archaeol Soc* **27**, 135–78.

Davies, J C, (ed) 1940, *The Welsh Assize Roll of 1277–84*. Board of Celtic Studies History and Law Series **7**. Cardiff.

Evans, D H, 1986, Further excavation and fieldwork at Llanthony priory, Gwent. *Monmouthshire Antiq* **5**(1 + 2; 1983–4), 1–64.

Fanning, T, 1976, Excavation at Clontuskert priory, Co. Galway. *Proc Roy Ir Acad* **76c**, 97–169.

Gilchrist, R, 1989, Excavations at the Dominican priory, Beverley, Humberside, 1986. The animal bones. Ancient Monuments Laboratory Report. Unpublished.

Kershaw, I, 1973, *Bolton Priory. The economy of a Northern Monastery 1286–1325*. Oxford.

Levitan, B, 1989, Bone analysis and urban economy: examples of selectivity and a case for comparison. In D Serjeantson and T Waldron (eds) *Diet and Crafts in Towns*, 161–88. Oxford Brit Archaeol Rep **199**. Oxford: BAR.

O'Connor, T P, 1981, The animal bones. p.34 in D H Evans, Excavations at Llanthony priory, Gwent, 1978. *Monmouthshire Antiq* **4**, 5–43.

O'Connor, T P, 1984a, Selected groups of animal bones from Skeledergate and Walmgate. *Archaeology of York* **15/1**.

O'Connor, T P, 1984b, Bones from Aldwark, York. Ancient Monuments Laboratory Report 4391. Unpublished.

O'Connor, T P, 1986, The animal bones. In Evans (1986), 40–2.

O'Connor, T P, 1988, Archaeological bones samples recovered by sieving: 46–54 Fishergate, York, as a case study. Ancient Monuments Laboratory Report 190/88. Unpublished.

O'Connor, T P, 1991, Bones from 46–54 Fishergate. London: CBA for YAT (Fascicule AY 15/4).

Poulton, R, and Woods, H, 1984, *Excavations on the site of the Dominican friary at Guildford in 1974 and 1978.* Research Volume of the Surrey Archaeol Soc **9**.

Raine, A, (ed) 1941, *York Civic Records* 2. Yorkshire Archaeol Soc Record Ser **103**.

Roberts, G, 1847, *Some account of Llanthony priory.* London.

Ryder, M L, 1961, Livestock remains from four medieval sites in Yorkshire. *Agr His Rev* **9**, 105–110.

Thawley, C, 1981, The mammal, bird, and fish bones. In J E Mellor and T Pearce, *The Austin Friars, Leicester.* CBA Research Report **35**, 173–5 and microfiche. London: CBA.

Whitaker, T D, 1878, *The history and antiquities of the deanery of Craven.* (3rd. edn; ed A W Morant) Leeds.

9   The monastic topography of Chester

Simon W Ward

The obvious significance of the church in the lives and attitudes of the population during the Middle Ages inevitably became expressed in the medieval fabric of Chester, as much as it did in any other urban centre. This is in many ways a paradox, since monastic ideals and urban life would appear to be mutually exclusive. This paper considers how the monastic houses of Chester shared in, adapted and perhaps even stimulated, urban development and expansion during the medieval period and consequently how the evidence from these houses can be taken as indicative of the whole city. This influence is not confined to the medieval period alone, for the former presence of these houses still continued to exert an effect after the Dissolution.

The information for this paper is derived from work undertaken by the Grosvenor Museum Excavations Section, and published in the Museum's monograph series (Ward, 1990). Grateful acknowledgement is made for permission to use this material here and for use of the figures (Figs 9.2, 9.3, 9.4, 9.5 drawn by P H Alebon and A Thompson, Grosvenor Museum Draughtsmen). I am also grateful to Dr A Thacker (V C H) for allowing free access to his research on this subject.

Medieval Chester was not richly endowed with churches compared to some cities. There were only nine parish churches, six religious houses (including an ephermeral community of the Friars of the Sack) and three hospitals (two with suburban locations and the third a very late foundation). This number reflects in part the city's relatively small population and poor economy. It is also due to the particular political situation of the county, in which patronage was concentrated in the hands of the Earls of Chester. This led to a small number of richly endowed houses (Kettle 1980, 124). Their number is, however, equivalent to that known in such comparable urban centres as Exeter or King's Lynn.

The earliest of the houses and by far the largest and richest, was the Benedictine abbey of St Werburgh's which was founded in 1093 by the first Norman Earl, Hugh of Avranches, from an existing college of secular canons. He and his retainers richly endowed it and gave it a precinct occupying the whole north-eastern quarter of the walled city. The abbey has a fairly normal history of good and bad abbots, building campaigns and financial difficulties. It was not dissolved until January 1540, amongst the very last of the major monastic house, and was refounded in August 1541 as the cathedral for the new diocese of Chester. It is significant that this establishment, with its large buildings and rich endowments, was considered more suitable as a cathedral than the original short-lived Norman cathedral: the parish church and college of St John's. Virtually no archaeological work has been done on the abbey, apart from the few observations made during 19th-century restorations. These extensive and drastic works, especially to the exterior of the building, tend to conceal the fact that this is one of the most complete abbey structures still surviving in the country.

The second of the religious houses to be founded was the Benedictine nunnery of St Mary's, again founded under the aegis of the earldom, in this case Ranulf II in c 1150. It was given a block of land on the castle demesne immediately to the north of the Norman castle in the south-western corner of the city. This was always a small and not wealthy house. It escaped dissolution under the 1536 Act by paying for an exemption, but was surrendered in 1540. The site of the nunnery was the subject of a short excavation in 1964 (Rutland 1965) before the erection of the Police Head Quarters' Building. This established the main layout of the church and cloister but discovered little regarding its structural history (Fig 9.2). We are fortunate to have a 17th-century ground plan of the buildings as then surviving, a Buck engraving of the ruins in the 18th century and even the chancel arch re-erected as a 'feature' in the Grosvenor Park.

The remaining houses were friaries. the Dominicans (Black Friars) were established first in c 1236, probably founded by Bishop Alexander de Stavensby on a block of land lying (provided by the earl), immediately to the north of the nunnery on the western side of the city. They were followed in 1237–8 by the Franciscans (Grey Friars) who were given, by permission of the king, a further block of land on the western side of the city, north of the Dominicans and on the other side of Watergate Street. The Carmelites (White Friars) had a community in Chester by 1277 but only in 1290 were they given seven houses by a citizen, Hugh Payn, on what became White Friars Lane, close to the city centre. They expanded their precinct considerably during the 14th century and by the time of the Dissolution were the most prosperous of the friaries. All three friaries surrendered without resistance on the same day, 15 August 1538.

Archaeologically nothing is known of the Carmelite friary. A tentative plan of the Franciscans has been drawn up (Fig 9.3) from discoveries made during building work in 1920 (Bennett 1921, 67–9) and from a 17th-century ground plot. Considerably more is known about the Dominicans, the subject of two and half years' excavation during the 1970's by the author on the confusingly named Grey Friars Court site (Ward, 1990), and a further short excavation in 1988 on the adjacent Nicholas Street Mews. These have revealed much about the church and the outer courts on its northern side, although the cloister to the south remains little explored (Fig 9.4).

Obviously, these religious houses by reason of their size and physical presence were an immensely important component of the medieval city. The abbey church was by far the largest building in medieval Chester and, indeed in

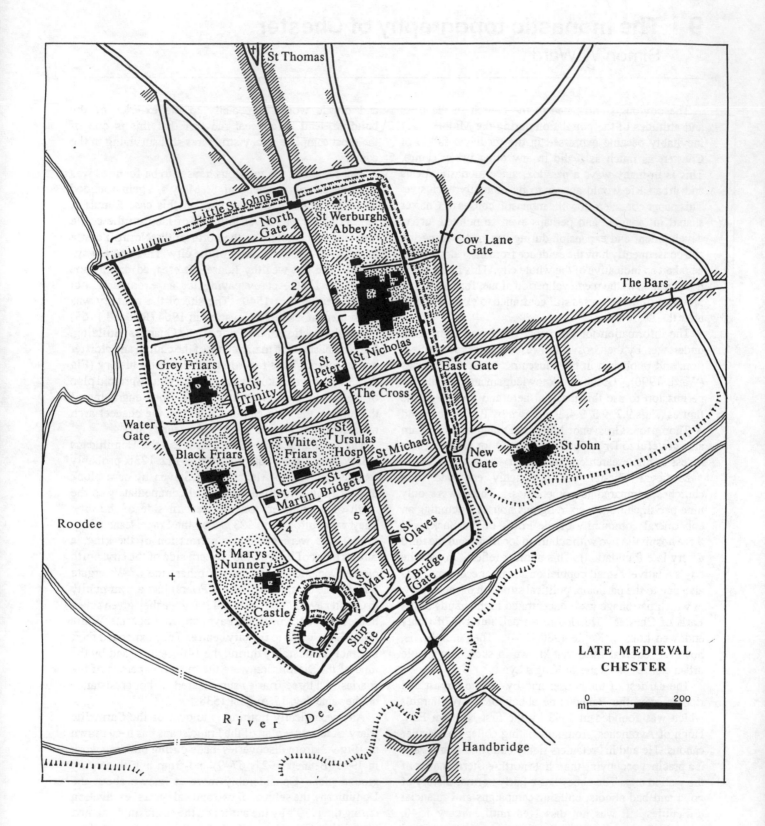

Figure 9.1 Map of late medieval Chester. Key to sites: 1. Abbey Green; 2: Princess Street; 3: 12 Watergate Street; 4: Cuppin Street; 5: Lower Bridge Street.

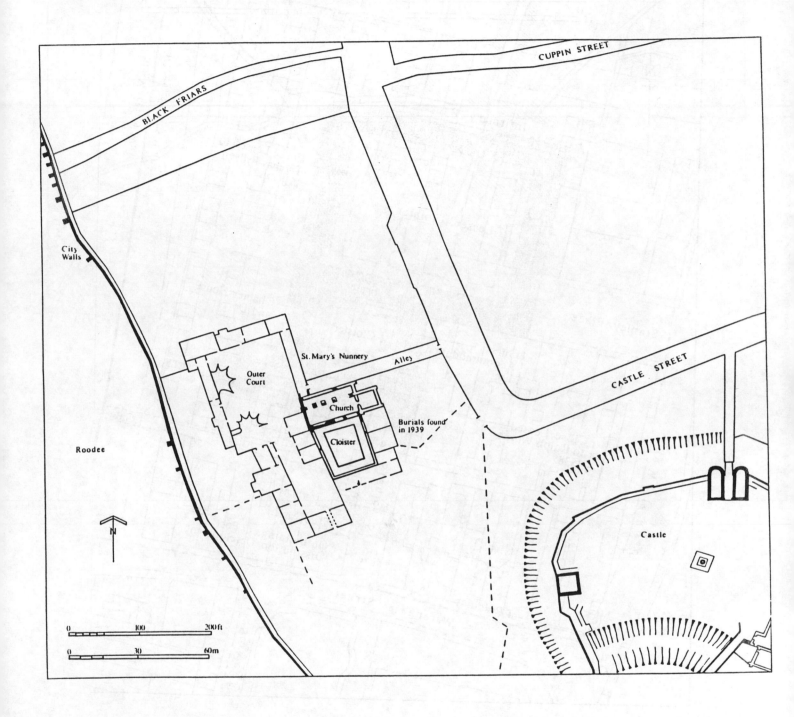

Figure 9.2 Plan of St. Mary's Nunnery.

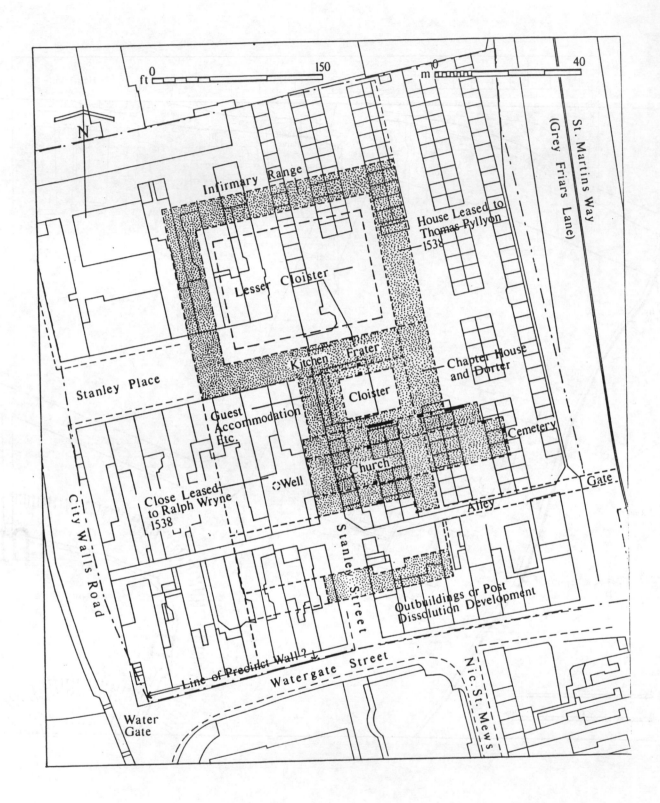

Figure 9.3 Plan of the Franciscan Friary.

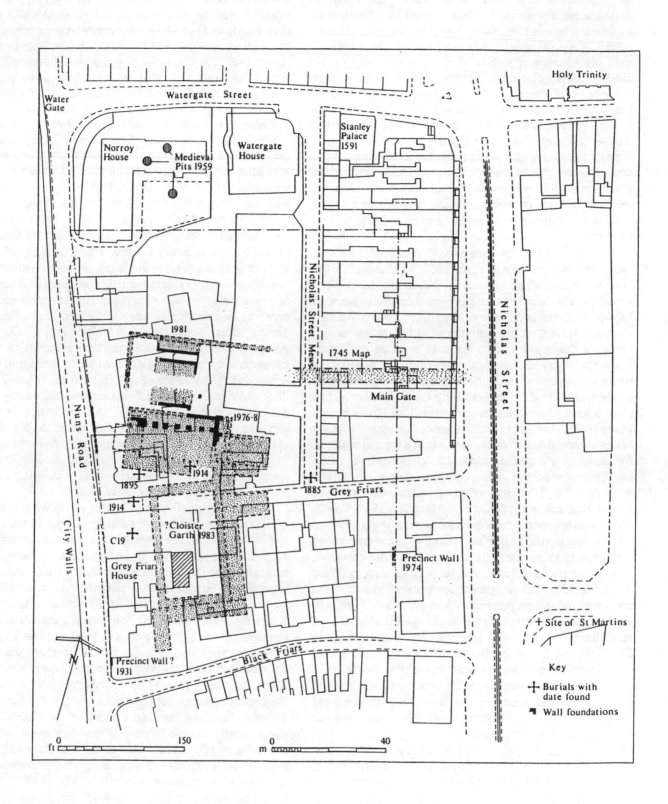

Figure 9.4 Plan of the Dominican Friary.

spite of modern developments is still amongst the largest today. Of those medieval churches whose plan is known, only one parish church, St John's, originally designed as a cathedral by the Norman bishop Peter, exceeds the size of the friary churches. Amongst the religious houses, only the nunnery church is of an equivalent size to the smaller parish churches. Their impact on the city is not only to be measured in the physical bulk of their buildings. By the late 14th century the combined area of their precincts totalled more than 25% of the walled area of the city (Fig 9.1). On the face of it, it would appear, therefore, that a considerable proportion of the area of the city was removed from the normal run of urban pressures and development by these precincts. A more detailed analysis of the foundation and development of the precincts, however, reveals more complex processes in operation.

As noted above, the abbey of St Werburgh's with its large precinct was founded in 1093 by the first of the Norman earls, Hugh, and it is worth considering the foundation in the context of the establishment of Norman rule on the city and county. In 1070/71 King William marched through Cheshire stamping out rebellion and ravaging the countryside. He built a castle at Chester and decided to establish a strong earldom there under his trusted companion and nephew, Hugh of Avranches. This castle was one of the series along the Welsh borders to form a strong bulwark against Wales. Earl Hugh, known as the Wolf or the Fat, initiated a series of major changes to his new capital which converted it into a typical centre of *Normanitas*. He and his successors completed the castle and commenced the construction of the southern and western sides of the city walls overlooking the river, thus completing the walled circuit (Alldridge 1981, 23–8). There also appears to have been a complete reorganisation and reallocation of land within the city. Excavations have consistently shown that there is no continuity between Saxon and post-conquest structures or properties (Ward 1985, 39–43). This reorganisation resulted in the typical medieval settlement pattern with structures concentrated along the street fronts with yards and open land behind. In addition, in 1075 the seat of the bishopric was moved from Lichfield to Chester by Bishop Peter. He commenced the construction of a new cathedral at the church of St John the Baptist, reputedly a 7th-century foundation and the most ancient church in the city. This status proved temporary, however, for in the early 12th century the see was moved back to Lichfield.

Earl Hugh's foundation of an abbey in 1903 at St Werburgh's, at Chester's second most ancient church, can be seen, as a significant stage in the *Normanisation* of Chester; the city was now provided with a full set of the institutions which epitomised Norman power and prestige — the castle, the city walls, the cathedral and the abbey. The secular canons were displaced and replaced by a community of Benedictine monks from Bec. The new abbey, however, still retained the parochial functions of the former college, an arrangement which was never a particularly happy combination and was a constant source of friction between the citizenry and the monks. Interestingly, this view of the foundation as a political

act, paying little regard to the previous history of the site nor to the interests of the inhabitants, receives supporting evidence from an excavation carried out at Abbey Green (Fig 9.1, 1) in 1975–7, near the north-western corner of the precinct against the city walls (McPeake, Bulmer and Rutter 1980, 21–31). In the Saxon period, from the 10th century onwards, light-scale manufacturing activity was carried out, including antler working and horn coring in association with a soaking pit, and probably also black-smithing connected to a light timber shed which was subsequently burnt down. This activity was possibly being carried out to the rear of a more densely occupied area adjacent to the major thoroughfare, Northgate Street, which lay to the west of the site. Perhaps more important was the occurrence of an intramural gravel track, laid down over the tail of the Roman rampart. This track has been located in various places inside the eastern half of the old Roman defences, but this is the first site at which it could be firmly dated to the Saxon period. Its existence around the western side can also be postulated because its line was preserved by a series of medieval streets which continue in existence to this day (Water Tower Street, Trinity Street, Weaver Street and White Friars). On the Abbey Green site neither the gravel intramural track nor the manufacturing activity survived the foundation of the abbey and the inclusion of this area within its precinct. The whole medieval period was represented merely by a build-up of cultivation soil. The foundation of the abbey in 1093 appropriated a whole sector of the city, thus extinguishing an urban and commercial development in its primal stage. It also perhaps confined the location of the commercial core of the city to the south of this area, a situation which still exists today.

The foundation of the three houses on the western side of the city, (the Benedictine nunnery and the Dominican and Franciscan friaries) reveals what is almost an opposite process in operation. To understand this, the stages through which this area became enclosed within the city walls need to be considered. During the Roman period the area lay outside the legionary fortress enclosure, between it and the harbour facilities now beneath the silt of the Roodee. Consequently, a thriving and important civil settlement grew up there. By the 10th century and the foundation of the burgh in 907, when this harbour area had silted, the major quays or hards had probably moved to the south of the city adjacent to the bridge. The burghal defences have not yet been located by excavation but the generally accepted theory is that they consisted of the northern and eastern sides of the legionary fortress together with two new spurs joining the north-western and south-eastern angles to the river (Mason 1985, 36–9). This defensive line, cutting off the peninsula on which Chester lay, considerably shortened the length to be manned and maintained as compared to the Roman fortress, although it enclosed much undeveloped land. Documentary evidence indicates that the Norman earls completed the circuit of walls by constructing the southern river front in the early 12th century and the western side shortly after 1250 (Alldridge 1981, 23–8). They can be considered, therefore, to have completed and ration-alised what they found, rather than simply enclosing the built-up area with a minimum length. By this process they also incorporated considerable areas of open land, especially on the western side. No doubt the earls hoped that proximity to the quays outside the Water Gate would lead to the profitable development of this area, but these hopes were not fulfilled. The silting of the river continued and new quays and out ports had to be constructed further and further down stream. Consequently, when the occasion demanded, there were large blocks of land on the western side of the city which could be granted to newly arrived religious communities. This land had been generally known as the Crofts and was given over to small-scale agriculture uses. On the site of the Dominican (Black) Friary it was demonstrated through excavation that when the friars received the site in 1236, the ruins of Roman buildings were still protruding above the ground surface (Ward 1990, 41). The friars avidly robbed out these buildings, removed the demolition deposits down to the latest Roman floor levels, dug out the hypocausts for tile and robbed the walls down to and even including the foundations. The sites of these buildings were then levelled and returned to useful occupation. The foundations of the earliest phase of the church included many large fragments of Roman mortar flooring derived from the suspended floors over hypocausts.

The creation of these monastic precincts in a great block all along the western side of the city can be seen, therefore, not as a negative event retarding or blighting urban expansion but as quite the opposite. Previously derelict land was brought into useful development and circulation. The grants to the Nuns and the Dominicans were on such a generous scale that apart from minor adjustments, their precincts remained unaltered until the Dissolution. The Dominicans' precinct adjoined two major thoroughfares, Watergate Street to the north and Nicholas Street to the east. The precinct boundary wall, however, did not lie along the street itself but behind tenements which occupied the street frontage. Presumably the Black friars were granted only the less valuable back lands.

In contrast, the Franciscans to the north of Watergate Street did occupy that frontage by the time of Dissolution. Their precinct wall survived till the 17th century when Speed's map of the city was drawn (Bennett 1921, 64). It is thought likely, although firm proof is lacking, that they expanded their precinct southwards to the street by a series of acquisitions. In 1332 and again in 1360 they acquired a messuage adjacent to their land. Although the location of these messuages is unknown, it was quite likely to have been on the Watergate Street frontage. In any case, it is clear that by the late Middle Ages, the friars had acquired this potentially valuable, but undeveloped frontage on the street immediately inside the gate which led to the harbour. It is a vivid indicator of the decline and silting of Chester's harbour.

The most extreme case of precinct establishment by accretion in Chester is provided by the Carmelite friars, the last house to be founded, who only acquired a small holding of seven houses in 1289 through the generosity of a wealthy citizen. In 1350 they acquired two lanes adjacent to their property. In 1354 the Black Prince (the

then Earl of Chester) pardoned the friars for acquiring further land without his permission and furthermore permitted them to acquire an additional plot, 200' by 160' in size, contiguous with their house (Bennett 1935, 11–2). As the final size of their precinct was only in the region of 400' by 250' this acquisition represents a considerable proportion of it — approximately one third. The Black Death of 1349–50 may have aided the friars in increasing the size of their precinct so dramatically in the 1350s. The aftermath of such a sudden fall in population must have left much property without heirs or economic viability.

The expansion of the Carmelite friary leads on to the next aspect: the way the religious houses participated in and reflected the general economic prosperity or decline of the city. The expansion and prosperity which was generally experienced at the end of the 13th and in the early 14th century is exaggerated at Chester by an historical coincidence. From 1277 when King Edward I opened his campaign in North Wales, until the first decade of the 14th century, Chester was the head-quarters through which all the men, supplies and materials conscripted from across the country were channelled to the war front. These, of course, included the personnel, both skilled masons and carpenters as well as labourers, who were engaged in building the great series of castles which enabled Edward to hold his conquests. It would not be surprising to find that this great outburst of activity was also reflected in the fabric of Chester. Not only did the demand for supplies and the large numbers of troops and workmen passing through the city give considerable business opportunities to the merchants of Chester, but also the presence of skilled workmen wintering in the city gave them the means to express their wealth in an out burst of new building. The series of sandstone undercrofts, colloquially known as crypts, which survive in many of the buildings on the main streets associated with the Rows, have long been known (Harris 1984, 13–5). Where they can be dated by architectural features, these undercrofts do seem to date to the late 13th century. More recently, work by the author (Fig 9.1, 3) (Ward 1988) and subsequently by the Rows Research Project, which was established by the City Council and County Council to survey and record all the ancient fabric in the Rows buildings, has revealed what a wealth of medieval timber and masonry fabric still survives; in some cases dendrochronology has supported the great Edwardian rebuild date (Brown, Grenville and Turner 1986, 132–4).

As would be expected the religious houses also participated in this activity. St Werburgh's Abbey commenced a major rebuilding of their church, starting with a new Lady Chapel in c 1250. By the 1270s the choir was under construction. They found, however, that King Edward's programme of castle building was a two-edged sword; in 1277 and 1282 the abbot's workmen were impressed for work in Wales. Consequently, the work on the choir seems to have been intermittent and undertaken by several master masons (Madison 1983, 39–41). Only after the turn of the century was the choir completed under the direction of Master Richard the Engineer who had been a major figure in the building of the Welsh castles. He also seems to have been responsible for the construction of the abbey gatehouse.

Elsewhere, there is archaeological evidence for contemporary building work at the Dominican friary. The church at the Chester house was found to have an unusual number of building phases (Fig 9.5). At other excavated examples of Dominican friaries, once the church was completed (a process which might have been achieved in one or two building campaigns), they seem thereafter to have remained relatively unaltered, for example at Oxford (Lambrick and Woods 1976) and Newcastle upon Tyne (Clark 1986, 170–1). At Chester there were apparently five phases, although the last one was overtaken by Dissolution, with the foundations only partly laid. The phase 2 rebuilding can be ascribed to the late 13th century. In that phase a wide aisled nave of seven bays and a walking place was added to the pre-existing aisleless structure which was largely retained to form the choir. A substantial foundation which lay at the west end of the north aisle is of uncertain function. It may have formed a porch or belfry.

It is clear, however, that building work was not confined to the immediate period of wealth and plentiful manpower generated by Edward I's Welsh campaigns, but extended over a much longer period. Dendrochronological dates on secular buildings have shown major reconstructions occurring in *c* the 1240s or 1250s (Ward 1988, 45–9) and the 1320s (Brown, Howes and Turner 1985, 149). The period of prosperity was followed by the Black Death and a period of economic decline and stagnation during the second half of the 14th century and early 15th century. This is most probably a major reason for the survival at least in part of so many medieval buildings of the preceding period in Chester. There was not the need, will nor resource to do much rebuilding for many years. The situation with the religious houses is not so clear cut. The stages by which the Carmelite friars considerably expanded their precinct at this time have been discussed above, and this can be seen as evidence of much reduced demand for land even in the city centre. They also, however, embarked on a major building campaign as is witnessed by gifts of oaks and money from the Black Prince, the then Earl of Chester, in 1353 and 1358 (Bennett 1935, 12–3), no doubt to make full use of their greatly enlarged precinct.

At St Werburgh's Abbey the rebuilding work continued from the choir to the crossing tower and the enlarged south transept during the 1350s and 1360s. Recent study suggests that the nave arcade was also rebuilt at this time (A Thacker *pers. comm.*), but work had probably come to a standstill by the end of the century, in a still very incomplete condition.

Conversely the Dominicans seem to have started rebuilding again around the end of the 14th century (phase 3). The nave was shortened by one bay, elegant octagonal piers were introduced in the arcade, a central crossing tower was built over the walking-place and for the first time decorated floor tiles were used extensively, all of which created a church of typical Dominican plan. The dating of this phase can be defined only generally

to around the beginning of the 15th century by the occurrence of floor tile fragments in the tower foundation.

The building activities of the friars would, therefore, appear to be running counter to the general slowing down and stagnation of activity in the city. Whilst admitting that this impression might be solely due to the incomplete state of the evidence, it is possible that it reflects the friars' continuing popularity and good work during the pestilence. Perhaps they also benefited from the period when plague had removed many potential heirs to local bequests which were in consequence left to the local popular religious institutions. Some support for such a view is perhaps gained from the number of chantries which were established in parish churches and at the nunnery in this period. The abbey seems never to have enjoyed such local popularity. It did, however, apparently have a brief upsurge of activity at the very end of the century when the south transept and tower were completed and the very important choir stalls were made. This was possibly associated with the patronage of Richard II who received much local support (A Thacker, *pers. comm.*). His deposition was associated with a corresponding decline in the city's fortunes.

Only towards the end of the 15th century is there widespread evidence of building activity and this evidence rapidly becomes abundant. New building work in a secular context has been located in both standing buildings, for example, the Old Leche House on Watergate Street (Brown, Grenville and Turner 1986, 122, 138–9) and during excavations. On excavated sites there is consistent evidence for infilling of open areas off secondary streets, a process which manifested itself in various ways. On Princess Street, (Fig 9.1, 2) in an area immediately west of the Market Square and, therefore, presumably of some commercial value, a series of property strips were laid out in the period following the Conquest (Fig 9.6). On the eastern half, a series of strips fronted onto the Market Square and stretched back some 93m parallel to Princess Street, which was known at that time as Parsons Lane. The rather shorter strips which fronted onto Princess Street, therefore, only commenced behind these, *c* 93m west of the junction with the Market Square. In the late medieval period two additional properties fronting onto Princess Street were created by cutting off the rearmost 23m of the five Market Square properties adjoining Princess Street. At 30 Lower Bridge Street (Fig 9.1, 5), excavated in 1974–5 by Dr D J P Mason, a late medieval cellared building was constructed behind the existing street-front building, using the side passage to provide access to the street in the absence of a convenient secondary street. As a final example, a site excavated by the author at the west end of Cuppin Street (Fig 9.1, 9.4) may be cited. Here there was no development for much of the medieval period; a thick cultivation soil attested to a long period of agricultural activity. Only at the very end of the medieval period were relatively extensive properties, occupying a street frontage of *c* 10m, laid out. During the 18th century these properties were further subdivided by cutting them in two. The presumed cause of this rebuilding activity and expansion onto previously open areas is a recovery of the population to its pre-

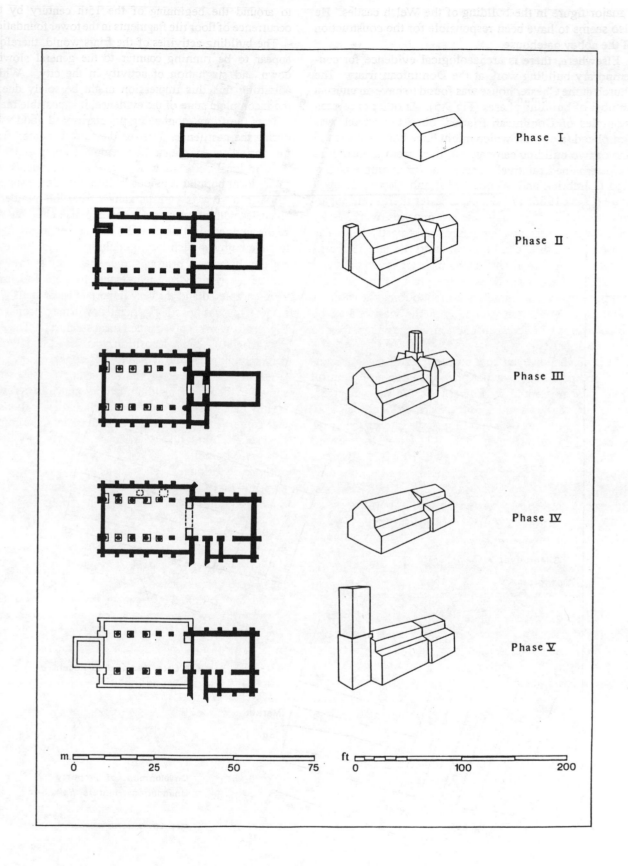

Figure 9.5 Phases of the Dominican Church.

Phase I

Phase II

Phase III

Phase IV

Phase V

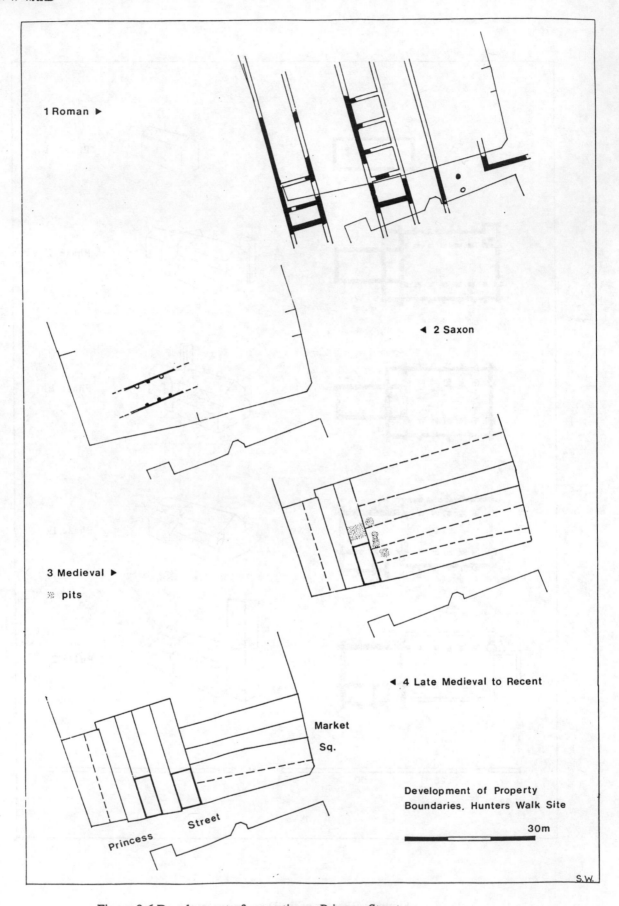

1 Roman ▶

◀ 2 Saxon

3 Medieval ▶

▒ pits

◀ 4 Late Medieval to Recent

Market

Sq.

Development of Property
Boundaries, Hunters Walk Site

30m

Street

Princess

S.W.

Figure 9.6 Development of properties on Princess Street.

plague level and also an economic revival (Platt 1976, 175–6).

This activity is matched by building work at the monastic houses. At St Werburgh's Abbey the list of structures which were rebuilt between the late 15th century and the Dissolution is extensive, including the completion of the nave clerestory, the west front, porch and south-western tower, the upper part of the north transept, the eastern aisle chapels and the cloisters. Consequently only on the eve of the surrender was the major rebuilding campaign, which had commenced with the eastern end in the mid-13th century, brought to a conclusion. The rebuilding bug also hit the friaries, but there rather more interesting developments were incorporated which subtly altered their role in the city. Rebuilding is well attested in the documentary sources at the Franciscan friary where the nave and aisles were newly built in 1528 (Bennett 1921, 28–9). At the Carmelite friary, in 1495 the church was given a western tower with a graceful spire (Bennett 1935, 44). At the Dominican friary, excavation has shown that the church was completely rebuilt in two campaigns, the choir in the 1480s followed by the nave during the 1520s and 1530s (Fig 9.5, phases 4 and 5). This latter work had come to a standstill with the foundations only partly laid in the trenches dug to receive them, before the Dissolution in 1538 halted it forever. Presumably the standstill was caused by lack of funds. The new work was to have included a large western tower which would have been an imposing sight overlooking the city walls and silted estuary immediately to its west. One is led to wonder if there was a certain spirit of rivalry over the Carmelites' new tower and spire. The nature of the Dominicans' church seems to have changed in this period, too. During phase 4, following the 1480s rebuilding of the choir, the nave aisles were increasingly subdivided by either light walls or large tomb structures which turned them into a series of chapels opening off the nave. This gives the impression that the original intention of providing space for teaching and preaching was being replaced by a pastoral, almost parochial role.

In this connection an important aspect of the function of the lesser religious houses in the medieval city was the provision of burial grounds. Anciently only the two original Saxon parish churches, St Werburgh's (which became the abbey) and St John's had the right to bury and they retained this duopoly after the Conquest. By the end of the 13th century, however, the friars had come to agreements which permitted them to bury citizens and strangers, although a proportion of the dues still had to go to the old mother churches. Funerals and their associated memorial masses were an important source of income to the medieval churches, probably of very great importance to the friaries by the 16th century. The friaries with their extensive precincts were well equipped to provide cemeteries. Although by the Reformation virtually all the churches in the city had acquired burial rights, the majority of the parish churches had very cramped and small cemeteries.

At the friaries, in the late Middle Ages, in parallel with the rebuilding programs, there went a gradual erosion of the principal of the secluded precinct, which was probably the result both of their financial difficulties and of the small number of brothers. The most extreme case was the Franciscans who in 1528 permitted the merchants and sailors of Chester to keep their sails, masts and other stores in the nave of the church as they had undertaken its rebuilding and would henceforth pay for its maintenance and repair. In 1538 (admittedly just before the surrender) they let out the western courts and guest lodgings in the western range of the cloister and a building abutting the dorter and infirmary (Bennett 1921, 37–8).

The Black Friars had leased out various orchards, gardens and buildings by the time of the surrender but retained control of the main buildings, the church and cloister (Bennett 1952, 50–1). With their tradition of work in the community, perhaps the intrusion into their precincts was not such a break for the friars as it might have been for other orders.

The spate of redevelopment at the end of the 15th century possibly resulting from the recovery of the population level, and the infilling and expansion of the occupied area, continued after the Dissolution. The population continued to expand and probably doubled during the 16th century. The Dissolution constituted the largest re-distribution of property since the Norman Conquest. Supposedly the passing of all this land into private ownership in a period of demographic burgeoning led to a great increase in property values and, therefore, in building (Platt 1976, 182). Certainly at Chester there survive many fine buildings which can be dated to the second half of the 16th century or the very early 17th century.

The effect of the Dissolution in Chester was considerably mitigated by the foundation of the cathedral. The old abbey precinct passed lock, stock and barrel to the new Dean and Chapter and has largely remained in their hands ever since. The other precincts, however, passed after a short period of uncertainly, into the hands of a small group of families, either wealthy citizenry or local landed gentry. The ownership of an old monastic precinct or a significant portion thereof, enabled these families to build large town houses in relatively extensive grounds. This was a new kind of development in the urban context, forming a significant break with the medieval tradition. Consequently, and in spite of later subdivision, a distinct settlement pattern on the sites of the old precincts is still discernible today.

The Franciscans provide the exception to these developments. In spite of passing into the hands of the Stanley's, a local branch of the family of the Earls of Derby, the site seems to have remained undeveloped. The friary buildings, no doubt becoming increasingly derelict and ruinous, survived until at least the early 17th century when the local antiquary Randle Holme drew a plan of them. Subsequently they disappeared and the site remained open until 1778. At that time the new Linen Hall was erected on the eastern half of the precinct, and the terraces of substantial Georgian town houses on the western (Fig 9.3). Even the place names on the site — Stanley Place and Linen Hall Place — record this period of occupation. The former presence of the Franciscan friary was forgotten and became in the last century the subject of some dispute.

The history of the sites of the other three houses, the nunnery, the Dominicans and the Carmelities, are more typical and show interesting parallels. The buildings of the former religious houses frequently survived for a century or so and the initial redevelopments occurred only on the sites of their outer courts. The Carmelites provide a good example of this. After the Dissolution, the site passed after a short interval to the Dutton family and then in 1583 to the Gamuls, both families being wealthy citizens. In 1592 it was bought by Thomas Egerton, the attorney-general. At this time the ruins of the church with the tower and spire were still standing and are indicated, for example, on Braun's map of Chester of *c* 1580. Egerton demolished the ruins in 1597 in order to build a new mansion. The loss of this tower was recorded by Randle Holme, the 17th century antiquary, in terms which in sentiment at least have a remarkably modern ring: 'It was a great pity that the steeple was put away for it was a grace or ornament to the City to see it. The curious spire steeple might still have stood grace to the City had not private benefit, the devourer of antiquity, pulled it down with the church and erected a house for man's commodity which since hath been of little use so that the City lost so goodly an ornament that times hereafter may more talk of it ...' (Harl, M S S 2125 F. 258, Bennett, 1935, 44).

The pattern of these developments is still visible today (Fig 9.7). Friars House is the site of the Egerton Mansion and occupies the western part of the precinct, presumably corresponding to the outer court of the friary. The area of the precinct which generally corresponds to the block of land bounded by Commonhall Street, Weaver Street and White Friars still only contains five major properties, which is in marked contrast to the much denser, medieval originated occupation on the southern side of White Friars and on the Bridge Street frontage.

The site of the Dominican friary was split into two from the beginning. This in effect continued the pre-Dissolution situation when much of the northern half of the precinct was leased out. In general, these leases continued in operation after the Dissolution. One, made to a certain Ralph Warynne in 1537, was of various gardens and a ruinous old building to the north and east of the church, adjacent to his mansion (Bennett 1952, 50–1). The position of this property corresponds to a building excavated on Nicholas Street Mews in 1988. Originally built in the late 15th century, this building was reconstructed at about the time of the Dissolution to incorporate a fine sandstone fireplace and a garderobe pit, probably associated with a first floor garderobe. The building was eventually demolished in the early 17th century. By which time the northern half of the precinct had descended to the Stanley's, who erected a house at its north-eastern corner, adjacent to Watergate Street.

The southern half of the precinct which contained the church and cloister was leased after the Dissolution to Thomas Smythe and Richard Sneyde. The Smith family, as they became, retained the site for several generations.

Although now much built up and subdivided, the former precinct still retains two 16th-century mansions, Smith's House at the south-western corner (now with a Georgian front and inappropriately known as Grey Friars House) which is thought to overlie the western claustral range and Stanley Palace at the north-eastern corner. Moreover, the central part of the site still retains some property boundaries which run eccentrically in relation to the orientation of the city, but which can be seen to correspond to the orientation of the friars' church which lay closer to a true ecclesiastical east-west line (Fig 9.4).

The nunnery has also had an interesting descent. The site passed to the Brereton family who were local gentry. An early 17th-century plan shows the ruins of the church and cloister and what appears to have been an extensive Elizabethan mansion ranged around the outer courts (Fig 9.2). In 1642 the then holder of the land, Sir William Brereton, was appointed commander of the Parliamentary forces in Cheshire. He was declared a traitor by the King and his house was seized and plundered by the Royalist council and garrison of the city. Thereafter, it seems to have remained in public ownership but was little used until the 19th century. At that time the remains of the nunnery were finally cleared as the Gothic ruins were thought to detract from the newly-built classical facade of the adjacent castle.

In conclusion, therefore, it can be seen that the religious houses of Chester continue to exercise an influence over the development of the city centuries after they were dissolved as institutions. They also provide an interesting counterpoint to the developments in London where the great magnates and courtiers acquired many of the monastic sites (Schofield, this volume). Much the same happened at Chester, but on a very much more provincial scale. The more prosperous citizens and local landed gentry taking the parts of the great and wealthy. I hope this paper has also demonstrated the value of the exploration and study of the religious houses in the understanding of the medieval city. Their number and size in proportion to the city as a whole inevitably means that development within them had a considerable impact on the rest of the settlement. Moreover it can be seen that these houses, especially the lesser ones which were closely tied to local sources of income, provide useful indicators of the general prosperity and activity in the city. This is a specific attribute of the urban monastery and offsets the better state of preservation frequently found on the sites of their rural counterparts.

Future work on the Chester houses is still likely to be prompted by developer threat, which obviously pays scant regard to academic research designs. Large parts of both the Franciscan and Carmelite friary precincts are potential development sites in the foreseeable future. The Dominican precinct is unlikely to see significant development in the near future apart from minor infilling. The nunnery presents the bleakest picture, for it is likely that the police headquarters building erected in 1964 totally obliterated the church and claustral ranges. The outer courts with its post-Dissolution mansion, however, may survive to its north-west. Undoubtedly, the best preserved remains and probably the most significant are

Figure 9.7 Plan of the site of the Carmelite Friary.

those of St Werburgh's Abbey which lie beneath and around the present Cathedral. They, however, are not likely to be disturbed by redevelopment, and so await an as yet unplanned programme of research.

References

Alldridge, N J, 1981, Aspects of the Topography of Early Medieval Chester. *J Chester Archaeol Soc* 64, 5–31.

Bennett, J H E, 1921, The Grey Friars of Chester. *J Chester Archaeol Soc* 24, Pt I, 5–80.

Bennett, J H E, 1935, The White Friars of Chester. *J Chester Archaeol Soc* 31, Pt I, 5–54.

Bennett, J H E, 1952, The Black Friars of Chester. *J Chester Archaeol Soc* 39, 29–58.

Brown, A N, Grenville, J C, and Turner, R C 1986, Watergate Street: an interim report of Chester Rows Research Project. *J Chester Archaeol Soc* 69, 115–146.

Brown, A N, Howes, B, and Turner, R C, 1985, A Medieval Stone Town House in Chester. *J Chester Archaeol Soc* 68, 143–154.

Clark, J, 1986, Medieval Britain and Ireland in 1985. *Medieval Archaeol* 30, 114–198.

Harris, B E, 1984, The Debate on the Rows. *J Chester Archaeol Soc* 67, 7–16.

Kettle, A J, 1980, Religious Houses. In The *Victoria County History of Cheshire* 3, London: Oxford University Press.

Lambrick, G, and Woods, H, 1976, Excavations on the Second Site of the Dominican Priory, Oxford. *Oxoniensia* 41, 168–231.

Madison, J M, 1983, The Choir of Chester Cathedral. *J Chester Archaeol Soc.* 66, 31–46.

Mason, D J P, 1985, *Excavations at Chester: 26–42 Lower Bridge Street 1974–6: The Dark Age and Saxon Periods.* Grosvenor Museum Archaeol Excavation and Survey Reports 3. (Chester) Chester City Council.

McPeake, J C, Bulmer, M, and Rutter, J A, 1980, Excavations in the Garden of No. 1 Abbey Green 1975–77; Interim Report. *J Chester Archaeol Soc* 63, 15–38.

Platt, C, 1976, *The English Medieval town.* London: Secker and Warburg.

Rutland, S M, 1965, St. Mary's Nunnery, Chester, 1964. An Interim Report. *J Chester Archaeol Soc* 52, 27–32.

Ward, S W, 1985, The Rows: the Evidence from Archaeology. *J Chester Archaeol Soc* 67, 37–46.

Ward, S, 1988, *Excavations at Chester, 12 Watergate Street 1985; Roman headquarters building to medieval row.* Grosvenor Musuem Archaeological Excavation and Survey Reports 5. Chester: Chester City Council.

Ward, S W, 1990, *Excavations at Chester: the Lesser medieval religious houses: sites investigated 1964–1981.* Grosvenor Museum Excavation and Survey Reports 6. Chester: Chester City Council.

10 Pottery and glass in the medieval monastery

Stephen Moorhouse

Pottery is the most common type of find which is likely to be made during the excavation of a monastic site; vessel glass is one of the rarest. Together they provide useful comparison for illustrating the problems of using archaeological material in order to understand the site on which it is found. Archaeological finds by themselves rarely proclaim how or for what they were used. For this one must use the resources of other disciplines, in particular the various types of written records. This paper will examine how these diverse strands of information can be deciphered and integrated, and how the results can be used to help bring the monastic house to life.

10.1 Pottery vessels

The form of a medieval pot and marks upon it will sometimes suggest or limit the range of uses to which it may have been put (Moorhouse 1986, 108–12). Documents are by far the most important source for evidence for how and where pots were used. These were never written with the future historian or archaeologist in mind; but when their individual characteristics are appreciated, they can be invaluable. For monastic sites the most important sources are the obedientiary accounts: accounts of income and expenditure which were prepared by each officer with responsibility for running one or more areas of the house's domestic, spiritual or economic life. Those best preserved come from the great Benedictine houses which enjoyed institutional continuity beyond the Dissolution, as at Ely, Peterborough and Durham. Even this did not guarantee survival. Accounts for most officers from Selby, for example, are scattered amongst eight repositories throughout the country (Tillotson 1988, 263–6), while those for Battle Abbey are found even further afield (Hare 1985, 197). Unlike charters, which recorded legal title to property and were therefore kept, accounts were domestic documents, and the need to retain them after the suppression of a house was slight. Hence while the greatest of all British Cistercian houses, Fountains, has bequeathed an extensive chartulary and a large number of charters for its estate, its surviving accounts amount to no more than a handful (Michelmore 1981, xii–xiii, xv–xvii; Wardrop 1987).

The most common type of reference is to the purchase of pots (*ollis*) without any qualification. It cannot be assumed that these were are all of earthenware, for pots of bronze, leather, pewter and wood are commonly referred to, and pot in the vernacular can refer to both a capacity and a form of cart. Earthenware pots are often referred to, but unless they are defined such references are of little help. Of more use are sources which mention earthen pots bought for a specified use, mainly as containers. A wide range of commodities was stored in them. Flour, salt, bread, milk, wine, beer, ale, honey, mustard, sugar, a variety of fats, and mince meat are some of the more common items (Moorhouse 1978, 7; Moorhouse in preparation). Earthenware was also bought for use in a particular room. At Bicester priory in 1412 three earthen pots were purchased for the prior's hall (Blomfield 1882, 169), while at St. Radegund's, Cambridge, in 1449/50, four earthen pots were bought for the lord's hall as containers for ale (Gray 1898, 150). The use of pots can also be inferred when they were purchased by particular monastic officers. Pots bought by the gardener are likely to have been used in one of the many horticultural uses for ceramic vessels (Moorhouse 1990), while those purchased by the Infirmarer are likely to have been for use in the hospital. On some occasions entries were more explicit: an unspecified number of earthen dishes was bought by the launderer at Merton College, Oxford, in 1297 (Highfield 1964, 258). The name given to a ceramic vessel can imply use. Dishes and pitchers are the most common, but occasionally something more specialised occurs, such as the earthen pot called a *spencepot*, probably a butter pot, bought for the lord's refectory at St. Radegund's, Cambridge, in 1450/1, for 1*d* (Gray 1898, 166). Elsewhere uses can be implied for otherwise non-descript earthen pots by their context. At Exeter Cathedral in 1412–13 one earthen pot and two earthern pans were accounted for amongst a large number of items bought for binding and fastening books in the cathedral library (Exeter Cathedral/Dean and Chapter Library/MS 2669, 'necessary costs'); the use of earthen pots and pans is well attested in late medieval size and glue making recipes (e.g. Thompson 1935, 422). The relative size of pots can be implied by successive entries. The Bursar's accounts at Durham in 1377/8 record twelve earthen pots for wine costing 6*d* and twelve earthen pots for ale at 3*s* 9*d* (Fowler 1901, 587). Here the difference in price implies pots of different size or quality. Six earthen pots cost the large sum of 20*d* at Wearmouth in 1412/13 (Raine 1854, 191). Standard earthen pots cost on average $\frac{1}{2}d$ each during the later Middle Ages; such a high unit cost suggests large pots, ones of a high quality or vessels made for a specialised use. Capacity is sometimes mentioned (Moorhouse 1981, 107, 120, n. 7). Posenet and quart occur, but the most common is the earthen pot of a gallon, a pot which could hold a gallon capacity. Eight gallons of earthenware are recorded in a Jarrow inventory of 1416/17 (Raine 1854, 91). Earthenware pots are implied in other ways. Weight is a rare instance. William Morton, Almoner of Peterborough 1448–67, records in his common account book the purchase of green ginger with a pot weighting $1\frac{1}{2}$ lbs, and treacle and a pot weighing $1\frac{3}{4}$ lbs (Mellows 1954, 154). Both were an important medical salve during the Middle Ages. The weight suggests that the pots were not of precious metal, but, on other evidence (Moorhouse 1981, 110, 120, n.9) were almost certainly of pottery.

The relative importance of some earthen pots can be gauged by their inclusion in inventories. Like many wooden vessels and utensils, most earthen pots were of insufficient value or importance to be included. Earthenware pots only tend to creep into inventories if the level of recording was very detailed. An incredibly detailed Wearmouth inventory of 1362 lists at the end of a very full pantry '2 earthen pots' of unspecified use (Raine 1854, 159). The most useful monastic inventories are those produced when the duties of an office were taken over by another person. Pots are occasionally mentioned because of what they contained. In the 'Stock-house for storing hard fish and cheese' at Peterborough Abbey in 1460 there were '3 earthen pots for storing flour' (Myers 1969, 1150). The high quality of some earthen pots can be implied by their presence. Hence in the larder at Finchale in 1411 there was listed 'one earthen pot for serving things' (Raine 1837, c/vii), probably a plate or bowl of imported maiolica. Other references almost certainly are to exotic imported vessels. At Jarrow in 1480 the Storehouse contained *1 payntyd plater* (Raine 1854, 227), while at nearby Wearmouth in an undated inventory made during the period 1501–06, a chamber contained *1 pantyd cupe* (Raine 1854, 228). The presence of pottery vessels in an inventory can reveal their relative importance in a different way. An inventory of the cell of Durham Priory at Lytham, Lancashire, in 1446, records a number of earthen pots in different rooms. The Pantry had four earthen pots, three of which were for honey, one being full; the Brewery contained one crock for fermenting beer and the Brewhouse one crock of salt (Fishwick 1907, 79–80). Pottery is not common from medieval excavations in Lancashire, and excavated deposits contain a higher proportion of pottery from outside the region than is normally found elsewhere in the country. It seems likely, therefore, that pottery vessels in the north-west were valued more highly than elsewhere in the country, and this seems to be reflected in the Lytham inventory.

References to earthenware pots cannot be taken at face value. Their mention at all is a product of the bureaucratic style in a particular house. It is clear that different houses, officers within houses, and even successive officers, could have varying opinions on the amount of detail that should be recorded, and the method of organising and presenting it. Some obedientiary accounts rarely mention earthenware in their expenditure, yet we know it was used in considerable quantities for a variety of purposes. It seems likely that some of the regular items, such as earthen pots, were accounted for within the gross sum given for 'other small or necessary items'. This all-embracing entry is a feature of the Durham accounts. Sometimes entries can be explicit. The sacrist at Ely in 1334/5 recorded an unspecified number of earthen pots costing $\frac{3}{4}d$ bought on different occasions for keeping tallow, salve, grease and verjuice (Chapman 1907, 69). One such reference can make it well worth the effort in methodically searching a run of documents. The published extracts from Durham Priory's accounts contain amongst the purchases of infirmarer in

1397/8 twelve earthen dishes for bloodletting (Fowler 1899, 267), the only such reference known anywhere. It is by accumulating such unique entries that a detailed and vivid picture of the many uses of medieval pottery is being built up (Moorhouse in preparation a).

While monastic references to earthen pots are more numerous and detailed than those found in lay accounts, they can only provide part of the evidence for understanding the uses of the vessels. Unique lay sources, like horticultural, veterinary, medicinal, craft and cooking recipes, are essential for understanding monastic usage (see Appendix 1). Written records relating to the uses of medieval pottery cannot provide a complete picture of how medieval pottery was used. The variability of information between accounts of even successive officers, the merging of duties between officials in some houses, and within the same house as the Middle Ages progressed, makes it unlikely that any statistical work on the types of entries referred to above will have any real meaning. But accounts do provide an important context in which to look at archaeological evidence. Perhaps more importantly they suggest questions which we can ask of excavated finds and can warn against irrelevant interpretation of site material.

10.2 Pottery from excavations

Pottery and the places where it is found can tell us a great deal about how it was used, and provide information which will help the excavator to understand the function and chronology of the site. The traditional role of pottery has been as a medium for dating. In fact, dating is one of pottery's least reliable characteristics. Pottery has an important contribution to make to medieval archaeology, but this lies in other directions (Moorhouse 1986; Moorhouse 1987a; Moorhouse 1990).

One of the most obvious types of evidence is the shape of the pot itself. Some forms may seem to be self evident, such as the bowl, jug, and 'cooking pot', but documents and illustrations show that all three, and particularly the 'cooking pot' were general purpose containers of a wide variety of foodstuffs and other materials. In fact, over one hundred and twenty purpose made shapes were produced (Moorhouse, in preparation b). Some are not obvious, like the fire-cover, an inverted bowl-shaped vessel with holes piercing its top and/or sides, and used to cover the hot embers at night. Their shape, like the more common forms already mentioned, was common to a number of forms which had very different functions, such as fish smoking (White 1984; Moorhouse 1983b).

Evidence left on the surface of the pot can betray much about what it was used for. Distinctive sooting marks, wear marks, residues, suspension marks, secondary holes and other less common features are beginning to tell us much about function, about the regional uses of vessels, and about their use in conjunction with vessels formed of other materials (Moorhouse 1986, 108–12). It is important to realise that such a joint use was common. Pottery cannot therefore be understood by looking at the ceramic objects in isolation. This point is discussed further below.

Pottery has much to tell when it is plotted spatially on a site. The plotting of forms is sometimes helpful. Plotting of all pottery dripping pans from the excavations of the southern ranges at Kirkstall Abbey reveals that the finds are all grouped around the places where they are most likely to have been used: the late medieval Meat Kitchen, the principal Kitchen, and the service quarters of the Infirmary (Fig 10.1). At Mount Grace Priory (North Yorkshire) the ceramic contents of the cell matched very closely the near contemporary recorded possessions of a Carthusian monk (Roebuck and Coppack 1987). More extensive excavations on the Charterhouse at Coventry have revealed that different types of pottery were in use in different parts of the site. Although similar types are found across the site, they occur in very different proportions from the excavated cells and the domestic buildings some distance away, suggesting that the differing proportions reflect considerations of function rather than chronology (Fig 10.2; inf. from I Soden). A feature found mostly on monastic sites, but not restricted to them, is the concentrations of ceramic urinals (Moorhouse 1986, 100–02). These are usually found in groups downstream of a garderobe outlet on the main drain. This occurs south of the surviving garderobe block of guest house at Kirkstall and in the main drain at Melrose Abbey. They are the discards of vessels which were used to separate the liquid and solid human waste in the toilet, the solid going down the drain and the liquid being stored. Urine had may uses during the Middle Ages (eg. Baird 1979; Jones 1937, 555–7), and there was a varied and constant demand for it, including an ingredient in medieval prescriptions, as a solvent in glass illumination and its use as a scouring agent in cloth production. Specific mention of monkish urine in medical and veterinary recipes suggests that it was thought to have special properties! The glass urinal was of a different shape to suit its very different purpose (see below).

The plotting of sherds as excavated is also helpful, but this relies more heavily on the quality of recording surface scatters during excavation. The value of such work on a monastic site is illustrated by the Infirmary at Kirkstall Abbey. Plotting the sherds as excavated confirmed that the interior of the first phase timber building had been floored when in use, that it probably had a pottery packed soakaway around the building, and that a garden existed to the east (Fig 10.3; Moorhouse and Slowikowski, 1987, 103–105).

Of yet more potential is the plotting of sherds from the same vessel. Many applications of this approach have been demonstrated at Sandal Castle (Moorhouse 1983c). The most notable contribution of the technique is in the recognition of the high level of residuality. Contaminated deposits are to be expected on confined sites which have been constantly occupied over a number of centuries. Successive building activity, especially in stone, is a common occurrence on monastic sites, disturbs earlier deposits and redistributes the material both vertically and laterally. In the second phase of the Infirmary at Kirkstall the internal stone arcade pier bases interrupted earlier levels. Examination of the distribution of sherds

of vessels from the first phase shows that where the pier foundations cut through, sherds from first phase vessels had moved upwards. While the first phase material was homogeneous, the second phase material was mostly contaminated (Moorhouse and Slowikowski 1987, 105–06). The clearest evidence for residuality comes from looking at the sherds of each vessel present in each deposit: the numbers of the sherds per vessel, their size and post-depositional abrasion. A combination of such evidence coupled with the evidence from the excavation, can reveal the extent of disturbed deposits. From over 3000 excavated contexts on the Guest House site at Kirkstall only a handful can be shown to have remained undisturbed. Not only can we be more realistic about the associated material, but such information dictates how the finds from those deposits should be published: those of proven reliable associations will be published as found, the remainder will be published as a type series of drawings.

The distribution of sherds from the same vessel can show how material has been moved around on site. The build up of deposits in urban tenements through pit digging and building foundations is well known. The same phenomenon occurs within a monastic precinct. Work at Kirkstall has shown that pottery can have both a local distribution from its original place of deposit and very broad one. Sherds were also scattered right across the precinct, shown here by three of many vessels (Fig 10.4).

Sometimes the limited horizontal distribution of objects can help support the idea that a group is contemporary. In Fig 10.5 the dispersed sherds from a large group of near complete pots is shown from Kirkstall. It is possible that such sherds may help to suggest where the pots had been used and broken, and which archaeological horizons may be contemporary. This could not be demonstrated at Kirkstall because of the incomplete site records, but it was suggested at Sandal Castle (Moorhouse 1983c, 193; 171 fig. 83).

Such observations have many implications. First and foremost they warn us that we have to prove that deposits contain homogeneous material rather than simply assume it.

Apart from domestic uses, pottery was used in many situations around the monastery. Documents show that most of the officers would have had some use of it, whether it be the Infirmarer using bowls for bloodletting, the Scrivener keeping ink, or the Sacrist storing the large quantities of oil which were needed to light the church and the numerous lamps which were kept burning before the altars (Cox 1896; Moorhouse 1987a, 179–82). A combination of evidence shows that even in the most obvious of places, ceramics had a wide range of uses unfamiliar to modern practitioners. The range of earthen pots in the medieval kitchen, and their uses, would be unfamiliar to modern cooks (Moorhouse 1987b). Elsewhere there is an unusual variety of uses for ceramic pots and tiles in the most unlikely of places, such as in the medieval garden (Moorhouse 1991).

Spiritual, ethical and economic differences may have influenced the range of material used in a house. Was

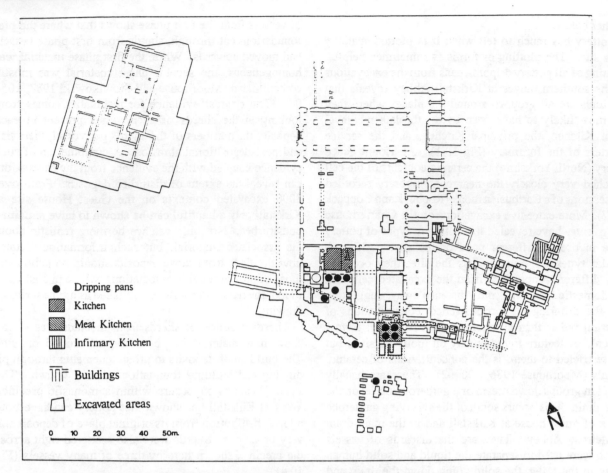

Figure 10.1 Distribution of ceramic dripping pans from excavation of the southern ranges of Kirkstall Abbey, 1950–64. They all come from the areas where they are likely to have been used (Moorhouse and Slowikowski 1987, 198 fig. 63)

there, for example, any difference between the Carthusian monks who ate in their cells, and the other more social orders who ate together in refectories? What effect did the assumed vegetarianism of the Augustininans have on their culinary and tableware as opposed to the meat-eating orders? Did the main urban-based orders such as the friars have a market advantage over the rural Cistercians in acquiring supplies?

It seems likely that there will be additional uses of earthen pots found in nunneries, because of the functioning of the female body. A body of literature on female ailments and diseases was produced during the Middle Ages (Robbins 1966, 402). One cure for ailments of the uterus was to sit the patient on a siege, a three legged stool with a hole in the middle, under which was placed an earthen pot containing coals and herbs (Rowland 1981, 103). Despite contemporary protestations about the value of such a remedy for this and other ailments, the number of times it is found in medical collections shows that it was widely practised (Moorhouse 1983c, 184, 209 n. 125). There were many 'remedies' for encouraging the menstrual flow, some of which involved the use of an earthen pot in the preparation of the prescription, and at least one where the pot had to be buried in the ground for a specified time (eg Dawson 1934, 122–6, nos 313–23). Many of these 'cures' were almost certainly ways of procuring abortions, which were outlawed by the church. That such practices would have been necessary within the nunneries is suggested by nuns having children, and visitation records, which suggest that some nunneries were run on far from purist theological principles.

10.3 Sources of the pottery

The status of a house and its connections within its own estate and beyond can affect the range of pottery found on a site. A wide range of pottery types from the Scottish border to the southern Midlands has been found at Kirkstall (Fig 10.6). It was thought initially that non-local provenance from the Guest House was explained by visitors to the complex. But examination of pottery from guest house excavations elsewhere, such as at Polsoe, near Exeter, and Elstow, Bedfordshire, has shown that this may not be the explanation. Placing the abbey in its medieval setting has probably provided the answer. Kirkstall lay on the major river crossing of an important trans-Pennine route which connected Ciltheroe and Pontefract. The position of the abbey, roughly a third of the way along the route from Pontefract, suggests that it was as a staging post — a medieval Hilton of the Pennines (Fig 10.7; Moorhouse 1983a, 49–50)!

Movement within the monastic estate for administrative and economic reasons was extensive and constant, providing many opportunities for pottery to travel, if only as containers (Moorhouse 1983a). One of many examples

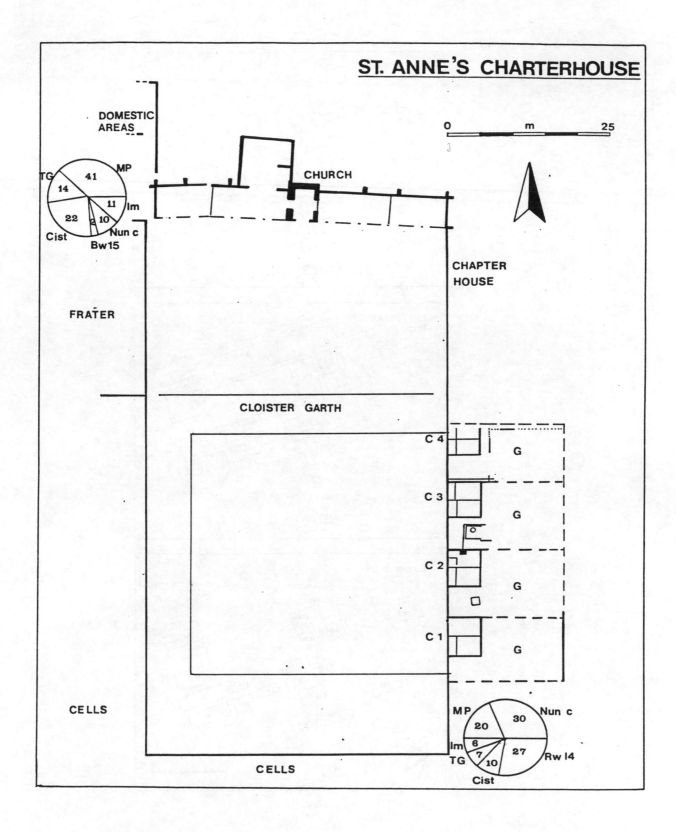

Figure 10.2 Excavations of the church and eastern cell block of the Carthusian house at St. Anne's, Coventry, showing the different proportions of contemporary pottery types from each area, probably reflecting their use for religious and domestic activity respectively.

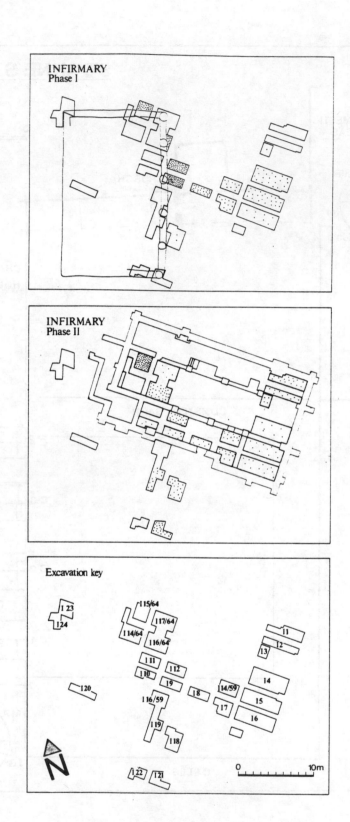

Figure 10.3 Distribution of sherds excavated from the two phases of the infirmary at Kirkstall Abbey (West Yorkshire). The varying concentrations and extent of the material outside the phase 1 building provided additional information about the use of the interior and its surrounding area (Moorhouse and Slowikowski 1987, 104 fig. 59).

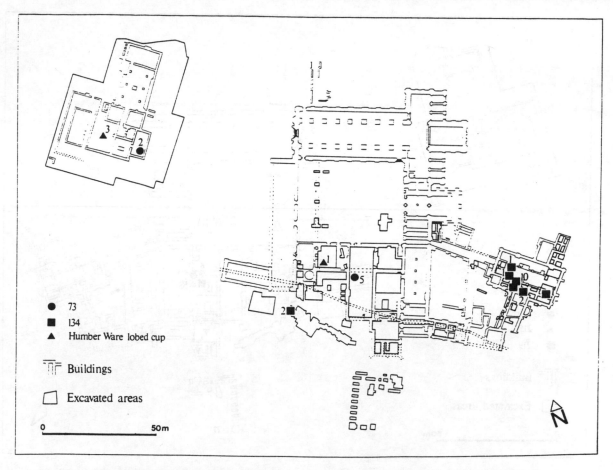

Figure 10.4 Widespread distribution of sherds from the same vessel at Kirkstall Abbey (West Yorkshire), illustrated by three of many vessels, showing their movement around the site caused probably by numerous phases of building activity throughout the site's life (Moorhouse and Slowikowski 1987, 107 fig. 62).

is the movement of milk. Most milk would be processed into white meat at or close to the place of milking. The extensive use of pottery vessels in the medieval dairy in the processing of milk into butter and mainly cheese is discussed below, but pottery was also used to transport milk. The 1416/17 Kitchener's roll for Selby Abbey records 3*d* for the purchase of two earthenware pots for collecting milk from its home grange at Stainer (Haslop 1976, 126; Tillotson 1988, 168). A number of other examples show that pottery vessels were used for moving milk over greater distances. The accounts of the honour of Pickering for 1325/26 record 3*d* for an unspecified number of earthenware pots for collecting milk, while the next entry gives 4*d* to a woman for 'collecting milk throughout the country' (Turton 1897, 226). That such a method was an accepted way of collecting milk is illustrated not only by the sheepfold scene in the Luttrell Psalter, an East Anglian manuscript of *c* 1330–40 (Millar 1932, fol. 163), but also from an unusual literary source. The first shepherds' play in the Townley cycle of Wakefield mystery plays include the story of Moll, her sheep and the broken pitcher of milk (Cawley 1958, 33 lines 152–60). The story has a long ancestry (Gerould 1904), but the version of collecting sheep's milk in earthenware pitchers must have been well known to Yorkshire folk of the mid 15th century, otherwise the allusion would have had little meaning. People who transported the milk

are occasionally recorded by occupational names, such as John le Melkberere, 'a milk bearer or carrier', who occurs in Essex in 1285 (Thuresson 1950, 199), and perhaps through nicknames, such as the two families called Sourmilk who occur in the West Yorkshire townships of Hipperholme and Sowerby by 1307 (Baildon 1906, 85, 86).

Perhaps one of the most constant factors concerning the movement of pottery was the market or fair. Obedientiary accounts show that officers in the larger houses frequently travelled large distances to acquire supplies. Durham monks often used the great southern fairs at Boston and Stourbridge near Cambridge. The more prosperous communities held town houses in important commercial centres many miles from home, mainly as bases for their commercial interests but also as accommodation when visiting markets and fairs. Kirkstall retained an interest in a town house in Pontefract for visits to the fairs there, and Furness Abbey had a similar arrangement in an urban property in Boston (Donkin 1959, 111–12). Apart from the occasional exotic wares which were purchased at such fairs, pots were also used as containers to carry things home, in much the same way as we use paper bags today (Moorhouse 1983a, 55–8). One of the commonest commodities carried was oil. The preference for earthenware as a material for storing oil is well documented (Moorhouse 1981, 115), but it was

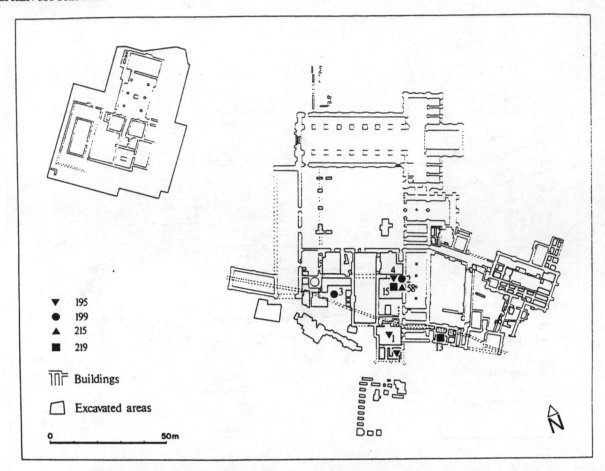

Figure 10.5 Distribution of sherds from an homogeneous group of near complete pots from the
Warming House cistern, Kirkstall Abbey: see text (Moorhouse and Slowikowski
1987, 106 fig. 61).

also bought at the market or fair specifically to carry the oil home. In 1415/16 the Cellerar at Bromholm Priory (Norfolk) bought two types of oil for the kitchen along with two 'pots of stone' to contain it from Yarmouth, twenty miles east along the Norfolk coast (Redstone 1944, 74). In 1450/51 the monks at St. Radegund's, Cambridge, purchased $1\frac{1}{2}$ gallons of rape oil 'with an earthen pot to put it in' at King's Lynn (Gray 1898, 166), thirty miles north of Cambridge.

The large quantity of pottery used on monastic sites that is revealed through excavation is not reflected in monastic documents: a mismatch which is also found on lay estates. The source of pottery is rarely given in documents. A rare instance occurs on Ramsey Abbey's manor of Elton (Cambridgeshire), where we are told not only where but precisely when: the 1307/08 accounts record that amongst the items of the dairy a bowl (gata) was bought on Ascension day at St. Neots (Ratcliffe 1946, 138), an important fair twenty-five miles to the north. Large consignments were bought in for special occasions such as inaugurations and funeral feasts. One of the most monumental of documented medieval feasts occurred when Ralph de Born was inaugurated as Prior of St. Augustines at Canterbury in 1309. The tableware bought in specially for a reputed 6000 people included 1000 earthen pots, 1400 wooden drinking bowls, and 3300 wooden dishes and platters (Fleetwood 1745, 67–71). Gatherings of such a size, in this instance probably

exaggerated, were rare. But visitations, important guests and prospective commercial clients may have made it necessary to buy in for the occasion, or, perhaps more often than is appreciated, to hire (Moorhouse 1981, 110).

The needs for such occasions would vary, as the social demands changed as the Middle Ages progressed. Although the heads of houses and their associates may have used vessels of precious metal or glass throughout much of the Middle Ages, ordinary inmates would have used treen bowls, a form of drinking vessel that was used well into the eighteenth century in some Oxford and London colleges (eg Herbert 1834, 442). By the end of the Middle Ages, pottery cups and ceramic ale stands were being used over much of the country. Thus in the purchases for the Lord Mayor of London's annual feasts for 1505, there are recorded under the heading of 'Ale pots and spigots (tapps)', 720 earthen pottes for wine and ale, 144 pitchers, 24 stenys (in this case stoneware pots), and 800 asshen, or wooden cups (Furnival 1868, 363). Although not monastic, the requirements of this lay feast illustrate the changes wich took place in the tableware dictated by the eating habits of the later Middle Ages. Such changes are evident in the organisation of the pottery industry, in the range and quantities of vessels produced, and in their distribution (Le Patourel 1968, 121–2; Moorhouse 1974, 54–6; Moorhouse 1987c, 184).

Although large quantities of pottery have been ex-

Figure 10.6 Distribution of non-local pottery from excavations at the Guest House, Kirkstall Abbey. It was initially thought that the material was a result of monastic visitors to the Guest House, but it is more likely to be a result of visitors using Kirkstall crossing the Pennines on the monorial route (Fig 10.7). (Moorhouse and Slowikowski 1987, 109 fig. 64).

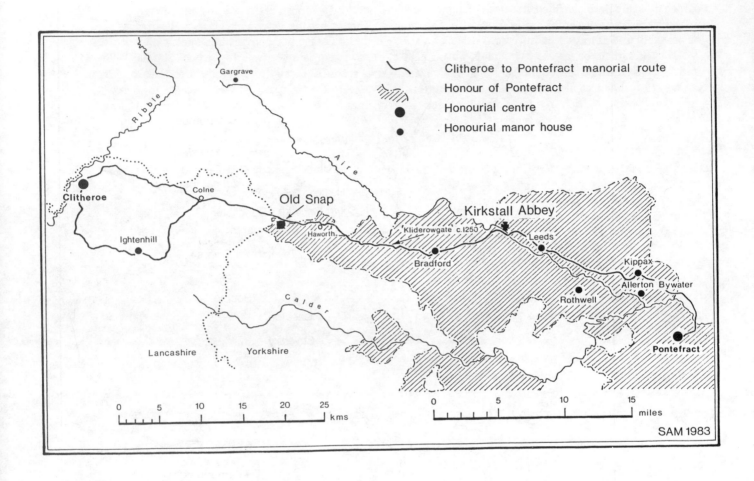

Figure 10.7 Manorial route across the Pennines, connecting the two important Lacy centres of Clitheroe and Pontefract. Kirkstall Abbey was probably one of two staging posts for overnight accommodation, the other being represented by a series of earthwork inn sites along the Old Snap, Stanbury. It is probably the siting of Kirkstall at a convenient position along the route, on the only major river crossing along it, which produced the wide range of non-local pottery from the Guest House excavations, rather than through its normal function (Adapted from Moorhouse 1983, 50 fig. 2).

cavated from monastic sites, no site has been excavated with sufficient completeness to assess the number of vessels used throughout its life. Sandal Castle was substantially excavated within the curtain wall (Mayes and Butler 1983). The site was in intermittent occupation for over 500 years, yet the near-total excavation produced sherds representing only 18,300 vessels, many of which were represented by a few pieces (Moorhouse 1983c). Notwithstanding the excavation of a major rubbish dump which filled the Barbican ditch, it seems evident that much of the rubbish was discarded outside the castle. The same is probably true of most monastic sites.

Quantities may be assessed in other ways. Bulk orders placed direct to potteries are well documented amongst royal and secular landlords, although curiously rare in monastic records. The large quantities recovered from excavations nevertheless suggest that consignments were bought regularly, and probably direct from the potteries rather that the local market. Such quantities are unlikely to have been lost amongst the miscellaneous small expenses, for which the total cost is the only thing recorded. One remote possibility is that pottery was acquired as payment in kind for rent. But Jean Le Patourel has noted only one such payment, at Worcester, about 1187, when six tenants owed the bishop two pots a week, amounting to about 600 pots a year (Le Patourel 1968, 106), and none have been noted in subsequent work. Such payments were nevertheless common amongst other craftsman, especially wood turners. A grant of 1193, again to the monks at Worcester, commutes an annual rent of 200 wooden dishes and 20 bowls to a payment of 2s (Darlington 1968, 133). Such payments might have occurred occasionally, but they were not the norm and could not explain the large quantities of pottery which were required by the larger houses.

The Elton purchase mentioned above illustrates a major difficulty when interpreting distribution maps. Again the evidence comes mainly from secular sources but can almost certainly be applied to monastic ceramic consumption. Documents show that customers did not always use the nearest commercial source, but would often travel many miles for some commodities (Moorhouse 1983a; Dyer 1989). They could deal direct with the supplier and bypass the middle men in the markets, fairs and commercial centres. On the other hand the manufacturer or trader would not always use his nearest outlet. The medieval potters at Toynton All Saints (Lincolnshire) travelled 40 miles south to stockpile their wares for sale at Spalding and Whaplode (Le Patourel 1968, 119). An account of Hereward the Wake infiltrating the Norman forces on the Isle of Ely in the late 11th century shows him taking on the guise of a potter peddling his wares, while the late medieval ballad of Robin Hood and the potter has Robin disguising himself as a potter at Wentbridge (West Yorkshire) and travelling the 60 miles south the sell his pots at Nottingham (Moorhouse 1978, 16). Such allusions would not have been used in the literature had they not been familiar to their audiences. Stall holders even at provincial markets could travel many miles to sell their wares, in much the same way as present-day stall holders move from market to market throughout the week. The origins of stall holders appearing before the market courts at Newmarket (Suffolk) between 1399 and 1413 show that fifteen came from beyond a 30 mile radius, and two from over 80 miles away (May 1981; Fig 10.8).

10.4 Glass

Pottery is robust, resists decay, and survives as rubbish. This is not the case with glass. The fragile nature of the glass and its composition means that it will only survive in damp or waterlogged conditions. Vessel glass is accordingly very rare in most archaeological deposits. Monastic accounts hardly mention glass vessels. The impression from both sources is that glass was rarely used. Yet in reality glass vessels were a common sight around the medieval monastery.

The documentary evidence is meagre. Only occasionally are glass vessels mentioned, and then very generally. A typical entry occurs in the Infirmarer's account at Abingdon in 1334–5, when 10d was paid for an unspecified number of glass vessels (Kirk 1892, 4). Only rarely are we told the vessel form. In 1457–8 the bursar at Fountains recorded 4d for an unspecified number of urinals (Fowler 1918, 50), a vessel form that had a number of very different uses (see below).

No synthesis of medieval English glass forms from excavation has yet appeared, except in a series of specialist papers in excavations reports (eg Charleston 1983; 1984; 1985; Fig 10.9 here). We can learn much more about the relative importance of glass and its uses in the monastery from lay sources, in particular from recipes. Vernacular recipes cover a variety of practical detail, listing the ingredients, the sequence of preparation and, of particular importance for our purposes, the vessels and implements used and their materials. Glass vessels figure prominently in some recipe collections, but occur throughout most (Appendix 1). A number of different forms are mentioned and descriptions given as to how the were used. The recipes, particularly for craft processes, show that glass vessels were deliberately broken to extract their contents after the process had been completed (Appendix 1, nos. 9, 11, 12, 13). The importance of recipes is that they were not written down as pieces of literature, but recorded practical use and experiment. The most common form is the bottle or flask, the 'phial' of the documents (Appendix 1), used either to hold liquids suspended in boiling water, or as a container for keeping medicinal cures. Their frequency in recipes suggests that they were in common use, a probability supported by the observation that the necked flask is one of the most common native forms found.

Most common of all is the high quality imported glass from various centres in Italy and northern Europe. These have been fully discussed by Robert Charleston and Donald Harden in a series of important papers (Charleston 1981; Harden 1972; Harden 1978; all with references). The locally made glass is less well represented, mainly because its composition does not allow it to survive as well as the imported material. The most common English

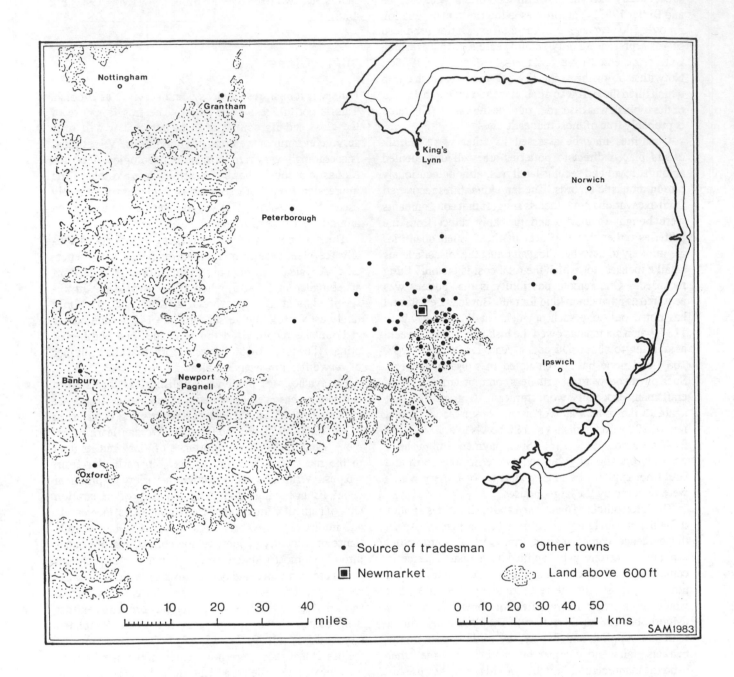

Figure 10.8 Sources of the stall holders fined in the market court at Newmarket (Cambridge-shire), 1399–1413. Apart from customers travelling many miles to particularly important fairs, traders also travelled great distances to sell their wares. A variety of documentary evidence (see text) shows that potters could travel up to 50 miles to sell their products, creating problems for understanding distribution maps (Moorhouse 1983a, 57 fig. 6).

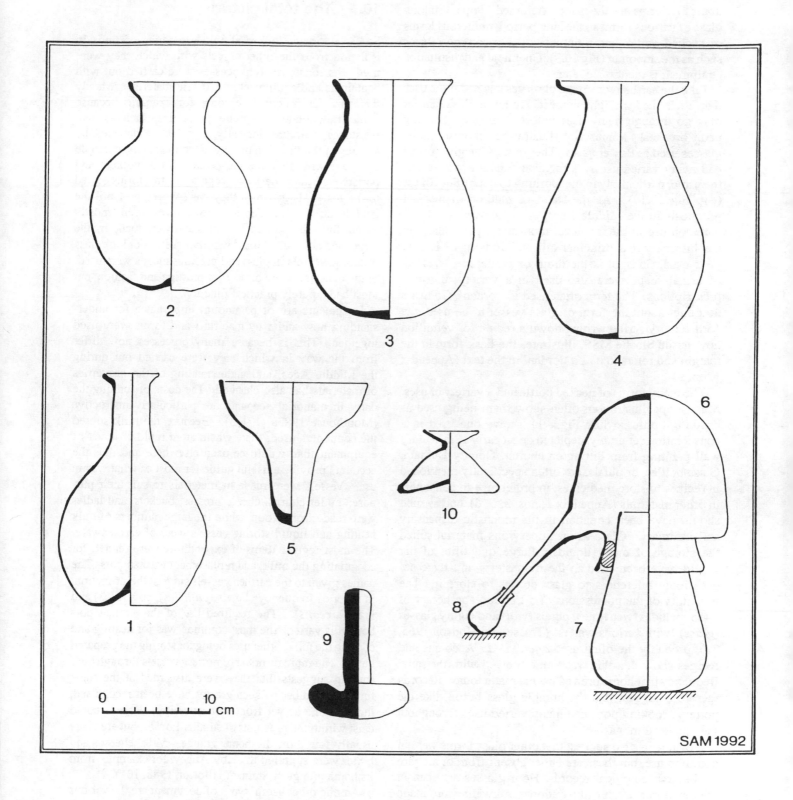

Figure 10.9 Range of English 'forest' glass recovered from excavation. The material does not survive in the ground as well as imported glass because of its composition, and is therefore much less common than the recipes suggest it was in use.

domestic forms are the urinal, stemmed lamps, drinking glass of various forms in the later period, numerous forms of necked bottle, and a number of less common forms such as the smoother (Fig 10.9). Chemical and distillation equipment is mentioned later.

Like the earthenware pots, glass vessels had more uses than their shapes might suggest. Today a glass jam jar may go through many uses before ending up cleaning paint brushes! Manuscript illustrations show drinking glasses used as flower vases. The form of the glass urinal had many varied uses. A medical function was to test the urine, particularly in the morning to determine illness (e.g. Fig 10.10). As the standard method of medical prognosis in the Middle Ages, such items would be in common use in the medieval monastery, particularly in the infirmary and principal officers' lodgings. Hence, their usual findspot is the drain or garderobe. Vessels of urinal shape were also used in a variety of recipe prescriptions. The term often used is 'jordan'. To make no doubt about the form of glass vessel to be used, the 15th century scribe writing down a recipe for vermilion now in the Sloane MSS, illustrates the flask form in the margin and refers to it as a 'jordan' in the text (Appendix 1, no. 9).

The many forms of necked bottle had a variety of uses. Manuscript illustrations often show them being used as drinking bottles, while Fig. 11 shows one used in a consecration ceremony, depicted on an early 12th century wall painting from Pittington church, County Durham. Glass bottles, or phials, are often specifically mentioned in recipes to store medicines, in preference to containers in other materials (Appendix 1, nos. 3, 5, 6), and as such should have been common in the monastic dispensary and infirmary. Glass as an impervious material suited the storage of many liquids. Large quantities of ink would have been used in the monastery, and there are occasional references to glass bottles to store it. The inventory of the possessions of a London apothecary of 1415 includes twenty new phials (*viol*) and eighty glasses (*glass*) 'with various waters' (Trease and Hodson 1965, 79), probably the often used *aqua vitea*. Accounts and recipes show that this was home brewed with the same frequency that home brewed beer is made today. Records therefore suggest that the humble glass bottle, like the pottery 'cooking pot', had many varied uses throughout the medieval monastery.

Documents also suggest that other glass forms were in common use, but these are either absent from or are rare in the archaeological record. Hour-glasses are seen in medieval manuscript illustrations. Inkwells were made from pottery, horn, most metals and glass, and are likely to be found in *scriptoria*. Glass distillation equipment used in a variety of distillation and fermentation processes is looked at in more detail below, but glass stills produced liquids for many other applications, ranging from fragrances of flower oils to medicinal waters (Appendix 1). They should not only be much more common on excavations but should have been used throughout many of the monastic domestic buildings, and particularly workshop ranges.

10.5 The total picture

So far we have looked at two categories of finds in isolation from the other objects with which they were used. As today, many processes were carried out with containers and equipment in different materials. Mostly this was for practical reasons, for example because a material contained special properties, such as heat resistance. Archaeologically, this can be detected by looking at the function of finds in context. One example of many will illustrate the point. Woodworkers and potters each had their own repertoire, the forms suited to the materials in which they were working. Until the later Middle Ages, cup and bowl forms were mostly absent form the potters' products and were made by the turner and other specialised wood workers. For high class drinking, vessels in glass and precious metals were used. Some materials were clearly for prestige and fashion, but most had a purely practical function.

Documents are of paramount importance for understanding how and why materials and forms were used together. This is because many processes now differ from the way in which they were carried out during the Middle Ages, and understanding of the properties of materials has also changed. The costs of running the dairy in manorial accounts are particularly instructive (Moorhouse 1987a, 171–3). Because the milk soured the containers used, there was a more rapid turnover of equipment than would be used elsewhere and thus the accounts provide a useful guide for most of what was in use. Vessels were made in materials to suit their purpose: butter churns, cheese presses, buckets, and ladles were made from wood, while the large numbers of milk heating and liquid storing vessels were of earthenware. The most regular items of expenditure were rennet, for coagulating the milk, and replacement earthen pots. The names given to the earthen vessels suggest their function, in order of frequency: bowls (*pattelies*), pots (*ollis*) and jugs (*urceolis*). The required use of the earthen pots bought is varied: the most common was for heating and cooling the milk, other uses being for storing the prepared butter. The rapid turnover of pottery vessels through their souring suggests that they were discarded at the same time. A number of such groups have been recognised, though none as yet from monastic sites. Dairies could exist within the precincts of smaller houses, but are more usually found on the home grange. Milk, cheese, and butter were supplied to Selby Abbey, for example, from its home grange at Stainer (Tillotson 1988, 101).

Among other useful types of document are the various treatises which describe industrial and craft processes (Thompson 1935). These describe procedures, materials and ingredients; they also give reasons lying behind parts of the processes and some are accompanied by detailed illustrations. These show more clearly than any other kind of evidence the importance of looking at finds as they were used. The most useful are alchemical treatises (Robbins 1966; Robbins 1970a; Robbins 1970b; Robbins 1970c). Commonly they illustrate many shapes which have not yet been found in the archaeological record (Fig 10.10). A number of groups of alchemical pottery

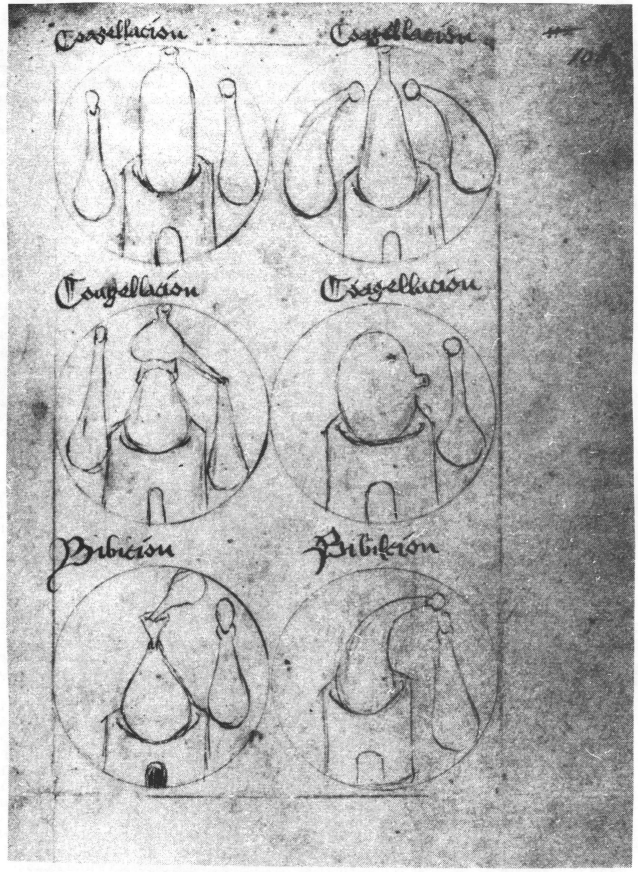

Figure 10.10 One of a number of illustrations from a late medieval chemical treatise showing various glass shapes and how they were used together in various sublimation process. Most of the forms have yet to be recognised in the flesh (BL Harley MS 2407, fol. 108).

and glass have been found, three from monastic sites: Kirkstall Abbey, Pontefract Priory, and Selbourne Abbey, Hampshire (Moorhouse 1972; Moorhouse 1987d). The best evidence for how these groups were used has come from Sandal Castle, where over 150 near complete pottery vessels of different shapes and purposes were found in a workshop clear out deposit, dumped in the Barbican ditch in the late 14th or early 15th century (Moorhouse 1983c, 191–4). The accompanying glass survived very poorly and only the thicker parts of the vessels — rims, bases, handles and alembic spouts — were present.

The way in which the Sandal material was analysed and published provides lessons for the way in which archaeological material could be handled in the light of the documentary evidence elsewhere. The Sandal group was first analysed before the documentary evidence had been looked at. The pots were examined for sooting, wearmarks, residues, incisions and other features. The results were then tabulated against the forms (Moorhouse 1983c, 192 table 13, 193 fig 81). These suggested which vessels had commonly been used together. Despite the large numbers and wide range of the pottery vessels, there were no ceramic alembics common in other similar assemblages. These were found in the glass fragments, along with a number of other forms which were not present in the glass (Moorhouse 1983d). These differences might not have been apparent if, as usually happens, the two materials had been handled by different people. When the documents for chemical and alchemical processes were examined, it was clear that much had been overlooked. The industrial ceramic forms had been separated from the assumed domestic vessels found in the same deposit in the publication. Accounts for the purchase of alchemical equipment and the treatises make it clear that ordinary domestic vessels were used in the processes, and as containers for many ingredients, including urine (Moorhouse 1987d, 367–9). The large groups of 'domestic' vessels and small finds found with the alchemical forms are therefore likely to have been used in the workshop and discarded together when the room or building was cleared out. The risks of making assumptions about functions of pottery and glass are shown by the pottery urinals which remain unpublished from the Pontefract Priory group, because at the time they were thought not to be associated (Moorhouse 1972, 97 fig 28). A bag-shaped vessel peppered with holes is to be seen in a number of illustrations accompanying late medieval treatises (Fig 10.11); an example was found in the Sandal chemical group, but was published along with the domestic pottery (Moorhouse 1983c, 145 fig 37 nos 411–12). Recipes and treatises show that ceramic sand baths were used to hold round-bottomed vessels, usually of glass, the idea being to spread heat more evenly around the glass and prevent breakage through localised exposure to heat. Re-examination of the solid straight-sided pottery bowls from the Sandal group (Moorhouse 1983c, 146 fig 38) showed discoloration around the inside, with many still having sand particles stuck to them. Documents make it clear that glass alembic heads were often used above ceramic bases.

These features are brought together in two 15th-century recipes. In the first, a medical prescription, the reader is told to 'mix them [the ingredients] well together and put them in a distillorie of glass, and lute the head of glass in a pot with sand' (University of Glasgow, Hunterian Library MS91, fol. 176a/b). The second, for 'silver water' given in Appendix 1, no. 13, describes a ceramic mantle of the type found at Lambeth Hill, London (Moorhouse 1972, 118 fig 33 no 13), or of the type found in Exeter (Allan 1984, 157 fig 72 no 1686). The industrial waste from such groups is also important, for some treatises speak of specially shaped ingots being used, of the type found in the Sandal group (Goodall 1983, 238 fig 3 nos 187–9). The use together of vessels and equipment in many different materials is summed up in David Tenier's mid-17th century *The Alchemist's Workshop*. It provides a salutary warning about trying to understand the function of artefacts by looking at them as art historical objects, in isolation from the process to which they contributed.

Appreciation of the need for a total approach is not altogether new. It was perhaps first adopted by Pitt-Rivers in the late 19th century (e.g. Pitt Rivers 1883). More recent developments have been at Penhow Castle, Glamorgan (Wrathmell 1987) and, most spectacularly, on the material from the fill of cellars to houses wich were destroyed by the fire of 25 March 1507 at Pottergate, Norwich (Evans and Carter 1985). No comparable interpretative study of finds from a monastic site has been carried out (but see Moorhouse and Wrathmell 1987).

10.6 Epilogue

This paper has looked at archaeological objects made in two materials and how they can be used to bring to life former processes and activities on the sites from which they come. The distribution of forms and of the sherds from them can provide unique information to assist in interpreting the use of a site as a whole. Monastic accounts provide a fundamental source of information on the range of things used in the monastery, by whom and what for, including many perishable items of wood and leather which are rarely present in the archaeological record.

Peter Sawyer's famous remark that archaeology is an expensive way of showing what we already know (Sawyer 1983, 44) can now be turned on its head: documentary work can provide the skeleton, for which the detailed covering and features can be supplied by archaeology. This is perhaps one of the most important roles that findswork can play; but it has to be interdisciplinary and the objects have to be seen as they were used then, and not implied from recent tradition or enthographic parallels (Moorhouse, in preparation c). Our concept of 'use' must centre less upon the individual object, and instead should embrace the *total assemblage*: that is, items, possibly in different materials, which were employed interdependently.

Examples of the successful application of this principle include the presentation at the Jorvik Centre in York, and Pottergate report from Norwich, which is a model of what can be achieved (Evans and Carter 1985). Finds monographs which are now beginning to follow from the

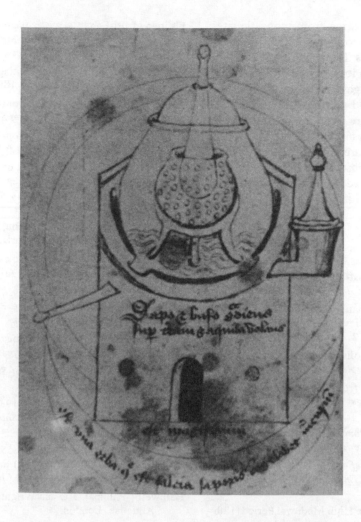

Figure 10.11 One of a number of illustrations from the same late medieval chemical treatise as Fig 10.10, showing a unit of vessels in glass, pottery and probably various metals, including the bag shaped vessel with many holes, a type found in the Sandal Castle group; see text (BL Harley MS 2407, fol. 106r).

work of the Department of Urban Archaeology in London are impressive (Cowgill, de Neergaard and Griffiths 1987; Grew and de Neergaard 1988).

Elsewhere, the picture is often less encouraging. The emergence of separate study groups for pottery, glass, small finds, tiles and bricks has tended to fragment rather than to unify. The study of different classes of material is now developing along different lines. Thus, while small finds and glass studies have been concerned mainly with function, work on ceramics has concentrated on dating the material and determining its source. Such aims are admirable, but are mostly unachievable with the analytical techniques that are currently in use.

Ceramic studies have developed little since the 1960s, with preoccupation on sherd counting, weighing material and describing often irrelevant clay sources, made seemingly respectable and up to date by a glossy veneer of computers and often meaningless statistics. This stagnation has many causes, but project funding must take the brunt, the newcomers to the subject re-inventing wheels which mainly turn out to have varying polygonal sides. Those working in the subject have failed to capitalise on the developments made in the 1970s, the kinds of approaches discussed in this paper, and lessons which

had been learnt before the creation of archaic systems which are now fossilised in most of our major units. The position will not alter until those working on the material ask the same set and sequence of questions, use the same vocabulary. Hence follow the same procedures, and work to the current knowledge of the subject. Work at Kirkstall has dominated this paper because similar work on other monastic sites was hard to find. The most sensible step forward is to establish permanent regional centres staffed by experienced people who can quickly assess all material from a site and carry out the appropriate level of analysis efficiently and to the highest standards, so that the experience gained can be used to good advantage and built upon, and work is not unnecessarily repeated from site to site. An initial step would be a small steering group made up of people from all aspects of finds work to put on paper many of the developing interpretative ideas which are now being practised. It is to be hoped that this will lead to finds being made to work for the often inordinate sums of money expended in excavating them from the ground.

Acknowledgements

I am grateful to the editors for refining a less than perfect text prepared during a long period of illness. The following institutions readily gave permission to produce illustrations: Curators of the Bodleian Library, Oxford, for Fig 10.10; the Yorkshire Archaeological Society for Fig 10.11. Fig 10.2 was prepared by Ian Soden, the remaning line drawings are by the writer. Finally, Dr Margaret Faull kindly edited the Middle English texts in Appendix 1 and saved the writer from several embarrassments!

References

Allan, J P, 1984, Medieval and Post-Medieval Finds from Exeter 1971–1980. *Exeter Archaeological Reports*: Volume 3.

Baird, J L, 1979, The Physician's 'urynals and jurdones': urine and uroscopy in medieval medicine and literature', *Fifteenth-Century Studies*, **2**, 1–8.

Baildon, W P (ed), 1906, Court Rolls of the Manor of Wakefield; II, 1297 to 1309. *Yorkshire Archaeol Soc Rec Ser.* **36**.

Bickley, F (ed), 1928, *Report of the Manuscripts of the late Reginald Rawden Hastings*: I. Historical Manuscripts Commission, 78.

Blomefield, J C, 1882, *The History of the Present Deanery of Bicester, Oxon: Part 2, The History of Bicester.*

Cawley, A C (ed), 1958, *The Wakefield Pageants in the Towneley Cycle, Old and Middle English Texts.* Manchester Universty Press.

Charleston, R J, 1981 Glass of the High Medieval Period (12th–15th century), *Bulletin of the International Association for the History of Glass*, **8**, 65–76.

Charleston, R J, 1983, Vessel glass. In A Streeten, Bayham Abbey: Recent Research including the Report on Excavations (1973–76) Directed by the Late Helen Sutermeister. *Sussex Archaeol Soc Monog* **2**, 112–16.

Charleston, R J, 1984, The Glass. In Allan 1984, 258–62.

Charleston, R J, 1985, Vessel glass. In Hare 1985, 139–46.

Chapman, F R (ed), 1907, *Sacrist Rolls of Ely (1291–1360)*, 2 volumes. Cambridge.

J Cowgill, M de Neergaard and N Griffiths, 1987 *Medieval Finds from London: 1. Knives and Scabbards*, Museum of London.

Cox, J C, 1986, The lights of a medieval church, In W Andrews (ed), *Curious Church Gleanings*. London, 36–64.

Darlington, R R (ed), 1968, *The Chartulary of Worcester Cathedral Priory*. Pipe Roll Society, 76 for 1962–63.

Dawson, W R, 1934, *A Leechbook of the Fifteenth Century.* London.

Donkin, R A, 1959, The urban property of the Cistercians in medieval England, *Analecta Sacri Ordinis Cisterciensis*, **15**, 104–31.

Dyer, C C, 1989, The consumer and the market in the later Middle Ages, *Economic History Review*, second series **42**, 305–27.

Evans, D H and Carger, A, 1985, Excavations on 31–51 Pottergate (Site 149N). In M Atkin, A Carter and D H Evans, Excavations in Norwich 1971–1978 Part II. *East Anglian Archaeology*, Report No. 26, 9–86.

Fishwick, H, 1907, The History of the Parish of Lytham in the County of Lancaster, *Cheetham Soc* new series **60**.

Fleetwood, Bishop, 1745, *Chronicon Preciosum: or An Account of English Gold and Silver Money, The Price of Corn and Other Commodities* .... London.

Fowler, J T, 1892, Mural painting in Pittington Church, *Yorkshire Archaeol J*, **12** for 1891, 38–41.

Fowler, J T (ed), 1899, Extracts from the Account Rolls of the Abbey of Durham: II, *Surtees Soc*, **100**.

Fowler, J T (ed), 1901, Extracts from the Account Rolls of the Abbey of Durham: III, *Surtees Soc*, **103**.

Fowler, J T (ed), 1918, Memorials of the Abbey of St Mary of Fountains. Vol. III consisting of Bursar's Books 1456–1459 and Memorandum Book of Thomas Swynton 1446–1458, *Surtees Soc*, **130**.

Furnivall, F J (ed), 1868, Early English Meals and Manners, *Early English Text Society*, original series **32**.

Furnivall, F J (ed), 1889, The Book of Quinte Essence or the Fifth Being, *Early English Text Society*, original series **16**, revised edition.

Gerould, G H, 1904, Moll of the Prima Pastorum, *Modern Language Notes*, **19**, 225–30.

Goodall, A R, 1983, Non-ferrous metal objects (except military finds, spurs and pins). In Mayes and Butler 1983, 231–39.

Gray, A (ed), 1898, *The Priory of St Radegund, Cambridge.* Cambridge Antiq Soc.

Grew, F and de Neergaard, M, 1988, *Medieval Finds from Excavations in London: 2. Shoes and Pattens*, Museum of London.

Halliwell [-Phillips], J O (ed), 1855, The craft of lymnynge bokys. In J O Halliwell (ed) Early English Miscellanies in Prose and Verse, *Wharton Club*, **2**, 72–91.

Halliwell [-Phillips], J O and Wright, T (ed), 1845, Religious Antiquae. London.

Harden, D B, 1972, Ancient Glass, III: Post-Roman, *Archaeol J*, **128** for 1971, 78–117.

Harden, D B, 1978, Anglo-Saxon and later medieval glass in Britain: some recent developments, *Medieval Archaeol*, **22**, 1–24.

Hare, J N, 1985, *Battle Abbey: The Eastern Range and the Excavations of 1978–80.* Historic Buildings and Monuments Commission Archaeological Report No. 2.

Haslop, G S (ed), 1976, A Selby Kitchener's roll of the early fifteenth century [1415–16], *Yorkshire Archaeol J*, **48**, 119–33.

Heinrich, F (ed), 1896, *Ein Mittelenglisches Medizinbuch.* Halle.

Herbert, W, 1834, *The History of the Twelve Great Livery Companies of London*: I London.

Highfield, J R (ed), 1964, *The Early Rolls of Merton College, Oxford*, Oxford Hist Soc, new series 18.

Jones, I B, 1937, Popular medical knowledge in fourteenth-century English literature: part II, *Bulletin for the Institute of the History of Medicine*, **5**, 538–88.

Kirk, R E G (ed), 1892, *Accounts of the Obedientiaries of Abingdon Abbey*, Publications of the Camden Society, 51.

Le Patourel, H E J, 1969, Documentary evidence for the medieval pottery industry, *Medieval Archaeol*, **12** for 1968, 101–26.

May, P, 1981, Newmarket and its market court, 1399–1413, *Proc Suffolk Inst Archaeol*, **35**, 31–40.

Mayes, P and Butler, L A S, 1983, *Sandal Castle Excavations 1964–1973.* Wakefield.

Mellows, W T (ed), 1954, The Book of William Morton, Almoner of Peterborough Monastery, 1448–1467, *Northamptonshiore Rec Soc*, **16**.

Michelmore, D J H (ed), The Fountains Abbey Lease Book, *Yorkshire Archaeol Soc Rec Ser*, **140**.

Millar, E G, 1932, The Luttrell Psalter ... from the Add. Ms. 4213, British Museum. London.

Moorhouse, S, 1972, Medieval distilling apparatus of glass and pottery, *Medieval Archaeol.* **16**, 79–122.

Moorhouse, S, 1974, A distinctive type of late medieval pottery in the eastern Midlands: a definition and preliminary statement, *Proc Cambridge Antiq Soc.*, **65**, 46–59.

Moorhouse, S, 1978, Documentary evidence for the uses of medieval pottery: an interim statement, *Medieval Ceramics*, **2**, 3–22.

Moorhouse, S, 1981, The medieval pottery industry and its markets. In D W Crossley (ed) *Medieval Industry*. CBA Research Report 40, 96–125.

Moorhouse, S, 1983a, Documentary evidence and its potential for understanding the inland movement of medieval pottery, *Medieval Ceramics*, 7, 45–88.

Moorhouse, S, 1983b, A semi-circular firecover from the Tyler Hill kilns, Canterbury, *Medieval Ceramics*, **8**, 101–07.

Moorhouse, S, 1983c, The medieval pottery. In Mayes and Butler 1983, 83–212.

Moorhouse, S, 1983d, The vessel glass. In Mayes and Butler 1983, 225–30.

Moorhouse, S, 1986, Non-dating uses of medieval pottery, *Medieval Ceramics*, **10**, 85–123.

Moorhouse, S, 1987a, The site distribution of pottery as evidence of function: a discussion and some case studies, in Vyner and Wrathmell 1987, 161–88.

Moorhouse, S, 1987b, Pottery vessels in the medieval kitchen. In S Moorhouse (ed), The Medieval Kitchen and its Equipment. Leeds, 21–28.

Moorhouse, S, 1987c, The composition and development of medieval potting tenements in the British Isles. In J Chapelot, H Galinié and J Pilet-Lemière (ed), *La Ceramique (Ve-XIXe S), Fabrication, commercialisation, utilisation.* Paris, 179–93.

Moorhouse, S, 1987d, Medieval industrial glassware in the British Isles, Annales du 10e Congrès de l'Association Internationale pour l'Historie du Verre. Amsterdam, 361–72.

Moorhouse, S, 1988, Documentary evidence for medieval ceramic roofing materials and its archaeological implications: some thoughts, *Medieval Ceramics*, **12**, 33–55.

Moorhouse, S, 1989, Monastic estates: their composition and development. In R Gilchrist and H Mytum (ed), *The Archaeology of Rural Monastries*, BAR British Series 203, 29–81.

Moorhouse, S, 1991, Ceramics in the medieval garden. In A E Brown (ed) *Garden Archaeology*, CBA Research Report 78, 100–17.

Moorhouse, S, in preparation a, Documentary evidence for the uses of medieval ceramics and its archaeological implications, PhD thesis.

Moorhouse, S, in preparation b, Defining Medieval Pottery: A Manual and Glossary of Terms for Ceramic Users.

Moorhouse, S, in preparation c, The Evidence from Documents for the Uses of Medieval Objects.

Moorhouse, S and Slowikowski, A M, 1987, The pottery, in Moorhouse and Wrathmell 1987, 59–116.

Moorhouse, S and Wrathmell, S, 1987, Kirkstall Abbey Volume 1: The 1950–64 Excavations; A Reassessment, Yorkshire Archaeology 1. Wakefield.

Müller, G (ed), 1929, *Aus Mittelenglischen Medizintexten: Die Prosarezepte des Stockholmer Miszellankodex X.90.* Kölner Anglistische Arbeiten. Leipzig.

Myres, A R, 1969, *English Historical Documents* IV: 1327–1484. London.

Pitt-Rivers, A H L F, 1883, Excavations at Ceasar's Camp near Folkstone, conducted in June and July, 1878, Archaeologia, 47, 429–65.

Power, D (ed), 1910, 'Treatises of Fistulo in Ano, Haemorrhoids and Clysters' by John Arderne, *Early English Text Society*, original series **139**.

Raine, J (ed), 1837, The Priory of Finchale. The Charters of Endowment, Inventories and Account Rolls, of the Priory of Finchale, in the County of Durham. *Surtees Society* [6].

Raine, J (ed), 1854, The Inventories and Account Rolls of the Benedictine Houses or Cells of Jarrow and Monk-Wearmouth, in the County of Durham. *Surtees Society* 29.

Ratcliffe, S C (ed), 1946, Elton Manorial Records 1297–1351, *Roxburgh Club* **208**.

Redstone, L J (ed), 1944, The cellarer's account for Bromholm Priory, Norfolk, 1415–15, *Norfolk Record Series*, **17**, 47–91.

Roebuck, J and Coppack, G, 1987, A closely dated group of late medieval pottery from Mount Gract Priory, *Medieval Ceramics*, **11**, 15–24.

Rowland, B, 1981, *Medieval Woman's Guide to Health: The First English Gynecological Handbook.* London.

Robbins, R H, 1966, Alchemical texts in Middle English verse: corridenda and addenda, *Ambix*, **13**, 62–73.

Robbins, R H, 1970a, Medical manuscripts in Middle English, *Speculum*, **45**, 393–415.

Robbins, R H, 1970b, A note in the Singer survey of medical manuscripts in the British Isles, *Chaucer Review*, **4**, 66–70.

Robbins, R H, 1970c, Signs of death in Middle English, Medieval Studies, 32, 282–98.

Sawyer, P, 1983, English archaeology before the Conquest: a historian's view. In D A Hinton (ed), *25 Years of Medieval Archaeology.* Sheffield, 44–47.

Smith, C S and Hawthorne, J G (ed), Mappae Clavicula: A Little Key to the World of Medieval Techniques, *Transactions of the American Philosophical Society*, **64**. Philadelphia.

Thompson, D V, 1935, Trial index of some unpublished sources for the history of medieval craftsmanship, *Speculum*, **10**, 410–31.

Thuresson, B, 1950, Middle English Occupation Terms, *Lund Studies in English*, **19**. Lund.

Tillotson, J H (ed), *Monastery and Society in the Later Middle Ages: Selected Account Rolls from Selby Abbey, Yorkshire, 1398–1537.* Woodbridge, Suffolk.

Trease, G E and Hodson, J H (ed), 1965, The inventory of John Hexham, a fifteenth century apothecary, *Medical History*, **9**, 76–81.

Turton, R B (ed), 1897, The Honour and Forest of Pickering, North Riding Record Series, 4.

Vyner, B and Wrathmell, S (ed), 1987, *Studies in Medieval and Later Pottery in Wales Presented to J M Lewis.* Cardiff.

Wardrop, J, 1987, Fountains Abbey and its Benefactors 1132–1300, *Cistercian Studies* **91**. Kalamazoo.

White, A J, 1984, Medieval fisheries in the Witham and its tributaries, *Lincolnshire History and Archaeology*, 19, 29–35.

Wrathmell, S, 1986, Observations on artefacts in ditch deposits. In Vyner and Wrathmell 1987, 189–99.

Wright, T (ed), 1844, Early English artistical receipts, *Archaeological Journal*, 1, 64–66.

Appendix 1

Vessel Glass in medieval recipes

The following thirteen recipes, translated from the original Middle English (except no. 8, from Latin) have been chosen to illustrate the various uses of vessel glass during the Middle Ages. Most of the recipes are the result of practical experience and the vessel material is specifically mentioned because of its assumed special properties. The frequent and often casual mention of vessel glass suggests that it was much more common than is suggested in other documentary sources, such as account rolls. It is likely to have been native potash glass and, because of its composition, is probably why, comparatively, so little of it survives in archaeological deposits. These and many other recipes show clearly how medieval man used his every day objects, which were often very different to their modern day counterparts (Moorhouse, in preparation c). They also stress the importance of looking at archaeological objects in context, rather then treating them as art historical pieces, an unconscious recent approach inherent in the way many artefact types are now studied and published.

Oil Preparations

1. Oil of Benedict

Take dry tile stones that have never touched water, well laid and new, and break them into small pieces, but not too small, and heat them in the fire until they become glowing red. Then quench them in olive oil or in laurel oil, but laurel oil is better. Then heat them again and quench them in the same manner till they become black. Then take a pot of earth that is big enough, or else one of glass, and put therein the tiles and oil, if there is any left, and make sure that the oil covers the tile sherds and is a fingerbreadth depth above them. Afterwards take spikenard, rue and castor and alecost that is called *menta greca*, and if you have no spikenard put in more of the *menta greca* as much as castor or of spikenard or of rue. All these should be ground and mixed with the tile sherds in the pot. The pot should be kept sealed for eleven days and for all that time it should be standing in horsedung. After that put it into a vessel and distil it. That which is distilled is called Oil of Benedict.

From a mid-15th century collection of Middle-English medical recipes and instructions, or 'leechbook', Müller 1929, 88–9.

2. Oil of roses

Another manner of making [oil of roses], and more cold. Shred your roses and put them into a vessel of glass with your oil, and stop it well. Hang it into a vessel with water up to the neck during two months, and every day stir it once and stop it again. After that strain it and throw away the rose petals (groundes). And this is more cold that the other [previous recipe].

From John Arderne's treatise on piles, haemorrhoids and clysters, issued in 1376, Power 1910, 92–3.

Medical Remedies

3. To make a man sleep that he may be treated or operated upon

Take three spoonfuls of the gall of a swine, three spoonfuls of the juice of hemlock root, three spoonfuls of vinegar and mix them all together. And then put them in a vessel of glass to hold to the sick men that you will treat or operate on, and take thereof a spoonful and put it to a gallon of wine or ale. If you want to make it strong, put two spoonfuls to it and give it him to drink and he shall sleep soon. Then you may treat him or operate on him as you will.

From a mid-15th century compilation, from various sources, of a general-purpose 'leechbook', Dawson 1934, p. 262, no. 852.

4. A medicine for the gout and ache that swells

Take a quart of olive oil and a quart of the juice of the berries of the woodbine of the kind of woodbine where the leaves are not serrated but like a man's heart. Gather these berries between the two feasts of Our Lady, and put the juices together into a double glass and shake them well together. Then set it in a pit a yard within the earth and let it be open, save for laying a board upon the glass [to keep off] the rain. Let it stand in the earth nine days and nine nights, the tenth day take it up and it will last twelve months.

Mid-15th century compilation, from various sources, of a general purpose 'leechbook', Dawson 1934, 310, no. 1022.

5. Water for the eyes

Take eight parts of fennel scales and one part of nettles and dry them in the sun and burn them all together and make fine ashes for them. Then take a quantity of fennel seed and grind it with the ashes. Then take the white of an egg, three parts of old ale, or red wine, and mix it well together until it passes through the eye [of a needle] and cast it onto the ashes. Make lye of it but strain it through a cloth two or three times, as barbers make lye. Make sure that you have two or three glass phials, or as many as you have water for. Then fill each [phial] half full of that lye, and no more. Then take flint stones or other stones, but not large stones, and lay them in a hot fire and make them very hot. Then take them out and set the phials with the water on the stones, as hot as they may be, but make sure that the phials are well sealed so that no air comes out. If any phial begins to curdle, unstop it, and if it does not curdle, leave it sealed. Heat the stone three times and always set them [the phials] on. When it is cold, put out the water into other phials and let them stand for three months, before you use it for any medical purpose. And this is the best water to make eyes clear.

From a mid-15th century collection of Middle-English medical recipes and instructions, or 'leechbook', Heinrich 1896, 217–18.

6. For the gout

Take leaves of henbane on Midsummer eve, and bruise them a little. Fill a great pot to the rim, and drill [holes in] the pot bottom, and cover it above with a tile stone. Make a hole deep in the earth under the hearthstone, and put the pot in. Set a little lead [pot] under the pot bottom to collect the oil that comes from the henbane through the pot. Fill up the hole all about the pot with earth and lay again the hearthstone. Make sure that you make your fire there on all the twelve months. Then take up what you find in the lead, and do it up securely in a vessel of glass. This oil is wonderfully good for the gout and for festering sores, and many other evils. If it is often painful anoint yourself with it by the fire. If you do not have this oil, then take oil that is made of the seed of henbane, or that which is made with other seeds, and anoint the gout with it.

From a 14th century Middle-English collection of medical recipes Halliwell and Wright 1845, p. 55.

7. General Purpose Female Remedy

... or else take 18 ounces of water of roses, 2 drachms of mastic, 1 ounce and 1 scruple of galingale, 1 drachm each of mace, cucumber, spikenard and cinnamon. Have them powdered and put all of them into a glass pot (*pot of glasse*). Stop it and let it boil in water for an hour. This water, if drunk, is good for all kinds of illness of the heart due to cold, heart attack, fainting, and for the flux caused by the cold.

From a 15th-century Middle-English treatise on female illness and hygiene, Rowland 1981, p. 82.

Colours

8. How to make vermilion: 12th century

If you wish to make vermilion, take a glass flask and coat the outside with clay. Then take one part by weight of quicksilver and two of white or yellow sulphur and set the flask on three or four stones. Surround the flask with charcoal fire, but a very slow one, and then cover the flask with a tiny tile. When you see that the smoke coming out of the mouth of the flask is straw-coloured, cover it; and when yellow smoke comes out, cover it again; and when you see red smoke, like vermilion, coming out, then take away the fire, and you have excellent vermilion in the flask.

A 12th-century recipe in a 12th-century compilation of craft recipes based on the much earlier *Mappae Clavicula*, which survives in its earliest form in an early-ninth century copy. Smith and Hawthorne 1974, p. 26 ch i.

9. How to make vermilion: 15th century

Take a pound a quick silver [mercury] and five pounds of live brimstone and put them in an earthen pot with a wide mouth, so that you can see right to the bottom. Make sure that you have a lid of wood tightly sealing the mouth of the pot. Then set the pot upon a few coals, constantly looking into the pot and stirring it. When you see a flash of fire fly out of the pot, immediately hold down the lid, and hold down the flash of light two or three times until the substance in the pot turns black enough, for then the quick silver is transformed. Then take it off the fire and grind the contents well on a stone. Then make a good coal fire. Take a good thick jordan of glass and good quality clay and horse-dung and make a good sealing mixture from it. Then daub the jordan all over half-an-inch thick, place all the ingredients in the jordan, and hang it over the fire by the neck so that the glass is almost a hands breadth from the coals. Take another glass jordan whose mouth is almost as large as the other, and set the mouth of this little glass against that of the hanging glass, with the bottom upwards. When you see the light of the ingredients streaming upwards into the upper glass, start with a slow fire, and then a good fire, always blowing it, all the while stirring the bottom of the jordan with a small rod of iron to make the heat rise out of the ingredients. Then you shall see many different colours of light rise into the upper glass, and when you see blood red, then the vermilion is made. Break the jordan and see what you find inside. Make sure that the jordan is not on the fire once the light begins to turn red, for if it is, all is lost. Make sure that the day on which you make it you are not fasting, for you will have wicked smelling breath, therefore eat a small amount and drink. Another thing, make sure that the initial fire is evenly distributed.

Early 15th-century, from British Library, Sloane 73, fo. 138v,

abstract in Wright 1844, 152–3. To make no doubt as to the form of vessel to be used, the scribe has drawn a vessel of glass urinal shape in the left-hand margin, a not uncommon example of the practical nature of many of the surviving recipes of all types.

Alchemy

10. Making quintessence

And another way of making quintessence is this. Take the noblest and strongest burning water that you have distilled out of pure mighty wine, and put it into a glass called an amphora, with a long neck and seal the mouth strongly with wax. Make sure that it is a half or a third full, and bury it all in horsedung, so that the neck of the glass is turned downward and the bottom is turned upward, so that by virtue of the horsedung, the quintessence rises up to the bottom, and the impurities descend down into the neck. After many days, when you take it out, gently lift up the glass as it stands and you shall see in thickness and clearness a difference between the distilled quintessence and the impurities in the neck... Take a sharp pointel, or a prick of iron, and pierce it into the wax that is in the mouth of the glass against the earth, and when you have pierced it fully into the water, take out the pointel or the prick. The earthly water will first come out of the neck, so that all [that is] left is the quitessence. When you see that the quintessence will run and melt after the earthly water has been removed, swiftly put your finger over the whole and turn the glass upright, and you have therein your quintessence.

From a late-15th century treatise on the quintessence, Furnivall 1889, p. 5. The text, typical of many others, is a long-winded account of making alcohol or spirits of wine, relying on the distillation of the alcohol from the heat of the horsedung. The treatise describes, in an indirect and flamboyant way, the processes of getting drunk: how to make it; getting drunk; and the illusionary (though thought to be real at the time) effect.

11. To make *aurum misticum*

Take a phial of glass and seal it well, or else a long earthen pot. Take 1 pound of sal-ammoniac, 1 pound of sulphur, 1 pound of crude mercury, 1 pound of tin. Melt the tin and then put in the mercury and all the other ingredients. Grind all these together on a stone, and then put them all together into a phial or into an earthen pot. Seal all the mouth, except for a little hole so that a spout of paper or of parchment may be set therein. Then put it over the fire in a furnace, but first a slow fire and then a good fire for the space of 24 hours, until no more air comes out the glass. Then take it form the fire and break the glass.

From a 15th-century collection of colour-making recipes, Halliwell 1855, p. 79.

12. To make a surprise (*musyke*)

Take a vessel of glass that will hold a quart and take red clay and temper it with horsedung, and daub the vessel more than half an inch thick, but put in the mouth as much as you can put therein [on] your little finger. Then take an ounce of gum ammoniac, an ounce of white brimstone, an ounce of quicksilver and an ounce of tin. First melt the tin in a goblet or vessel and when it is melted put the quicksilver into the goblet on the fire. Quickly stop the mouth of the vessel with a handful of fresh grease [so] that the quicksilver does not jump out. Soon take them from the fire and let it cool, and then you may crumble them between your fingers. Then take all four substances and grind them on a stone together and then put [them] into the vessel together and stop the mouth well, save the little hole. Afterwards hang the vessel over the fire for the amount of two hours till you observe no steam come out of the vessel over the fire. First you must

make a slow fire and afterwards more and more and always
blow the fire until the glass has stopped steaming. Then take it
away and break it and look what you find inside.

Amongst 16th-century additions to a late medieval volume on
alchemy and practical household prescriptions and instructions,
Bickley 1928, 428–9.

13. To make water of silver

Take green copperas and saltpetre, powder them and put them
in an earthen pot. Set [the pot] on a still made of glass, and put
them in [another] pot and make a fire under it. Take the second
water and *graven* inward with it. Take the third water and put
a little fine silver in it and stop it with wax and let it stand a
day and then take it and lay it on a sword and let it lie for 20
minutes. Then wash it off and it shall be silver. Then take the
fourth water and put gold into it and let it stand until it is cold,
and with this water you shall write gold as fast as with ink. Take
the same fourth water and put into it pewter made of tin and of
quicksilver and put them in and stop it with a paper leaf until it
is stable, and then leave it for five days.

From a 15th-century commonplace book containing usual
range of entries, including many English recipes for alchemy,
medicine and pigments, Bickley 1928, p. 431.